JUMPING mouse
a story about inner trust

JUMPING
mouse

a story about inner trust

Mary Elizabeth Marlow

 HAMPTON ROADS
PUBLISHING COMPANY, INC.

Cover design by Matthew Friedman
and Jonathan Friedman

Interior drawings by Louis Jones

Inside front flap drawing by
Joseph Rael (Beautiful Painted Arrow)

For information write:

Hampton Roads Publishing Company, Inc.
134 Burgess Lane
Charlottesville, VA 22902

Or call: (804) 296-2772
FAX: (804) 296-5096
e-mail: hrpc@hrpub.com
Internet: http://www.hrpub.com

If you are unable to order this book from your local
bookseller, you may order directly from the publisher.
Quantity discounts for organizations are available.
Call 1-800-766-8009, toll-free.

Library of Congress Catalog Card Number: 99-94474

ISBN 1-57174-147-X

11 10 9 8 7 6 5 4 3

Printed on acid-free paper in Canada

Dedication

To Ann Maria,
My Dear Friend,

Whose Heart is Open
Who Walks in Total Trust
Who Sees with the Eyes of an Eagle

Contents

Preface

An East Indian teacher once challenged a group of students to share *one truth* that they knew. Immediately, hands went up. Each person, in turn, confidently shared impressive bits of knowledge and information, for these were students with academic accolades and advanced studies in metaphysics. The teacher listened patiently as each person took his turn, then spoke with a piercing clarity. "What you have shared is not what you know. It is only what you have learned from someone else. It is borrowed truth. Go off by yourselves. Take as long as you need. Re-examine your lives, your experiences. Come back only when you have discovered something you personally know."

What this teacher knew, and perhaps what we all sense at some inextricable level, is that to know and to trust our own truth is probably the single most challenging issue any of us ever face. We long to have the courage to trust within.

On a personal level, men and women alike are confronted with the dilemma of not knowing how to trust. As a society, we are sobered by the reality that much of what we have trusted in our political, religious, economic, and social world is in flux. If, as a people, our trust is solely in external form, we are in jeopardy. If, on the other hand, we know and trust our own inner truth, it is easier to sense what is trustworthy in our outer world. We are less likely to be misled, or thrown off balance, or pulled in conflicting directions. Both personally and collectively, we need to re-examine who and what we trust. We want to know when to, whether to, and how to trust.

Some years ago, I heard a story that spoke about trust in a voice all its own. The story, *Jumping Mouse*, is an ancient legend from the Native American tradition. I felt as though I had been waiting for this story my entire life; it touched my soul with a resounding chord of resonance. I wept from a deep place within. I knew it was my story, for the issue of trust has been a major theme in my personal mythology. And I knew it was not just my story; at some level it is everyone's story.

Jumping Mouse is ancient in origin but timely in concept. It is a compelling story of initiation told in the language of the heart. It is whimsical, yet profound. In this legend, a mouse leaves the familiar, undertakes heroic tasks, meets overwhelming obstacles, makes difficult choices, and resolves paradoxes. As Jumping Mouse faces the mosaic of challenges demanding more and more courage to trust within, we journey alongside him and interface with our own obstacles. We face confusion, doubt, and fear and reawaken innocence and trust in the moment and in ourselves. In the end, we are empowered, for *Jumping Mouse* is a triumph of the Soul.

Perhaps your experience with this story will be similar to mine. Once heard, this story becomes an integral part of the listener. It never leaves. It continually calls us to remember who we are. With each telling, there are new discoveries, and the heart is opened a bit more. It may be that the full disclosure of its deeper mysteries is a lifetime task.

I tell the story as it speaks to me, and continues to speak—with a plethora of feelings, memories, images, and metaphors, and with other stories which juxtapose themselves alongside *Jumping Mouse.*

As you read, I invite you to pause along the way. Sense your own inner alliance with the collective wisdom of the story. Allow your spirit to take flight and soar far beyond the pages of this book to the heart of your own truth.

Acknowledgements

I wish to acknowledge the following people for their invaluable contributions to this book:

The Plains Indian People of the Native American tradition for their gift of this sacred story;

Corrine, a beautiful Seneca Indian woman, who came to be a part of our family when I was born, who nurtured and cared for me, and imparted in me a love for the Native American people, their songs, and their stories;

Joseph Rael (Beautiful Painted Arrow), without whom I may have wandered the world over without ever being introduced to the wisdom of the Ancient Ones;

The late Paul Solomon, who awakened in me a love for the unifying Spirit in all traditions;

John Nelson, author and long-time friend, invaluable sounding board and critic throughout the writing of this book, who insisted on more when I would have settled for less;

Kathy Grotz and Jean Reeder for painstaking and careful editing and proofing;

Lynne Paine, dear friend and fellow therapist, for encouragement and empowerment;

My many friends throughout the world, representing diverse traditions from many different countries, who have honored me with their sacred stories and in so doing have demonstrated that amid diversity there is the One Great Spirit.

Mouse Village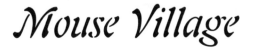

Life In Mouse Village

Once there was a mouse named Jeremy who, like all the other mice, lived in a little village hidden away in the woods. He was always busy, running and jumping, hurrying and scurrying to and fro. It seemed he was always in motion. In fact, he hardly ever stood still. And, like the other mice, he couldn't see very far. Nor was he able to see very clearly. For mice, as you may have noticed, usually have their whiskers in the ground.

Several years ago, I was asked to conduct a day-long counseling session with a "very busy" family of seven. This was a particularly prestigious family. Every member of the family was academically distinguished and highly accomplished. As they entered the therapy room, my first impression was that they were one of the "busiest" families I had ever seen. They quickly began rearranging furniture, fluffing pillows, talking non-stop all the while. Eventually, we sat down and began our day together. It became obvious that the busyness was more than a momentary attempt to camouflage their nervousness about the upcoming session. It was a coping mechanism to which they were accustomed, one they used frequently to avoid having to relate at deeper levels. The family had been so frenzied over the years that they had often overlooked some important needs. For mice are always busy, hurrying and scurrying with their whiskers in the ground.

One daughter had married a man the family considered beneath their standards. As a result, he was given only polite acceptance. The daughter reacted by stuffing anger under a polite exterior. A second daughter had been plagued with an eating disorder. The severity of the problem had been denied; it was time to own the fact she was anorexic. A third child, the son, had been actively gay for five years. Three of the family members had never noticed.

For that one day, at least, they all took their whiskers out of the ground and stopped and listened and noticed.

Jeremy, like the other mice in the village, stayed very busy, doing the things that mice do. He was always looking and searching, hurrying and scurrying, to and fro.

Mice work forty-hour, sixty-hour, eighty-hour weeks. Does that sound familiar? One self-acknowledged workaholic justified his schedule by saying, "Well, you do what you have to do!"

Mice tend to worry and scrutinize. Mice analyze and nitpick. At times, they become obsessive. They go over things again and again, and then one more time again, just to be sure. Sometimes this activity reflects a genuine expression of the inner self, but all too often the busyness is used to avoid dealing with the real concerns. We allow the innate conflicts of the conscious mind to drive us into activity. The busyness is displaced energy which perhaps would be better used were it directed to quiet the conscious mind, in order that we may hear the whisperings from the deeper self.

In time, we tend to become disconnected from our authentic selves. We lose touch with our spontaneity, playfulness, joy, imagination, and creativity. We lose our ability to be in the moment, and to experience wonder, sorrow, surprise, hope, vulnerability, love, and trust. In essence, we lose our connection with the Soul.

We identify, instead, with the ego self, that part of our identity which was shaped by parents, community, and culture. We become a reflection of the outside world. We are prompted by a false sense of duty and obligation and driven by a desperate emptiness which cries out to be filled with the approval and acceptance of others.

A scene from my childhood comes to mind. I remember a specific incident when my father discovered that we three children, Joanna, John, and I, had been sleighing down our sloping driveway, which led directly to the street. To emphasize his point about the dangers inherent in this kind of sledding, Dad called the three of us together to ask us each the same straightforward question: "What would you do if, when you got to the bottom of the hill, a vehicle came down the street?"

Joanna, the oldest, promptly answered, "I would lie real flat on the sled."

My father countered her response with, "You wouldn't have to worry about that. A car would make you flat, indeed!"

My brother was next. "I would roll off my sled," John said, with a confident look in his eyes. His statement got a definite nod of approval from Dad.

Now I, as the youngest of the three, had my turn. I didn't think I could give the same answer as John.

And surely Joanna had been off track. I was a such a careful little mouse (and safe answers are so very important to careful mice). After some hesitation, I said, "I am not sure," which was not the right answer at all!

The truth was that I knew exactly what to do. Just the week before this conversation, the exact situation which my father had anticipated had occurred. I had been sledding down the driveway, when suddenly, as I approached the bottom of the hill, a car quickly sped from around the corner and whizzed in front of the driveway. I rolled off the sled and managed to veer the unmanned sled away from the path of the car. In a moment of crisis, I had instinctively responded and averted danger. But when questioned later by my father, I was more concerned about the approval of others than I was in honoring my own truth.

Dad cautioned us to sled instead in a safer place, and the whole matter was dropped. No doubt, the incident has long been forgotten by all the other family members. But the memory stays with me because it signaled a theme which would later play out in my life in countless ways: seeking the courage to express feelings and thoughts without overconcern for pleasing others.

An even more challenging theme than being afraid to express thoughts and feelings is one of not even knowing what our thoughts and feelings are. Some of us have been so traumatized that we are still frozen in earlier experiences, cut off from our feeling and thinking reality.

Kari, a woman in Norway, recalls painful memories of the Nazi occupation of her small village during World War II. Before then, there had never been soldiers in her village; suddenly, with no explanation, soldiers arrived. Too many of them. Overnight, everything in her village changed. There was the eeriness of strangers in strange uniforms, speaking harsh words in guttural sounds her young ears could not understand. Kari remembers the clinking sounds of boots on pavement and the ever-prevailing presence of guns and weaponry. Ugly, giant machines were everywhere. Nothing felt safe anymore.

Her family and friends looked and talked and acted differently. There were worried looks and hushed voices, mumblings overheard late at night behind closed doors. There was scarcity. Not much food. Not much of anything. Adults had secrets. Many secrets. And children weren't told what they were. It was frightening, and no explanations were given. Kari's whole world changed. And she didn't know why.

The village had always been governed by a non-verbal consensus of what life was and how life was to be lived. Once that consensus was disturbed, fear gripped the village—not just the fear of what would happen under occupation, but the fear of not knowing what, collectively, to trust anymore.

One incident stands out above all the rest. It was twilight and the villagers gathered auspiciously on the bank of the river. Overhead, there were planes. So many planes. The whole sky was ablaze with light. Kari was terrified, and everyone else seemed to be afraid, too. She remembers her father picking her up and pointing frantically up to the sky. Then the bombing started. In the distance was the ugly, piercing sound of explosions ricocheting in the night. Much later, she learned that it was the night of the first Blitz, a devastating German air raid which affected much of Western Europe.

The night seemed to go on forever. She covered her ears and wanted to cover her eyes. Her father, in his well-meaning attempt to comfort her, told her how beautiful the sky was and that she should look at all the lights. What Kari needed was for him to tell her it was all right to be afraid. That he was frightened, too. War is terrifying for both adults and children. She needed to know that she could come to him when she felt apprehensive. She could talk to him and he would listen, and his love would make her feel safe. But he was too consumed with his own fears and too disturbed by the collective mania to be of any real comfort.

Instead, her father kept talking about the beautiful lights. Kari became afraid that who she was, as well as what she felt, was not acceptable. She tried to feel what he told her she "should" feel. She couldn't. She was a scared little mouse, paralyzed with fear. She became numb. No feelings.

Years later, Kari married an insensitive man. Her husband, as her father before, denied and controlled her feelings. She longed for children. She endured three miscarriages and four operations with no emotional support, and still, no baby. Her husband told her it wasn't hard. Still paralyzed in the frozen grief of her childhood, and still the scared little mouse, Kari obediently listened to what she "should" feel and, once again, numbed her feelings.

With the passage of time and with the help of extensive therapy, she is beginning, slowly, to trust her own thinking and feeling reality, even when it differs with that of others.

The Mousetrap Called "Consensus Reality"

Even without childhood trauma, how easy it is to allow ourselves to be governed by outer authority—the rules, beliefs, and opinions of others—without giving them our careful consideration. We accept what sociologists call "consensus reality," the reality agreed upon by most people as the way things "should" be.

If that consensus reality is one based on deep family, cultural, and spiritual values, we are likely to have an intrinsic sense of self and the confidence and courage to trust ourselves. If, on the other hand, that consensus reality is lacking in values, we may survive by dovetailing inconspicuously with the status quo. We obey the *shoulds* and *ought-tos* and *have-tos* which, in many cases, are blindly alluded to not so much because of their value, but because they exist. A grey dullness pervades. It becomes easier to blend in, to go along with what is, to be mediocre. We weigh and measure our responses, and in the process we become numb to our authentic selves, to genuine feelings and original thoughts. And then, years later, we one day find ourselves with the sobering awareness expressed so well by T.S. Eliot in *The Love Song of J. Alfred Prufrock*: "I have measured out my life with coffee spoons."

It may seem that an outer consensus reality does not rule us. But with careful scrutiny, we may discover we have internalized our consensus reality. Inside us, there may be a demanding, inner patriarch that keeps us stuck in Mouse Village just as effectively as any external pressure could ever do. We judge and criticize ourselves. We lavish guilt on ourselves because of our shortcomings. And we fall prey to limitations of family systems and generational patterns which we unconsciously perpetuate.

We may feel obliged to live out our parents' unlived lives, or we may feel trapped in roles assigned to us in our families of origin. Ann, for example, has an idealized view of her mother. She must "break the spell," as John Bradshaw so clearly puts it in his book *Creating Love*. Ann's mythologized view of her mother is that her mother sacrificed her life to give Ann the opportunity to be the ballerina she could never be. The truth is that her mother martyred herself, making Ann responsible for her own unlived life. Mom gave Ann opportunities but controlled her choices. As fate would have it, Ann grew too tall to fulfill the dream of becoming a ballerina. At fifty, there is a sad resignation that life somehow just happened. Because the child Ann didn't get to choose, the adult Ann has difficulty with the choices of everyday life. She doesn't trust herself. She doesn't know herself. She vacillates over decisions and second-guesses herself once choices are made. Her inner patriarch makes harsh demands. Since she failed to live her mother's dream, everything is on hold in her life. It is as though nothing can be enjoyed totally. Ann waits for permission to begin her dance of life.

Tom's inner patriarch is quite different than that of Ann's. He is governed by internal rules which keep him stuck in the same roles which were assigned to him as a child. As the youngest in a large family, Tom found his place by being funny and making everyone laugh. The very roles that once gave him power as a child now rob him of his identity as an adult. He has so over-identified with his role of clown and caretaker that much of his more authentic self has been discounted. As a man, he now seeks the purity of his deeper, more honest feelings.

We can live a lifetime as little mice, hurrying and scurrying, running to and fro with our whiskers in the ground, not really seeing very far, searching desperately for the self we never find. We can believe that this is how life was, how life is, and how life will always be. . .and so it is. . .just that. . .I call this living in Mouse Village. I believe all of us have lived there part of our lives. Some of us still do.

Many of us go back and forth from time to time. In fact, few of us have changed our permanent address.

Think about yourself and your Mouse Village. Be candid. Get a graphic picture of the scene. You might even be mildly amused. Describe yourself. What do you look like? How do you "busy" yourself? What are your feelings? Your thoughts? What beliefs dictate you and your Mouse Village? Take time to complete the sentence "When I am in Mouse Village, I. . ."

Hearing the Call

One day Jeremy began to hear a new strange sound, one he had not heard before. It was a roar coming from somewhere out in the distance. Now Jeremy was used to the sounds of the forest. He knew the different sounds of the two-legged and the four-legged and the winged and the hoofed. But this was unlike anything he had known.

Sometimes, he would stop everything and lift his head to the direction of the roar. He would strain to see what might be there, and he would wiggle his whiskers, hoping to sense something in the air. What could it be, he wondered?

And so Jeremy did what most of us do when we are not sure about something. He asked someone else. When we don't trust ourselves, we need confirmation from an outside source to validate our reality.

Jeremy scurried up to a fellow mouse and asked him, "Brother Mouse, do you hear a sound, a roaring in your ears?"

The other mouse didn't even bother to lift his whiskers out of the ground. He was too busy. "No, no, I don't hear anything. And besides, I don't have time

*to talk." And off he went before Jeremy had a chance
to say anything more.*

*Not to be easily discouraged, Jeremy decided to
ask another mouse the same question. Maybe this
mouse had heard the sound.*

*The second mouse looked at him in a most peculiar
way. "Sound? What sound?" And before Jeremy could
stop him long enough to describe what he had heard,
the second mouse scampered off, disappearing behind
the pines.*

The sound which Jeremy heard comes from the
Unknown. It is the voice of Spirit, the Higher Self,
the Inner Voice. It communicates to us in a number
of ways: a hunch, a feeling that persists, a revealing
dream, an inner knowing, an intuitive flash, a chance
meeting which has particular relevance, an experience
that has metaphorical significance, or a sensing that
defies the rational process. We can experience any
number of these "calls," even within the course of
a single day. For life is always calling to us, even
though we may not always hear that call.

Sometimes, the call from our inner world is confirmed with an experience in the outer world. It is
those moments of exquisite synchronicity that serve
to keep us in awe of life. Gina, in England, recalls
an experience in which her inner and outer worlds
converged in a most meaningful way. She was sitting
on her bed reading a letter from her ex-boyfriend,
painfully reviewing what had been a most difficult
relationship, one in which she found herself continually
longing and hoping for more connection, more commitment. It was a futile wish for the improbable, a
fantasy built on a dream of what might be, rather
than a realistic view of what was. The letter was
his final exit, although in many ways he had never
entered the relationship.

As Gina read the letter, she glanced up to see a butterfly trapped inside her bedroom window, struggling to free itself. As it fluttered unsuccessfully against the glass, she was reminded of the many times she had struggled for a sense of self but felt trapped in her willingness to endure unnecessary hardship and pain. As she finished the final words of the letter, simultaneously the butterfly found its way to freedom. A resonating rush of energy surged through her body. The butterfly served as a powerful metaphor. It was the call to give up her pleasing-passive role, a childhood pattern learned early to gain approval from disinterested parents and one which she continued in relationship after relationship. It was time to free herself and take flight.

The sound of the inner voice has a distinctive quality, like no other voice we may hear. A mother can distinguish her child's voice amid the voices of a hundred other children on a busy playground. She knows her child's voice because she has listened to it countless times. Likewise, the more we listen to our inner voice, the more certainty there is in distinguishing the sound of the true self from all the other voices that may be crying out to be heard (the voice of ego, the voice of fear, the voice of anger, etc.). And the more we listen to the inner voice, the more it speaks to us.

At first, the call comes in a gentle fashion. We may have a dream, for example. And there may be an incident in our outer world which parallels the message from the dream. We listen to the dream, notice the metaphor in relationship to what is occurring around us, and make the necessary changes. But when we ignore or discount those messages, the communication becomes more faint. The voice becomes less frequent, less distinct. It is as though our Higher Self ceases its struggle to get through to our denser reality. We forgo the option of conscious choice, and life becomes the tough taskmaster. Instead of gentleness, we are given the "divine boot," kicked out of our complacency or resistance into difficult challenges which demand change. There may be illness, loss, separation, or other trauma, experiences which serve to wake us up to a deeper reality.

There are many kinds of authentic calls. On a practical level, the call may be the impulse to respond to a want ad in the newspaper, a strong feeling that propels you to re-connect with a friend you haven't seen in years, or a sudden knowing that it is time to make a geographical change, go back to school, change jobs, or end a relationship.

Or the call may be of another kind altogether. A particular story or poem might call out to you. A particular area of the world may call you to come visit or even to make a geographical move. Creative self-expression may suddenly beckon. Grandma Moses didn't begin painting until she was in her eighties!

We may, at times, sense the unspoken call from another person. A stirring story is one about Suzanne, who talked long-distance to her friend one Sunday afternoon, as was her custom. There was nothing distinctive or particularly different about that conversation to alert her in any way to any special concern for her friend. Later that night, however, she found herself dialing the number of her friend again. There was no logical reason to call, since she had already talked to her that day. Suzanne was startled at her own reflexive action, but continued to dial anyway. This time when her friend answered, her speech was heavy and slurred. Suzanne sensed what had happened. Her friend had overdosed on pills. Immediately, she dialed 911, an action which saved her friend's life.

From another perspective, a call may beckon the hero or heroine to a quest, an undertaking, a mission, or a journey. These calls, which come from the very depths of your being, enlist you in mythic tasks: to pursue a lifetime dream, to serve in some capacity, to undertake some historical undertaking, or to follow a spiritual pursuit. For example, Orville and Wilbur Wright answered the call to adventure. They dared to explore new horizons with their contributions in the field of aerodynamics. President Clinton's story about the impact of his meeting with John F. Kennedy is an example of a call to public service. Or the call may come from nature. There may be the sudden impulse to mountain trek in Tibet or river raft in Colorado.

The call, of course, need not literally be a sound, as it was for Jeremy, for the murmurings of the heart make their voices heard in a variety of ways. But the fact that Jeremy heard a sound is significant. Sound demands attention. As David A. Cooper states, "Certain sounds evoke deep stirring in the unconscious realms, stimulating mysterious and powerful urges that transcend intellectual concepts. These are sounds that lure us into the domain of the sacred."

In many of the ancient traditions, sound is used to awaken the individual. The sound is a call to Spirit. Sikhs blow blasts of a trumpet to announce the arrival of the Holy Granth, their sacred text. Muslims sound the vocal call to prayer: *Allah Hu Akhnar* ("God is most great"). Christian worship often begins with bells, the chords of an organ, the voices of a choir. In the Jewish tradition, the blowing of the shofar, the ram's horn, is the call to prayer. And shamans and other spiritual healers use rattles, chants, whistles, bells, howls, grunts, and other sounds.

The call that Jeremy hears is the call of Spirit, or what is known in many traditions as a Sacred Call. It is the call of the True Self, which calls out, from deep within, to be recognized as our true identity. The false self, the ego, the "I," made up of the thoughts and reactions that we have allowed to rule our lives, is no longer in charge. Each time we experience a Sacred Call, we are instantly drawn into our true nature, which Joseph Campbell describes as "that interior, ineffable source of being, consciousness, and bliss."

What distinguishes a Sacred Call from any other kind of call? According to Cooper, "The Sacred call is transformative. When such a call occurs and we hear it—really hear it—our shift to higher consciousness is assured. A decision is made and a turn in direction is taken. The one who receives the message recognizes a new sense of reality, and follows, as if by intuition, in a way that may elude verbal explanation."

Leaving Mouse Village

When none of the other mice knew anything about the sound, Jeremy decided that the best thing he could do would be to forget about the whole thing and get busy. He knew how to be a busy little mouse. And so he started hurrying and scurrying to and fro once more.

But no matter how busy he was, he would still hear the sound. He tried to pretend that it had disappeared. But even when he tried not to hear it, he knew it was still there!

Jeremy became more and more curious about the sound. So one day, he decided to go off by himself and investigate. It was easy to scurry off from the other mice. They were too busy to notice he had gone, anyway.

When he was off by himself, the sound was stronger and much clearer. Now he could sit quietly and listen hard.

Heeding the call heralds a moment of spiritual passage, a dying to the old and birth of the new, the mystery of transformation. The familiar life horizon has been outgrown, and the old concepts, ideals, and emotional patterns no longer fit; the time for the passing of a threshold is at hand. Leaving Mouse Village marks the shift from an identity with the unauthentic self, dictated by consensus reality, the reality most people accept, to an identity instead with the authentic self, the central point within the psyche to which everything is related. The departure is not without its anxiety. For, as Freud has suggested, all moments of separation and new birth produce anxiety similar to the original birth trauma and separation from the mother.

Leaving Mouse Village has two requirements. The first requirement is the courage to venture into the unknown. How many times do we have a strong intuition but fail to follow it, either because we don't trust that feeling enough or we don't have the courage to follow what we feel?

There is an often-told story about a woman who loses a key. She stands under a brightly lit lamp post and searches for it there. A stranger comes by and asks her what she is looking for.

"I am looking for my lost key."

"Oh," he replies. "Did you lose it here under the lamp post?"

"No, I lost it down there," she answers, pointing to the darkness ahead, "but I can't see there."

To find the symbolic key, we must be willing to go from the known into the unknown, with no guarantees, no assurances, no certainty of where our venture into the unknown might lead.

I am reminded of an earlier period in my life when I first moved to Virginia Beach. My seventeen-year marriage was over. I had left a comfortable life, a large home appointed with beautiful antiques situated on four acres on the James River, and the accompanying lifestyle that goes with being married to a professional and doing all the "right things." The decision to leave had clearly been mine, but the consequences of that choice had not been squarely faced. I was left reeling from the aftermath of having exchanged safety for uncertainty. The abrupt and drastic changes in lifestyle left me overwhelmed and burdened with too many choices. My life had taken on a surrealistic overtone. The truth is I was terrified.

I called a dear friend in New York, a seventy-plus "young" woman to seek her sage advice to deal with what I was experiencing as my great travail. "Suzanne, I don't know what I am going to do, or even where I am going to live."

I was totally unprepared for her response. "How fascinating!" she exclaimed. "I will have to try that some time!" So much for my sob story! I started to chuckle. Thanks to Suzanne, I was jolted into seeing my situation from quite a different perspective. It was the push I needed to move out of my limbo and to begin facing the unknown with affirmative action, by making conscious decisions about my new life in Virginia Beach. Travesty or opportunity, the choice was mine!

A willingness to venture into the unknown is one thing. Successfully confronting the mythic task of "leaving home" is quite another. Both are required if we are to successfully leave Mouse Village. Leaving home does not necessarily refer to a geographical move, for we can move geographically but remain in a limited awareness. Leaving home means severing the umbilical cord to all that prevents us from experiencing our true identity.

In many of the ancient myths and legends, there are three underlying segments around which a story

is woven: leaving home, facing challenges, and returning home. The hero (or, of course, heroine) may
leave home voluntarily, as in the case of Jeremy, to
go off to a foreign land on some quest or adventure.
Or he may be cast out from his homeland for any
one of a variety of reasons. Next, the hero must
face his challenges, or aspects of self, mirrored in
the people and experiences he meets along the way.
By people, we include monsters, demons, witches,
trolls, animals, tricksters, helpers, guardians, etc. Finally, there is the return home. The hero, having met
the various aspects of self, returns home. It is not
necessarily the literal home to which the hero returns,
but "home" in the metaphorical sense of returning
to the real self.

In the more ancient traditions, rites of passage
served to help those crossing difficult thresholds of
transformation. The ceremonies were concrete
metaphors that severed conscious and unconscious
patterns and then introduced the participants to the
forms and feelings of the new stage.

Our modern world provides few such opportunities
for these kinds of experiences. However, the need
for support in making life transitions is evidenced
in the number and variety of support groups which
have sprung up everywhere. These groups often provide the deep interpersonal connection which were
formerly found in family and community. Sometimes,
these groups include ceremonies of various kinds to
ritualize major life transitions and to celebrate both
the beginning and the ending of significant cycles.

A meaningful ceremony for me is the Drum Dance,
a three-day, dry-fast dance, held annually in locations
both in the United States and Europe under the
guidance of Joseph Rael. The Dance contains the
three essential elements for any ceremony: movement,
sound, and purpose (or intent). In this particular

ceremony, the movement is the dance itself, a metaphor for the expansion of light; the sound, the beat of the drum, takes one deep into the inner self; and the purpose for the Dance is personal as well as planetary healing. Although the experience for each participant is unique, one thing is assured: at the completion of the Dance, every dancer is in a different place inwardly than when he began. The very nature of dance expands the psyche, severing conscious and unconscious patterns. Just the act of participating in the Dance automatically causes a shift in consciousness.

At times, the Dance is physically grueling. Somehow, you endure and wait for those resounding moments of triumph, those exquisite moments when you know you have danced through and beyond some blockage. In that moment, you are lifted into stillness where you are no longer dancing; instead, you are *being danced*. Your feet become the drumstick and the Earth the drum. You slip into those spaces "where God hides," in Rael's words, and, for a lingering moment, you touch the transcendent.

Whether or not you choose to use a ceremony to facilitate making a shift in consciousness is purely a personal matter. What is imperative, if you are to "leave home," is that you separate from the mosaic of identities you have settled for and begin, instead, to trust the true self.

Saying Goodbye to Other Mice

When we stand ready to cross the threshold and leave Mouse Village, we review the people and experiences in our lives. We place the people and events in our lives with a new perspective by beginning to understand their deeper significance. We relinquish judgment and become gentle with ourselves and with others.

If you have ever examined the underside of a homemade quilt, you are struck by what seems to be a hodge-podge of knots, hanging threads, and raw edges. How could anything beautiful be made from such randomness and confusion? But when you turn the quilt over, you see a beautiful, intricate, delicate pattern. Each piece is an integral part of the whole design. Each piece is placed deliberately in relationship to the other pieces. Placing people and events in your life is rather like turning a guilt over to the right side. You begin to see how each part of your life is an integral part of a far grander design.

Pamela, a woman in England, received a letter from her former husband that stirred a whole range of feelings. After many years of estrangement, receiving a letter from her ex was a mixed blessing. Years before, when she was in her early forties, he had left her for another woman. At the time, it was a devastating experience. He was her world, her Renaissance man, accomplished in the world of finance, involved in humanitarian concerns, and recognized as a connoisseur of art. In addition, he was her best friend and constant companion and was dashingly handsome, energetic, passionate, and sensitive. She had lived life with him and through him. Without him, all seemed empty.

Life had booted her out of Mouse Village. At forty-plus, she was forced to go back to school to earn a degree and begin a career. And so she did, at first with great effort, then with great success. The world of art, to which her former husband had introduced her, changed from being a world she could only appreciate in a detached way to becoming her world, her own place of unique expression.

In retrospect, all of her years of struggle seemed somewhat remote, for she had gained depth and definition through it all. Now, as a mature woman, she enjoyed a "significant other" relationship, a supportive and interesting circle of friends, a successful and meaningful career, and a comfortable home.

In sharp contrast, the letter from her ex spoke of loneliness (the relationship with the younger woman had long ago ended), of ill-health, of changes in finance, and of estrangement from their children. He was leading a life of quiet desperation. At an earlier time, she would have felt triumph, a sense that in the end she had won. But no such feelings surfaced. Instead, there was a sense of deep compassion, of wanting to see him one last time, to somehow place him in her life and to acknowledge all he had been for her.

They had first met on the River Seine. It seemed appropriate that their final meeting be there as well, at the familiar café, to sit together once again and share a bottle of Chardonnay. She wanted to thank him for being the one who had given her children, for opening her eyes to art and beauty, for being the most passionate lover in her life, and for the special moments that transcend words. For all of this, she was thankful. And even his leaving had, in retrospect, been a gift, for she had learned, in time, to love and trust herself. At any rate, a toast and a fond farewell. . .

Once we place the people and events in our lives, we are no longer restricted by our history; we are empowered, instead, by a deeper understanding and a sense of honor about our past.

Jeremy stood on the edge of Mouse Village and took one long look back at the only life he had ever known. He sat listening to the sound for a long time, and he knew he could no longer be content to just listen. It was time to discover more about this sound. He turned to face another direction. He looked out into the darkness of the vast unknown and boldly left Mouse Village.

CHAPTER TWO

Leap of Faith

*J*eremy was listening hard to the sound in the distance, when suddenly he heard someone say, *"Hello, Little Brother."* Jeremy was so startled he almost ran away. *"Hello,"* again said the voice. It sounded friendly enough.

"Who are you?" asked the timid little mouse.

"It is I, Brother Raccoon. You are all by yourself, Little Brother," said the raccoon. *"What are you doing here all alone?"*

Jeremy was embarrassed. He didn't want to have to talk to anybody about the sound. Especially not after what happened in Mouse Village.

"I heard a sound," he said timidly. *"A roaring in my ears and I am investigating it."*

"A roaring in your ears? You mean the River," said the raccoon, without any hesitation. *"Come, walk with me. I will take you there."*

Reflections From the River of Life

Jeremy was amazed! No sooner had he ventured out of Mouse Village than immediately he met someone who not only knew the sound in the distance but would take him to its source! Jeremy was determined to find out once and for all what this sound was about.

"Once I find out about this River, I can go back to my work and my life in Mouse Village," thought Jeremy. "Why, I will even ask Raccoon to return with me. If the mice in the village don't believe me, they will surely believe a raccoon."

Little Mouse walked close behind the raccoon, so as to be sure not to lose his way. His heart was pounding. He had never known such excitement. They wound their way through a cathedral forest of tall evergreens. There was an intoxicating smell of pine and cedar. As they drew closer to the River, the sound became louder. There was a sense that something important was about to happen. The air became cooler, and there was a fine mist. Suddenly, they came to the River! The mighty River! It was so huge that Little Mouse could not see across it. And it roared, loudly, rushing swiftly on its course, coming from some other place, going to the great unknown.

For one long, sacred moment, Jeremy was one with the river. He watched the river in reverent silence, inspired by its awesome beauty and the mesmerizing sounds. Western cosmology begins with, "And God said, Let there be light." God created light with his own voice—with sound—signifying that sound is the essential matter of the universe. Sound touches us deeply. It nourishes our most primal needs and reassures us, keeping us in harmony with life. Certain sounds, such as the roar of the river, evoke deep stirrings in the unconscious realms. These sounds, according to David A. Cooper, call to us in soulful ways that "stimulate mysterious and powerful urges and transcend intellectual concepts."

A friend recalls a peak experience when just hearing the pure sound of the river was a much-needed healing balm. Like Jeremy, he experienced a timeless moment when he became one with the river. John had made a trip to San Diego to reconnect with a female friend, hoping to build a permanent relationship. His dream soon turned into bitter disappointment. It was clear that any long-term relationship with her was simply not to be. To find solace from his pain, he sought refuge in an enchanted spot which he often visited in National Park, San Diego. It was a remote place where he could stretch out on a large river stone and comfortably lie, sometimes for hours, transfixed by the roar and rush of water cascading over rocks. In this secluded spot, a diverse group of onlookers would regularly congregate. Here, differences would disappear. Each person would sense which special stone was his and claim it as a private sanctuary. The one commonality was the shared reverence for the river.

To my friend John, the art of listening to the sound of the river is a high form of Zen meditation, a way to slip into the gaps and go beyond time. On this particular day, he lay on a rock by the river in a total state of bliss, completely absorbed by sound. What seemed more like five minutes extended into five hours and left him wondering, later, where time had gone. The sound lifted him out of his emotional pain and restored his Soul. He regained his equilibrium and was able to satisfactorily complete the relationship with his friend instead of slipping back into old abandonment issues. His experience with sound made him keenly aware that he had been neglecting his inner self; as a result, he made a commitment to designate time each day for meditation. The sonorous sound of the river called him back to himself.

An interesting point in our story is that the mouse went to a river. If Jeremy had gone to a mountain instead of a river, he would have begun to climb, for mice can maneuver in earth. But mice can't manage in water. His mouse self was rendered helpless before something he was unable to manipulate and master. He could only surrender to the song of the river and listen to its many voices, which together make up the music of life.

When we live in Mouse Village, our identity is determined by who and what others tell us we are. Once we look in the River, we no longer need to depend exclusively on the opinion of others for self-knowledge. The River of Life gives us a more profound way of knowing ourselves. The River, which is Life, is a mirror. The people, the situations, the symbols in our life merely reflect inner aspects of self. The mirrors in our outer world reveal messages we would otherwise not be able to hear.

When we look in the River of Life, we begin to see our inner selves. We begin to take responsibility for our underlying issues which determine why we attract certain people and particular situations in our lives. In time, we can detect our weaknesses, the aspects of self we are most afraid of, reflected in life around us. We see our greatest strengths mirrored and face those fears as well. What would happen if we claimed all our power? What would happen if we allowed ourselves to be all that we are? What would happen if we did not undermine or sabotage ourselves?

When we listen attentively to the many voices of the River, as did Jeremy and John, in time we may discover the oneness in it all and realize that the voices in the River belong to each other. We no longer distinguish the merry voice from the weeping voice, or the childish voice from the manly voice, or the lament of those who yearn from the laughter of the wise. All the voices are interwoven and interlocked, entwined in a thousand ways. All of them together are the world.

We enter that transcendent state of oneness, described so poetically by Herman Hesse in *Siddhartha.*

When he listened to this river. . .to this song of a thousand voices: when he did not listen to the sorrow or laughter, when he did not bind his soul to any one particular voice and absorb it in himself, but heard them all, the whole, the unity; then the great song of a thousand voices consisted of one word: Om-perfection.

"It's powerful!" the little mouse said, fumbling for words.

"Yes, the river is a great thing," answered Raccoon, "but here, let me introduce you to a friend."

In a smoother, shallower place was a lily pad, bright and green. Sitting upon it was a frog, almost as green as the pad it sat on. The frog's white belly stood out clearly.

"Hello, Little Brother," said the frog. "Welcome to the river."

"I must leave you now," cut in Raccoon, "but do not fear, Little Brother, for Frog will care for you now."

The Role of the Raccoon, the Guide

As soon as the raccoon completes his task of guiding Jeremy to the River, he leaves quietly, unnoticed. He will return to the edge of Mouse Village and await the next person who needs a guide to the River. It may be a long wait, for few have the courage to venture out of Mouse Village. But when the next seeker crosses the threshold, leaving the confines of the village behind, the raccoon will willingly serve as a guide to whomever it might be. True teachers have no preferences. The raccoon gladly took Jeremy to the river. The truth is he would have taken anyone who was interested. But then, no one else had asked.

Raccoons are midwives who assist in the birth of consciousness. Although the role of the midwife is critical, the focus is the birth, not the midwife. Once the birth process is complete, the midwife is often forgotten. As soon as the raccoon safely delivered Jeremy to the River, he appropriately averted Jeremy's attention away from himself and his role as a guide and directed attention, instead, toward the next phase in the mouse's journey. The raccoon's timing was impeccable. He knew when his task with Jeremy was complete. He sensed when to introduce Jeremy to the frog and when to slip away unobtrusively.

All animals, including raccoons, represent the instinctual self. Meeting with the raccoon was also an indication that the little mouse was coming face-to-face with his own instinctual self and was beginning to trust inner impulses.

Jeremy was indeed fortunate that his particular guide was a raccoon. For it is the unique nature of raccoons to wash everything they eat in water. They wash in the River of Life and they understand its mysteries. What they take into their physical, emotional, mental, and spiritual bodies is purified, or washed in water (or light). Raccoons have no need for control, no need for adulation, and no attachment to outcome.

No limit is placed on the number of Raccoons we can have in our journey. And our Raccoons need not only be people. Raccoons can be turning-point experiences which can appear in any number of forms. A book, for example, can appear at a critical juncture and serve as a guide to the next stage of our journey. But no matter how many Raccoons we may have, the experience with our first Raccoon is always a cherished memory.

One of my first significant Raccoons was a book entitled *There is a River*, written by Thomas Sugrue. It is a story of a transpersonal explorer, Edgar Cayce, who shed light on other lifetimes and other realities. The book was a Raccoon waiting on my path, ready to take me to the River. It came during a period of deep introspection when I was exploring answers to some rather perplexing philosophical questions. The material from the Cayce readings clarified previously unanswered spiritual questions and confirmed the validity of many of my personal experiences. The book was life-changing. My entire perception of reality shifted. (There is nothing so strange as the way the strangeness wears off the strange.)

Pause a moment and reflect on a significant Raccoon in your life. Who was that person and/or experience waiting on your path once you left Mouse Village? In what way did that Raccoon guide you into the next phase of your journey?

Leap of Faith

"Who are you?" Jeremy asked.

"Why, I am a frog."

"A frog?" questioned Jeremy. He had never seen a frog before. "How is it possible to be so far out in the mighty river?"

"That is very easy," said the little frog. "I can go both on land and on water. And I can live both above the water and below in the water. I am the Keeper of the Water."

Jeremy was astonished! He tried to think of words. But no words came. He had never met the Keeper of the Water.

Without hesitating, the frog said, "Little Mouse, would you like some Medicine Power?"

"Medicine Power? Do you mean for me? Yes, of course. What do I do?" asked the eager little mouse.

"It is not that hard. All you need to do is crouch down real low and jump up as high as you can."

"That's all?" asked Jeremy.
"Yes. Crouch down as low as you can and jump up as high as you can! That will give you your medicine!"
Little Mouse did exactly what the frog told him to do. He crouched down as low as he could and jumped as high as he could. And when he did, his eyes saw something even more powerful than the mighty River. He saw the Sacred Mountain.

The jump that Jeremy took is what is known as the Leap of Faith. Faith is an unquestioning trust in someone or something. In this case, Jeremy trusted the frog. And what the frog told him was that if he wanted his power, he would need to leap. He had to go beyond himself, take new risks, move beyond limited perceptions and beliefs of who and what he was, to experience new levels of consciousness. Growth is a continuum that spirals upwards. A leap of faith, on the other hand, is an awakening characterized by a quantum shift in consciousness.

When Jeremy made his leap, he saw the Sacred Mountain, which is even more compelling than the River. The Mountain is the Heart of God. When we see the Mountain, we are stirred by that which is sacred to us, by that which has depth and genuineness. To see the Mountain is to connect with the Soul, to be nourished by what we feel and know and dream.

We begin to remember our real selves. We remember our spontaneity, playfulness, joy, imagination, creativity, and the ability to be in the moment. We awaken new possibilities. We remember our ability to experience wonder, sorrow, surprise, hope, love, and trust.

A young man made a spiritual pilgrimage to the Southwest to visit the Anasazi ruins. The decision to make the trip was definitely a leap of faith. He was at a critical juncture in his life, a time in which personal decisions were delayed until he sorted out his relationship with his father. Alan knew he couldn't be like his father, nor could he be who his father wanted him to be. And it would be futile to continue in his rebellious stage, acting out with drugs and alcohol. Instead of freedom, these addictions brought more despair and left him with a deeper sense of helplessness.

The sacred land of the Southwest had called him in some mysterious way and he had responded. Deciding to take the trip wasn't a logical decision; it meant putting his education on hold and spending his last bit of hard-earned money. But it seemed necessary. Alan trusted what he felt. When we are willing to make a giant leap into the unknown, as did the little mouse and this young man, we open ourselves to mountaintop experiences.

Three months later, Alan found himself exploring the ancient ruins of the Anasazi Indians in Bandelier, New Mexico. Perhaps he was feeling, at some non-verbal level, the need to search out ancient roots and, in so doing, search out his own roots.

Exploring the ruins was a somber experience. He sensed the silent wisdom of the Ancient Ones and the blessings being passed on, somehow, to those fortunate enough to walk time-worn pathways of sacred land. At such places, the invisible energy fields and the tangible worlds interface. The effect on the psyche is nonverbal and most profound.

Needing quiet time to reflect, Alan decided to hike up a nearby mountain. What this young man did not know was that, in the Native American tradition, vision questers traditionally go to a mountaintop. Symbolically, they enter the center of the Medicine Wheel, which is the Heart of God.

Once on the mountaintop, Alan noticed a circular design in the ground. Someone who was there before him had carefully chosen stones and meticulously placed them to form a perfect circle in the earth. It seemed that this Medicine Wheel was waiting just for him. It was a gift from Spirit and an auspicious opportunity for personal ceremony. He reverently entered the circle and sat directly in its center. He said prayers to honor the four directions, the East (mental), the South (emotional), the West (physical), and the North (spiritual). Before him was an exquisite panorama of desert beauty. The artist in him wanted to seize the moment. He reached for his camera and was concentrating on loading film when, all of a sudden, a large bird whooshed over his head so close he could feel the wind from the flap of its wings. He was startled! It took him a moment to collect himself before he could follow the magnificent bird with his eyes. He could identify it, now. . .a giant golden eagle! He watched it soar majestically, making a wide circle, and then, as though to make a definitive statement, the eagle completed the circle and flew breathtakingly close over his head once again.

To this young man, all life is a metaphor of the mind of God. The deeper significance of this event would not go unnoticed. It was significant to him that an eagle, a metaphor for Great Spirit, flew from the East, the place where wisdom enters. He knew Great Spirit would give him wisdom and it be would forthcoming. This was a moment of deep communion with his Soul. He had reclaimed himself. Tears streamed down his face. He could feel his heart and all within him that was authentic, connected, powerful, and real. Simultaneously, he knew his relationship with his father would no longer be a paralyzing issue. He could cease the struggle of seeking his identity through conflict with his father. Instead, he could boldly step into his life and move toward his goals which, heretofore, had been delayed. He had a renewed trust in Great Spirit. He was assured now that he would be given the strength he needed to live out his dream. When he came down from the mountain, his eyes glistened. This mountain would always be his mountain, his place for reclaiming his power.

Once we glimpse our Mountain, in the symbolic sense, as did the little mouse and the young man in New Mexico, we have an inextricable sense of who we are. Even if our view of the Mountain is fleeting and the experience is momentary, we are empowered to trust our inner truth, and to honor what we feel and know and dream.

We do not necessarily need to go anywhere physically to experience the leap of faith. Eric Butterworth, a well-known Unity minister, tells a story about one man's shift in consciousness which occurred while he was simply sitting in a chair! The man, who was a middle-aged, middle-management executive, similar in many ways to many other men, was suddenly given his final notice. The company which had employed him for twenty-some years was downsizing and there was no longer a position for him. The news was devastating. At his age, job marketability was not promising. Not only that, but he had three children, two of whom were college-age. There were educational costs, mortgage payments, car payments, etc., to consider. He was stunned! He had never anticipated or planned for anything like this. He sat staring blankly into nowhere. He could not move. When office hours were over, he continued to sit and stare. Numb. Overwhelmed.

As he sat staring into nothingness, suddenly a tiny spider caught his attention. It was hanging on a thread hooked in at the ceiling and inching his way downwards, very close to the man's desk. At a certain point, the spider began meticulously to spin a web.

The man had never watched a web in process. It was fascinating. Minuscule silvery threads were magically being woven into an intricate design. Suddenly, he felt an empathetic connection between himself and the spider. Like the spider, he was hanging on a thread. If a divine intelligence is able to communicate with a spider and let it know how to spin a web with such perfection, then surely he could trust that same intelligence to guide his life. He started thinking about all the things he had really wanted to do but had postponed. Writing, for example. He had been so busy being "responsible" that his creativity had been pushed aside. Other options and possibilities came to mind. He could begin reclaiming important parts of himself he had previously disowned. He began to experience a glimmer of hope. His life could have so much more depth and value. It was a leap of faith to consider the possibility of living like the spider, to be in the moment, to listen, to trust, and to know that he would be given the knowledge to weave his own unique design.

Rediscover the Sacred Mountain

When Joseph Campbell was asked by someone in an audience what he should do with his life, the reply was the oft-quoted, "Young man, follow your bliss." Certainly, the advice from Campbell is sage wisdom. The difficulty, however, lies in knowing what our "bliss" is. How can we catch a glimpse of our Sacred Mountain, even if it is only for a fleeting look? How can we touch, taste, sense, feel, re-awaken, re-kindle, stir, remember, that which is sacred within us? How can we tap our intuitive source of spirituality and wisdom and be nourished by what we feel and know and dream?

Certainly, life itself can provide the catalysts we need to enable us to see the Sacred Mountain. Such was the case for Jeremy, for the young man in the Southwest, and for the middle-aged executive. Life is the indisputable teacher and is capable of creating the precise situation needed for us to return to our deeper selves. But is it possible to see the Sacred Mountain without the need for external events to catapult us into shifting to our more soulful selves?

Over the years, I have been privileged to be present during the sharing of the diverse life stories of many people throughout the world. Those stories are told in a variety of ways. They may be dramatized, drawn in spontaneous drawings, molded in clay, or expressed verbally. As I look and listen to each story with a particular interest in appreciating its sacredness, I am struck by some remarkable similarities. It would seem that during childhood, all of us, without exception, have had at least one moment in which we felt connected to the divine, although we may not always consciously remember the experience. For it is in childhood, when we are most innocent, that God's thumbprint is indelibly imprinted on our souls.

I find that these early experiences can be placed in three distinct categories. In the first category are the fortunate few who have had experiences in childhood so compelling that they never lost their connection with the sacred dimension of life. Eileen and Aaron are examples of persons who undoubtedly belong in that first group.

Eileen recalls the first years of her life when she heard the heavenly sounds of celestial music four or five times a day. What she heard defies the parameters of language's ability to adequately describe, for these sounds originate in another dimension of reality. Eileen describes the music as an ethereal blend of tinkling bells, each varied in tone and pitch, accompanied by the lilting sounds of harps and other stringed instruments; it was indeed heavenly music! Eileen could hear those delicate sounds more easily when it was quiet and she was alone. For in solitude the veil between this third dimension and the higher dimensions lifts somewhat. In particular, Eileen could hear the music while sitting alone eating, or walking down the sidewalk, or before drifting off to sleep at night. And in those quiet times Eileen would be comforted, as God and all His angels would sing, especially for her.

Although different in nature to the childhood experiences of Eileen, Aaron's early memories are equally compelling. Aaron describes his first childhood memory as one in which he was on the ceiling in his bedroom, looking down at himself, a tiny infant in a crib. According to Aaron, he spent a great deal of his time as a child in an out-of-body state. Not only was he able to move in and out of his physical body, but he was able to see auras, or the colors, shapes, and images around a person, and to accurately interpret those symbols.

In the second category of special childhood experiences, the persons felt a connection to the sacred dimension of life, but their experiences were discounted. They were either denied, ridiculed, or criticized by those around them. Or they minimized their experiences themselves because they were afraid to trust their own truth.

Persons in the third group have no conscious memory of any special moments in their early years. Their childhoods were so soul-severing because of trauma or abuse that they feel permanently disconnected from any loving Source of life. With help, they can be assisted into recalling or at least imagining one pleasant moment.

One way to reconnect with our Sacred Mountain is to revisit magical moments from your childhood by recalling childhood experiences when you felt loved, or joyful, inspired, happy, carefree, whimsical, creative, playful, safe, etc. Any number of incidents might come to mind, incidents which might appear to be insignificant. For example, you might recall the heavenly scent of jasmine on a hot summer night, or baking gingerbread with grandmother in the kitchen, or watching the play of light on treetops, or making costumes out of crepe paper with a best friend, or daydreaming under a giant oak tree. These experiences may seem trivial, but they have significance because they are selectively recalled and because they are scenes, or moments, which stir mysterious chords of memory. Within those memories are important clues which reveal that which, for you, is sacred in life. Those experiences often foreshadow a life's work, an avocation, a call to serve in a particular way (as opposed to a vocation, which may simply be a job to produce income). Most important, you learn what gives life meaning, that which calls uniquely to you. With a bit of creative detective work, you can decipher metaphors and draw inferences which could give important clues to your deeper nature.

An artist recalls a early scene when, as a two-year-old, he silently took his aunt by the hand and ceremoniously walked her over to stand with him, reverently, in front of a brightly lit Christmas tree, decorated with balls of every color. Years later his art would simulate that early imprint. His artistic signature would be his ability to skillfully reflect the play of light amid brilliant color.

Jean's special childhood moment was a time when she danced on the sidewalk to the nodding approval of her adoring grandfather. It was not necessarily that life was calling her to be a dancer, but it was affirming her innate ability to create her own unique movement in life. As a woman, she would need to call on her dancing spirit, her creativity, spontaneity, and liveliness, to weather some demanding challenges. It is interesting to note that now, as a therapist, she has added arrhythmic movement to her repertoire, teaching others to be at ease with their movement in life.

The father of a well-known minister, whom we will call Caleb, recalls an experience when his son did not come home from first grade at his normal time. It was at least an hour past the scheduled time when his son returned home to the father who was now very concerned. Caleb very matter-of-factly explained that one of his classmates had forgotten how to get home, and there was no parent to assist. Caleb knew the way and so he took his friend Lauren by the hand and walked her home. Later in life, he would know how to take many people "home."

Whether or not we choose to explore the symbolism of special childhood moments as a way to explore our own sacred dimensions, no doubt life will present additional opportunities which will serve to reconnect us with our Sacred Mountain. The experience can be one of a transcendent nature, a vivid dream, an out-of-body experience, an experience with light or sound, etc.; or we can be awakened by experiences on the opposite end of the paradigm—by death, loss, pain, struggle, hardship, etc. In either case, we have the opportunity to surrender to an unseen reality and reclaim the real self.

An example of a woman who is awakened through facing and overcoming obstacles is beautifully presented in the compelling story "Weaver of Worlds," by David Jongeward. In the story, Carolyn Jongeward accompanies her husband David, an archeologist, into Navaho country while he does writing and research. At first she watches with mild curiosity as the Navaho women weave their Javah. In time, Carolyn becomes intrigued with the weaving of the Navaho women, who are the recognized masters in this ancient art form. She develops a strong desire to learn the ancient ways and asks to be taught, not knowing what she is really asking.

Thus begins a story of initiation, an intense inner journey which is paralleled by a demanding outer journey. At times Carolyn's teachers treat her with kindness and teach her with patience. At other times, she is laughed at, ignored, ridiculed, and shamed. She is given a decrepit loom which frequently breaks down, not told how to thread her loom, given old rotting threads which break easily, and made to clean up the hogan while others casually sit sipping Coca-Cola and leafing through catalogues. She experiences anger, resentment, frustration, and many tears. Carolyn struggles to deal with her inner turmoil; meanwhile, her apprenticeship continues in other areas. She must learn a high level of mastery in the principles of sacred geometry, number symbolism, Native American philosophy, and creation mythology.

There comes a day, though, when she makes a leap of faith. The mental struggle and the emotional struggle cease. She moves through her inner turmoil into her sacred center. For the first time, she is able to sit down at her loom with no anger. She sits in total stillness. Then, like Spider Woman in the creation myth from the Native American tradition, she weaves together the cords of Heaven and Earth. From that still, sacred center, wherein lies the creative center of her being, comes the knowing to weave intricate, beautiful designs. She sits in the place of no thought, no concern about the past, no worry about the future. All she needs is given to her. She is both weaver and the one being weaved. Only the moment. Only trust.

How long Jeremy gazed at the Sacred Mountain, we can't be sure. For such moments exist in a space somewhere beyond time.

CHAPTER THREE
Death of Trust

All of a sudden, everything changed. Instead of landing on familiar ground, the little mouse splashed down in water. And mice, as you know, can't swim very well. Jeremy was terrified. He flailed his legs about, trying to keep head above water, choking and sputtering, struggling for his very life. He was frightened nearly to death. Finally, he managed to make his way to the river bank.

"You tricked me. . .you tricked me!" Little Mouse yelled at the frog.

Feeling Betrayed

Jeremy felt betrayed! Betrayal is the death of trust. We feel betrayed when our expectations are not met, when someone or something we trusted turns out to be different than what we had hoped for or what we anticipated. We, in turn, lose trust in others and in our ability to know whom and what to trust. In the ultimate sense, however, no person or experience can ever betray us. There is nothing anyone can do that can ever change who we are or alter our worth as a person. Our worth is never dependent on anyone else's action or evaluation. Our value is simply not negotiable.

The lesson is not to stop trusting. Instead, it is to *always trust others and to trust who they are in reality,* rather than who or what we want them to be. We create images of who we think others are and are disappointed when the images are not real. The more we love and trust ourselves, the less need there is to project those parts of our ourselves we have disowned onto others.

Jeremy was furious with the frog! The frog was not who Jeremy wanted him to be, and his experience with the frog was not what he expected. Jeremy never thought he would land in water! The frog gave him no warning of what would happen once he took his leap. No need, really, to blame the frog, for the frog was simply being the frog! But Jeremy could not yet clearly see the frog, for he was just beginning to discover his own true identity.

Initiators as Tricksters

The role of the Frog in our lives is decidedly different from that of the Raccoon. The Raccoon is a guide, one who shows the way. The Frog, on the other hand, is an initiator, one who demands change. The concept of *initiator* is ancient in origin but is still relevant in our modern world.

In the past, certain cultures provided Mystery Schools for those students committed to the understanding of Universal Laws and the deeper mysteries of life. These schools, located in secluded settings in Greece, Egypt, Persia, India, Syria, China, and elsewhere, were opportunities for students to disengage from ordinary consensus reality and to focus instead on ancient spiritual truths. The teachings were revealed in the language of the Soul: through myth, metaphor, literature, music, art, and ritual.

These Mystery Schools provided the perfect opportunity for the student to study the microcosm in the macrocosm. They were places of special initiatory experiences in the sacred mysteries. Initiators crafted the specific initiation, or lesson, appropriate for each particular student. Initiations were opportunities to alter perception. Passing an initiation signaled the moving from one state of consciousness to another, the comprehension of the esoteric—inner—principle behind the exoteric—outer—form. It indicated that the student discerned the deeper meaning of an experience in his (or her) life. In practical terms, it meant that the next time that student was confronted with a similar situation, he would not be triggered; he would *respond* and not *react.*

Although we may never be in an official Mystery School or may never have a spiritual teacher as our initiator, we are, nonetheless, enrolled in the Mystery School called Life. And we most certainly have initiators in our lives, even though they bear no official title and may be totally unaware of how effective they are in their roles. Our initiators are those persons who challenge us, push our buttons, get in our way, participate in our dramas. Any mother-in-law, former husband, difficult child, cantankerous boss, or demanding friend will do! Initiators help to shape our characters. They show us our weaknesses and throw us back on ourselves. And they challenge us to sink beneath confusion to deeper levels of wisdom.

In the Mystery School of Life, we experience both minor and major initiations. Minor initiations are lessons in single areas of our lives, such as relationships or money or self-worth, etc. (There can be an infinite number and variety of these minor initiations.) Major initiations occur usually once, sometimes twice, in a lifetime. They are across-the-board experiences, signaled, on the outer level, by simultaneous changes in almost every aspect of our lives, which can include changes in self-identity, location, career, relationship, money matters, friends, interests, goals, etc. A major initiation, such as the one Jeremy must confront, requires a major shift in identity from the Ego Self to the Soul Self.

The task of the initiator is to break down all the former notions of "self." Initiators take us beyond the limitations of ego to the Soul, that part of us which has always been connected to the eternal. Jeremy, on his own, would never have made the leap of faith. It is only by the tricking of the frog that Jeremy was willing to go beyond his limited ego self. And even when he did jump, seeing something beyond the parameters of what he had always known almost caused him to drown.

Initiators perform their tasks in a variety of ways. The frog, in our story, played the role of trickster. Tricksters are shape-shifters. They wear disguises; they deceive. One never knows when they will pop up or what forms they will take. In the East, there are many stories of gurus who purposely disguise themselves as beggars to test the limits of their unsuspecting students and see how they will treat a nameless beggar on the street. These gurus shape-shift, or trick, their *chelas,* their students, in order to push them beyond their ego boundaries into the deeper mysteries of life. The ego, the structure we build to give us our self-identity, knows there is something else beyond itself but is hesitant to let go. The ego wants to be immortal, to be safe from all suffering, to be successful, prosperous, and loved. Above all, the ego wants the world to make sense in a way that the rational mind can comprehend.

Although tricksters can appear at any time and in any form, they seem to appear especially at those times when the ego becomes over-identified with the Innocent or the Orphan archetype. At this point in the story, Jeremy was very much an Innocent. Carol Pearson describes this archetype as wanting "to deny unpleasant truth and just have faith and follow blindly." The frog awakens the little mouse, the Innocent, to depth and discernment, to paradoxes, and to the wholeness of life.

Most of us do not consciously choose a major initiation. It seeks us out. Jeremy saw the Sacred Mountain because he was tricked, or shocked, into that sacred space. We may be shocked or disoriented through any number of ways: physical pain, sudden loss, a paranormal occurrence, a vivid dream, an out-of-body experience, an experience with other dimensions, etc. The ego will struggle to figure the experience out by analyzing and rationalizing and by trying to control. But those strategies are not adequate to understand life at a Soul level. Passing the initiation has little to do with the amount of trauma or disorientation we experience. Initiation has to do with our willingness to be awakened by the experience. We must be willing, even, to *not* understand immediately what an experience means, and to trust the process, knowing that in time the learning will come.

And in time, insights would come to Jeremy, and he would continue his journey a much more seasoned traveler.

Confronting Paradox

Again, Jeremy shouted, "You tricked me!"

Undisturbed by Jeremy's screaming, the frog said calmly, "Wait. No harm came to you. You saw the Sacred Mountain, didn't you? Let go of your anger and fear. It can blind you. What matters is what happened. What did you see?"

The little mouse, still shivering from the fear or landing in the water, could hardly speak. He stammered, "The. . .the Sacred Mountain!"

"You are no longer just a little mouse. You have a new name. You are Jumping Mouse."
"Oh, thank you," said a startled Jumping Mouse.
"Thank you, thank you."

On the one hand, the frog was the one who encouraged him to take the leap which allowed him to see the Sacred Mountain. On the other hand, the frog tricked him. He landed in water! Is the frog trustworthy or is he deceptive? Who is the real frog? Divine paradox at its best!

In the Mystery tradition, the student was challenged repeatedly with paradox and required to resolve it. The resolution of the paradox is never in choosing either extreme. It is not that the frog is either deceptive or trustworthy. Either/or thinking does not bring resolution. Nor does resolution come in denial or suppression of feelings in pretending, for example, that there is no anger. Neither is there resolution in compromise, in some lukewarm midway point between the two extremes. Nor can there be resolution in trying to transcend the paradox and questing for that state of bliss beyond all experience. Certainly, we are able to transcend this third-dimensional reality, but transcendence is at a later stage in the journey, not at the beginning.

The only way out of the paradox is through it. We must accept and embrace the opposites, deal with the pain and open to the joy. On the one hand, Jumping Mouse was tricked. From another perspective, the experience was a gift. The frog was both deceptive and trustworthy. Once we accept the opposites, we can see the whole of which paradoxes are the two opposite ends. We accept light/dark, right/wrong, joy/pain, sickness/health, rich/poor, being/non-being. To embrace paradox is to learn about death, dissolution, dismemberment, sex, passion, and ecstasy, and to see the beauty in it all. To embrace paradox is to see the divine interplay between life and death, confusion and harmony, matter and spirit. It is to come to terms with the conflicting forces in nature within ourselves and within others. In the end, it is to acknowledge the divinity within paradox, to open our hearts and embrace it all.

Before he gives Jeremy his new name, the frog says, "Let go of your anger and fear." Emotions must be owned and dealt with. The challenge is to deal with them and not get stuck in them. Letting go of disturbing emotions is often a very delicate and painful process. A Zen story illustrates the point.

> Once a Zen Master and his disciple were making a long journey. When they approached a stream, there was a young woman standing there, bewildered. She could not cross on her own and did not know what to do. Without any hesitation, the Master bowed to her respectfully, picked her up in his arms, and carried her across the stream. He put her down on the other side, bowed once again, and continued on his way.
>
> Nothing was said about the experience. By the time night came, the disciple could stand it no longer. He broke the silence of the journey. "Master," he said, "I have something I must say to you."
>
> "Speak," the Master replied.
>
> "You are a Zen Master," the disciple observed. "It is not permitted for you to carry a woman in your arms."
>
> "My son," the Master replied, "I put her down on the other side of the stream, many hours ago, but you are still carrying her in your heart."

The disciple was being challenged to move through paradox and *let go*. . .and Jumping Mouse was asked to move through paradox and *let go*.

Once there was a Frog who I was convinced had betrayed me. Through him, I had definitely seen the Mountain, but I had also spent a great deal of time flailing around in the water. In retrospect, it is clear that the Frog was a perfect mirror for where I was, a reflection of what was inside me. Again, it was just a Frog being a Frog! For several years I had carried anger about this Frog, feeling quite justified about my position. But no matter how much self-justification I felt, I was the one still stuck. Like Jeremy, I was blinded by anger and fear. It was time to *let go*.

I went to a Native American Sweat Lodge Ceremony, an ancient purification ritual for healing. I entered the lodge, a small dome-shaped structure, and took my place with others around the circle and sat cross-legged on the ground. In the center was an open pit with a glowing fire of hot, volcanic rocks. The Sweat Lodge is paradoxical in its very nature. There is hot and cold, light and dark, pain and joy. If one can embrace the opposites, a greater truth enters. I sat silently for a long while in the inky darkness of the lodge and waited for clarity. I began to understand my paradox: first exalting this man who had played the role of Frog, and later discounting him. He had been both deceptive and trustworthy, a mirror for the duality within me. The more important question was: had I seen the Sacred Mountain?

When it was my turn to pray to the grandfathers of the North, South, East, and West, I asked for healing. I was told to do a ceremony: to take a clay pot and to hold it five feet above a rock and then drop it. Shattering the pot would shatter the pattern.

I waited several weeks for an auspicious moment for the ceremony. Easter Sunday morning seemed the appropriate time. I carefully selected a particular clay pot, one given me many years before by a close friend. The small earthenware vase had been my friend's first effort as a potter; at the time, we both had considered it beautiful. Over the years, her work had matured, and that same pot now seemed awkward and unrefined; it had had its time and was now outmoded. The pot was a perfect metaphor for the occasion.

I walked five miles or so down the beach, watching the ocean tide rolling in and out, nodding at an occasional passerby. After an hour or so of walking, I reached the north end of the beach, the isolated sector of the oceanfront, silent and private. Immediately I was drawn to a rock of sizeable dimension, lying in the sand. It was as though it had been waiting for this moment to give itself to ceremony. With the clay pot in my right hand, I raised my arm high above my head. I called out to Great Spirit and dropped the pot onto the rock below, where it shattered into many pieces. Instantly, I was filled with amazing sounds—beautiful, full, rich tones and counter-tones, euphonious and melodious. The music was not of this world. I knew it to be the music of the spheres. I wanted to spread my arms wide and fly like an eagle.

Scenes from childhood flashed in my mind—the many times when I would go to the precipitous edge of a steep hillside, open my arms expansively and wait with hope for the time I could fly. On the beach, I was flying, except this time it didn't matter whether my body lifted off the ground. What mattered was that my spirit was soaring.

Resolving Paradox

The frog points Jumping Mouse beyond the paradox to the greater truth. "What did you see?" If we get stuck in either/or thinking, deciding that the frog is either trustworthy or deceptive, we stay stuck in duality. Whole truth contains opposites. If we can hold the opposites, and not get stuck in either the first or second condition, we allow room for the third condition, a higher truth, to reveal itself.

It is not insignificant that this *third* condition is such a vital step in our journey. In numerology the number three symbolizes unity, the trinity, the place of harmony. In the Native American Medicine Wheel the number three is also significant. The Medicine Wheel is a metaphor for the mind. There are corridors that lead out to the four directions, the East (the mental), the South (the emotional), the West (the physical), and the North (the spiritual). Inherent in the Medicine Wheel is a five-step process that Nature gives us to make decisions. (Sometimes the entire five-step process occurs in a split second. Other times, we get stuck for months, or even years, at some place within the Medicine Wheel.) The East—the mental—is first on the wheel. It is the direction where there is unity in all things, where wisdom enters. In the direction of the South—the emotional, the second step—we deal with duality, with paradoxes. The direction of the West—the physical, step three—is the place of reconciliation of the opposites. Then we go to the North, the spiritual, to find direction and purpose and finally to the Center, which completes the circle and is the place of transformational possibilities.

It was the third step—the West—that Jeremy encountered at the moment the frog answered the accusation that he had betrayed Jeremy.

"Let go of your anger and fear. . .What did you see?" asked the frog. What did you learn from the experience? Focus on new wisdom, not old pain. Move through duality. How were you changed? In what way have you been enriched or deepened by the experience? Are you more compassionate, more genuine, more aware, more feeling? Don't waste the experience. Let it serve you.

Jeremy saw the Sacred Mountain and in so doing gained a new name. In the beginning of the story, he lived as Jeremy in Mouse Village, on the periphery of the Self. Next, he progressed to the River, which was closer to who he was. But when he saw the Mountain, metaphorically he saw the Heart of God. He caught a glimpse of his real self and his own sacred dimension.

"You have a new name," said the frog. "You are Jumping Mouse." When what we learn from any painful experience, whether it be an initiatory experience, a re-birth, a betrayal experience, or simply a difficult time, is greater than the amount of pain we have invested in it, we know that we have successfully moved through and beyond the experience. The new name is the indication that Jumping Mouse has indeed passed his initiation.

In the ancient traditions, initiations were often accompanied by physical trauma, such as physical scarring or having the Medicine Man knock out a tooth. Such shocks were the outer manifestation of an inner change. Jeremy is plunged into water. Emersion in water is associated with baptismal rites, the symbolic death to the old life and the birth of the new. As soon as the little mouse is immersed in water, the frog immediately gives Jeremy his new name, Jumping Mouse. New names often are an integral part of ceremonies and rites of passage. The new name carries with it a new vibration, a new identity, a new sense of self. Jesus re-named his disciples; gurus give spiritual names to their devotees; and Catholic nuns are given new names when they take their vows. And naming is often an integral part of both confirmation and baptismal ceremonies. The name Jumping Mouse is a reminder to the little mouse of a new identity. His former self has been transformed into a newborn being. He is no longer a little mouse limited to hurrying and scurrying with his whiskers in the ground. He is *Jumping* Mouse. He will see all of life from a much different perspective.

The Inflation Stage

Jumping Mouse stood up and shook off the water. And he shook off the anger and fear. He thought instead about the beauty of the Sacred Mountain.

He thought, "I must go back and tell my people what has happened." He couldn't wait to share. Surely, they would be eager to hear his stories of the river and the mountain.

With great excitement, Jumping Mouse set off for Mouse Village. Everyone would be so pleased to see him. And surely they would be interested in his story. Why, there might even be a celebration in his honor!

Most of us have had the experience of having a transformative experience and wanting to share it, immediately, with others, whether or not they want to hear it and whether or not it is appropriate to share! Jumping Mouse fantasized a triumphant return to Mouse Village. It would be obvious that he had had a unique experience because he was still wet from the river. Everyone would be curious about what happened to him and would insist he tell them his story. No doubt they would sit spell-bound in amazement. They might even have a party, or a celebration, just for him!

Carl Jung warns about getting over-identified with the transcendent realm. Jumping Mouse had had a glimpse of the Mountain. For a moment, at least, he had seen the other side. When the ego becomes inflated, it assumes and absorbs the manna of the transcendent realm as if it were a part of itself. This inability to differentiate *other* from *self* is called the Inflation Stage. In this state, we are similar to the infant who cannot differentiate himself from others; the ego assumes the mountain is part of itself, too. In this stage, we are attached to the result of our action. It matters what others think. We must have impact. We have to impress. We want to be noticed, to be special, to be separate.

Jumping Mouse was still new to the journey. In time, he would gain spiritual maturity and learn discernment. Some spiritual experiences are best not shared or at least not shared for some time. They need a period of incubation. We need to hold them a while in our hearts. With maturity, we eventually realize that our experiences are both highly personal and very impersonal. We don't need to be "separate" from others in order to experience sacred moments. Our experiences are unique to us and available to everyone.

> *When Jumping Mouse arrived, he was still wet. But it hadn't rained in Mouse Village and everyone else was dry! There was great discussion as to why Jumping Mouse was wet. Could it be that he had been swallowed by some horrible beast and then spit out again? That would mean there was something horribly wrong with this mouse. Fear took hold; who knew what could happen once you left Mouse Village?*
>
> *No one wanted to spend time with Jumping Mouse. His stories about the river and the Sacred Mountain fell on deaf ears.*

Jumping Mouse was crushed. We love to be valued, to be acknowledged, to be able to share who we are and what we experience and to have our identity and our experiences validated. But the real test comes when the outer world, or those persons whose responses we value, cannot or do not understand our truth. Do we give up our reality? Do we change it slightly so it can be acceptable? Do we become bitter and critical of the inadequacies of others? Do we insist on convincing others of our actuality in some desperate effort to win their favor and in so doing regain their acceptance?

Trusting Your Own Truth

Some years ago, a group gathered for a "forty days in the wilderness" experience. It was a program designed for deep inner work. Midway through the program, a young woman named Anna experienced what she considered to be a profound visionary experience. During group time, she began to describe her revelation in vivid detail. Her friends sat listening intently to the story, enthralled with her every word, inspired with the hope that they might one day have a similar experience. Everyone was captivated— everyone, that is, except an East Indian teacher who sat crossed-legged in the back of the room with his gaze focused downward. When she finished sharing her vision, he spoke in a sharp tone. "Your story, though interesting, is far from being a true visionary experience. It is pure projection and fantasy. Such experiences are born out of ego, and the ego dies hard."

There was a hush in the room. Everything changed. Suddenly, no one was interested in her experience. Her former friends suddenly were suspicious. No one believed her anymore. She felt betrayed, but she never gave up her truth. . .her belief that hers was truly a visionary experience. In her heart, Anna knew what is so well expressed in *A Course in Miracles*: "Nothing real can be threatened; nothing unreal exists."

We usually look to those closest to us for our validation. Because they matter the most, these are the ones who hurt us the most. If we depend on validation of self from others, invariably there comes a time when outside approval is withdrawn. Such experiences ultimately help us become aware of our need for healing. We are faced with our own shadows. We must confront our deepest fears. We are required to test the depth of our trust in our own truth.

Months later, that same East Indian said to Anna, "I always knew you had a true visionary experience, but I didn't know if you had the courage to trust your own truth."

> *Even though no one in Mouse Village believed Jumping Mouse, in time it didn't matter. He never forgot his vision of the Sacred Mountain. Jumping Mouse stayed in Mouse Village, but of course now life was different. But then, he was different.*

The familiar Buddhist story says it well:

> "What did you do before you became enlightened?"
> "I chopped wood, and I carried water."
> "What did you do after you became enlightened?"
> "I chopped wood, and I carried water."

CHAPTER FOUR

Facing Doubt

Jumping Mouse settled quietly into life in Mouse Village. For a while, that is. But there came a day when he knew he must leave. The memory of the Sacred Mountain was not one he could forget. He knew that somehow he must find his way there.

Once again, Jumping Mouse went to the edge of Mouse Village and looked out onto the prairie. This time, there was no raccoon waiting. There was no path, even. He knew that now he must find his own way. He looked up in the sky for eagles. It was full of many brown spots, each one an eagle. At any moment, they could swoop down from the sky. Even though his heart was pounding with fear, Jumping Mouse was determined to go to the Sacred Mountain. And so, gathering all his courage, he ran just as fast as he could onto the prairie.

Trusting the Unmarked Path

When Jumping Mouse first left Mouse Village, he was motivated more by curiosity than by conviction. He relied on the knowledge of the raccoon, a seasoned guide, to lead him to his discoveries. In the beginning of our journey too, we may need to follow the footsteps of another in order to find our way. Reliance on others is both acceptable and expected. But as the journey continues, we must make the transition from depending on others for direction to trusting within ourselves. We must find our own way on the unmarked path.

This time, when Jumping Mouse left Mouse Village, no raccoon was waiting. Jumping Mouse had to search out his own truth. Curiosity had to give way to conviction; doubt had to yield to inner certainty.

At this stage of our journey, we may be hesitant to proceed on our own. We may decide to wait for yet another Raccoon to lead us to the River. . .or remain on the banks of the River transfixed by the roar of the River. . .or retreat to the life we once knew in Mouse Village. Once we return to the status quo of Mouse Village, we can discount the significance of the River. We can convince ourselves that we never saw the Mountain. Or we can minimize the impact of the experience by reducing it to a minor incident. We can choose from a plethora of options. And we are free to stop at any point along the path.

If we want to continue on our journey, we must be willing to proceed without a Raccoon. For if we insist on depending on outside help when it is not needed, we may face dramatic consequences. The very sources which once proved reliable may suddenly become erratic and give misinformation, perhaps quite unintentionally. Or perhaps the sources we seek simply cannot, or are not, willing to assist. It is as though there is a conspiracy of a higher order which insists we pass this initiation of confronting doubt so we can move to a deeper level of inner trust.

A young American whom we will call Gordon traveled all the way to France, hoping to receive guidance from a Raccoon of his own choosing, a revered teacher. As so often happens, guidance was given, but it was far different from what Gordon had expected.

Gordon, who had been a student of ancient wisdom for a number of years, had been, during the course of his studies, particularly impressed with the works of Frederic Lionel, a Frenchman who authored a number of books on esoteric subjects. The trip to France was, in a sense, a spiritual pilgrimage; Gordon was at a critical juncture in his life. He had reached an impasse. Even though he had sensed his Sacred Call during a much earlier period, had made his way to the River, and had even glimpsed the Sacred Mountain, now he was suddenly doubting. He was indecisive. He did not know where to turn or how to take the next step.

Gordon decided to enlist the help of Frederic Lionel. If that meant a trip to France, so be it! He was determined to seek out sage words of advice from a man he considered a spiritual giant. After a series of letters and phone calls to France, an appointment was arranged. As a way of introducing himself, Gordon forwarded copies of several readings which had been given for him by well-known psychics.

At the arranged time several months later, Gordon knocked on the door of a charming Parisian flat. He was greeted cordially by Frederic Lionel's wife and then ushered into a room and seated at a small wooden table across from Frederic. In his eighties, Frederic had an imposing presence which spoke of aristocracy and nobility. He was tall and regal, and a shock of thick white hair framed his finely chiseled features. His eyes riveted Gordon with a quick glance that shot through him all the way down to his toes. Frederic made no effort to engage in small talk or social pleasantries. Instead, there was a deafening silence. Gordon inadvertently began to compare himself with the commanding presence of this legendary man and found himself lacking in the comparison. Both men sat silently, pensively, as moments extended into some indeterminable length of time. Then, with great precision, Frederic clasped his hands together, as though to gesture the coming together of thoughts. Slowly, ceremoniously, he placed his hands on the table and proceeded to look into Gordon's eyes with a penetrating gaze. His questions were equally piercing.

"Why are you here?" he asked.

Gordon gave a carefully measured response. "I want to get in touch with a voice inside that is truth, one that I can always hear."

"What are you afraid of?" responded Frederic. "Young man, do you know that your insistence on seeking outside sources has gotten you nowhere?"

He then referenced the readings which Gordon had sent ahead. "Yes, I read them. Your reliance on others has imprisoned you. Get rid of your atavism, your need to put others on a pedestal. I don't even want you to believe what I am saying. Go inside yourself. What makes you think others have better access than you do? You are looking everywhere except right where you are. How can you advance spiritually if you don't dare to become a free state of being?"

Gordon quickly responded, "I see. What you are saying is that I need to be in the center of my circle."

"No" was the answer. "You are not understanding what I am saying at all. You *are* the center of your circle. Take this project that you are beginning. It is good to have a final vision. But you make a mistake in letting the vision get in the way. You must start to let the flower unfold, without picking at the bud. Become quiet each morning. Listen to your intuition and follow what it says *now*. It may only be a small thing, like writing a letter or making a call. The important thing is that you trust what comes. Listen to what you feel. Trust it totally, and do it right away. If no response comes, it means you are not supposed to receive anything. It means your phone is busy. At those times, even if you were to listen, you could not hear. Your ego would argue and get in the way, somehow. The river is always in progress. Be in the river. It is all up to you. Do you have any more questions?"

Gordon was quiet for a moment and then said, "Nothing more."

"Good," said Frederic. "Then maybe you have understood something of what I have told you."

Gordon fell silent as he sat looking at a man who knew unequivocally that of which he spoke. Frederic's knowledge of esoteric wisdom had been fully tested in the arena of life. Gordon had heard numerous accounts of his heroic deeds during World War II, when Frederic was a recognized leader of the French underground resistance. For four years, he had managed to stay ahead of the Nazis by doing precisely what he now passed on to Gordon: Listen within—to hunches, feelings, visceral responses, intuitive flashes, and inner knowings, and trust the response.

Certainly, any lingering tendency Gordon had to continue waiting for a Raccoon had been dispelled. He had his answer—not the one he had come to hear, but the one that was needed to continue his journey.

Listening Within

With no Raccoon to guide, we, like Gordon and Jumping Mouse, must learn to listen within. How is it that most people go through enormous struggles to acquire inner trust while others seemingly have a natural propensity to trust, instead of doubting, their inner voice?

Perhaps there is no easy answer to that question, no formula or identifiable cluster of characteristics which can clearly designate what ensures inner trust. But I have noticed a striking commonality in those persons who have a natural ability to listen within. As children, they listened to and trusted outer authority which was trustworthy—outer authority which deserved their trust. As adults, they were able to shift gracefully from listening to outer authority to listening to inner authority. Children who trust false or unreliable authority, however, find it more difficult to make that graceful shift in adulthood. Consider German youth who, during World War II, listened obediently to the existing authority, or children of abusive parents who listen to also-untrustworthy authority. As adults, these children have a much more challenging task of learning to discern what is trustworthy in both their outer worlds and their inner worlds.

My father is an example of a person who had a natural ability to listen within. He not only was gifted intuitively but also had an amazing power of discernment. As a child, I observed time and time again as he would look at a person or a situation and just *know*. He had a profound, natural wisdom. No hesitation. No confusion. No vacillation. Just *knowing*.

I loved listening to his heartwarming stories about growing up in the foothills of the Blue Ridge Mountains. The tales, told in a charming Waltonesque style, reflected a love of the land and portrayed the delightful and amusing antics of his brothers and sisters. Somehow, though, I took lightly his insistence that he had always been obedient to his father. Perhaps it was the choice of the word *obedient*, which felt terribly old-fashioned and uncomfortable to young sensitive ears. But at family get-togethers, when childhood anecdotes were often retold in this family of gifted storytellers, his brothers and sisters would invariably affirm that indeed Guy, my dad, was the most obedient child. He had always listened and had done what he was told "right away."

The correlation between my father's obedience and his trust in his inner self escaped me until years later when I had a conversation with Joseph Rael, who has an indisputable link to Spirit. I was struck by the realization that this theme ran through the childhoods of both men. While Joseph and I co-authored *Being and Vibration*, we would talk about the events in his childhood. In our discussions it became clear that an essential part of his early training was to "pay attention" and "listen" to how all of life was speaking to him. Paying attention included obedience to the elders. Joseph listened well. His response to authority was always the same: immediate and consistent. That capacity to listen would prove to be critical later.

In 1984, Joseph asked Spirit for a vision which might show him how best to serve the earth and honor all life. The vision came in a flash of light. In linear time, it may have lasted only two or three minutes, but in the place where visions appear, time, as we know it, does not exist. In this vision, Joseph was told to build Sound Chambers around the world. These chambers would be places where people whose spirits and voices resonate in absolute harmony would come to balance the present, the future, and the memory of how the cosmos is oriented through the use of sound.

I was curious as to why it was he, not someone else, who was chosen to receive the vision for the Sound Chambers. Joseph says, with a glint in his eye, that he asked the grandfathers on the other side that same question. "Was it because I am talented? Because I am deserving? Because I am worthy?"

The answer was surprising and disarming. "It isn't any of these reasons. It is because you listen. We knew you would do what you were told."

Resisting Country Mouse Comfort

Jumping Mouse ran until he came to a mound of sage. He was safe now, out of view of those brown spots in the sky. He was resting and trying to catch his breath when he saw a kind old mouse, a country gentleman. This patch of sage, which was home for the old mouse, was a haven indeed. There were plentiful seeds, varieties which he had never seen, and material for making nests. So many things for a mouse to be busy with.

"Hello," said the kindly old mouse. "Welcome to my home."

Jumping Mouse was amazed. He had never seen such a place. Or such a mouse! "What a wonderful place you have. You have everything here. And you are even safe from the eagles. I have never seen such a place like this before."

"Yes," smiled the kindly old mouse, "it is safe here. And from here, you can see all the beings of the prairie. Why, there are buffalo and rabbit and coyote and fox and. . ."

Jumping Mouse listened in amazement as the old mouse named every animal of the prairie. Why, he knew all their names by heart!

"Sir, what about the river and the mountains? Can you also see them?"

"Well, little friend, you can certainly see the river. I know of the river. But as to the mountain, I am afraid that does not exist. It is just a myth, a story that people enjoy telling. Young man, take my advice and forget about the mountain. Everything you could want is here. You can stay with me for as long as you like. And besides, this is the best place to be."

For a moment, Jumping Mouse questioned his decision to go to the Sacred Mountain. He was tempted to stay put and make a life here with Country Mouse. This was such a comfortable place. And cer-

tainly it was far greater than the life he had known in Mouse Village.

There is a temptation, once we leave Mouse Village and discover Country Mouse, to become satisfied with our initial breakthrough. We decide we have found *It*. We know we have grown beyond where we were. We rationalize that we don't really need to take more risks or strive to extend our inner or outer limits. *It* is comfortable and *It* is safe. We stop growing. We become stuck in form. We settle for a mental system and forgo the heart journey.

There was a time when I, like Jumping Mouse, had to decide whether to stay with Country Mouse or leave. I was deeply involved with a spiritual organization, and, for the most part, my association with the group had been a fruitful one. But I had reached the inevitable crossroad. Change was imminent, but I conveniently avoided a decision about my future by staying in doubt and confusion. Deep down, I knew there were only two choices. Either I must make a clean break and leave the organization altogether, or I could stay. But if I stayed, it must be in a decidedly different capacity. It wasn't an easy decision. For one thing, there was a strong emotional pull from other group members, people with whom I had bonded by sharing important steps in our mutual journey. They seemed satisfied to be Country Mice and were quite convincing as they sought to encourage me, as well as others, to stay put. Country Mice want others to stay where they are. Their insistence stems both from their genuine satisfaction in the existing form and, partly, from their own fear of moving beyond the familiar.

I had to reconcile the murmurings of my heart, which were calling me to other horizons, with the loyalty I felt toward this organization, which had become my Country Mouse. The concepts learned in this organization, which had once freed me from the limitations of Mouse Village, I now found limiting.

I had vacillated long enough. It was time to make a decision. Early one morning, from that still place deep inside, I asked Spirit to give me a clear answer within twenty-four hours, one that could not possibly be missed. This ancient form of prayer, called *precipitation,* is based on the universal law which says that we create (precipitate), or draw to us, anything that our consciousness is capable of believing we deserve. The process of precipitation involves first "putting out a thought in Spirit," then letting go of all anxiety surrounding that thought, and, finally, letting go of any expectations as to the specific way the request will be answered. In this way, a void is created for something new to enter—a new thought, a new insight, a sign or a symbol.

That evening, I went to a restaurant with a group of fifteen or so people who were members of the organization. We were in a rather jovial mood, laughing and talking with an ease born out of long-term friendship and mutual experience. Halfway through the meal, something became lodged in my throat. I was choking. I could not swallow. I could not breathe. It happened so quickly that no one even noticed.

Suddenly, I was aware of two realities at once. The Physical-I was choking; the Observer-I was in another reality, witnessing the scene from above with absolute calm.

Eventually, the person sitting on my right noticed that something was wrong and began to gently pat my back. The Observer-I thought, "That is nice, but a pat on the back is not going to do it!" I tried to take a sip of water. There was no relief. I bent over in an effort to dislodge whatever it was that was stuck. That didn't work, either.

The Observer-Self was curious about the physical phenomenon of oxygen deprivation. I wondered how long a person could live without air. Did a person turn blue, pass out? Exactly what was the sequential order? Maybe it had been a long time already. Somehow, from that observer space, linear time had little relevance and certainly there was no anxiety about anything. The seriousness of the situation some- how eluded the Observer-Self. In fact, it all seemed rather amusing. Here was a table full of healers, and not one of them knew how to handle this emergency!

The Observer-Self suggested I stand up. Immedi- ately, the waiter, who happened to be a friend, sensed my difficulty. He rushed over to where I was and said, "Mary Elizabeth, you can't breathe, can you?"

I shook my head no.

Without wasting a second, he skillfully placed his hands around me in the position of the well-known Heimlich maneuver. With a quick jerk, he lifted me off the ground and dislodged the piece of food from my throat. All of a sudden, I could breathe again! I took several long, deep breaths. The oxygen was welcomed by every cell of my body. It wasn't until sometime later that I discovered my waiter friend had learned the Heimlich technique only the night before!

I had my answer. No more doubt. Spirit had responded in no uncertain terms! I was choking in this organization. My throat, the fifth chakra, the will center, the metaphor for self-expression, was being shut off. It was time for me to be on my own and make my way to the Sacred Mountain.

It is never easy to leave Country Mouse, especially when he tells us that the Sacred Mountain is only a myth! If we listen to our hearts, however, we can hear the message and know when and if it is time to leave. It is seldom that the message is given in such dramatic form as a literal choking! But if we listen, we can hear the message nonetheless.

Facing Doubt

Jumping Mouse listened carefully to the words of Country Mouse, especially what he had to say about the Sacred Mountain.

"How can you say that the Great Mountain is only a myth?" challenged Jumping Mouse. "Once I saw the Sacred Mountain, and it is not something one can ever forget."

Jumping Mouse had his own answer. He knew he must go. He thanked Country Mouse for making him feel so welcome and for sharing his home. "I cannot stay longer. I must go now, to seek the Mountain."

"You are a foolish mouse, indeed, if you leave here. The prairie is a dangerous place, especially for a little mouse! Why, just look up in the sky. The old mouse pointed dramatically to the sky. See up there? Those spots are eagles, just waiting for a little mouse. They can see for miles. And they will catch you!"

The fear that those brown spots would swoop down was actually a much greater fear of Country Mouse projected onto Jumping Mouse. What if Great Spirit were to swoop down out of the sky and take Country Mouse out of his limited ego self? What if those eagles were to lift him up to see from another perspective?

No doubt, Country Mouse had already risked once, when he left Mouse Village years ago. Now he is comfortably situated in a lifestyle and a philosophical system which works. He has gone far beyond what he knew in Mouse Village. . .You mean there might be more?

To confront Country Mouse is to confront that part of ourselves that doubts our journey to the

Sacred Mountain. How committed are we to following that which, to us, is sacred? What is it that we will not compromise? What are we willing to risk? Once we are certain about our path, the doubts and fears of Country Mouse will not matter. What we hold sacred will determine all else in our lives.

The I Ching, the Oriental book of changes, contains ancient philosophical wisdom. The book is composed of sixty-four hexagrams in which the Oracle counsels about action and attitudes that are appropriate in the midst of outer change. *The I Ching* emphasizes holding to inner values and living in harmony with the Tao in the middle of a continually changing universe.

According to the teachings, when heaven and earth come together, they give birth to the first son. The first son's name is Intuition. Intuition is the flash of inspiration, a certainty which defies the rational mind, a feeling that persists, a deep sense of inner knowing.

As soon as we give birth to our first son, Intuition, another son follows on his heels. This second son's name is Doubt, the linear, rational, reasoning mind. He tests our trust in our own truth. Doubt is the questioning thoughts which cause us to second-guess our original knowing. He is the chattering voice of our Monkey Mind that discounts and denies. And Doubt is the critical and skeptical voices of the people in our outer world who serve as mirrors to reflect our inner confusion.

Doubt comes again and again to challenge our certainty about ourselves and our choices. When we doubt, we settle. We settle for our fears, and we settle for the fears of others. We settle for beliefs which limit. We settle for the truth of others. We settle for less than what we are, for less than what could be. We settle. . .rather than trusting our in-nermost feelings.

Resolving Doubt

The I Ching tells us how to resolve doubt. Once the second son Doubt (the rational mind) is born, we must go to the High Mountain (Higher Mind). It is then that the third son, Stillness, is born. In this place we discover direct knowing.

Marie was a single woman in her late thirties in Norway who was faced with a critical choice. A highly educated professional woman, she became pregnant with a much-wanted child. Because of her age, which placed her in a high-risk pregnancy category, she was required to undergo amniocentesis.

She was stunned to learn that her unborn child carried Down's Syndrome! Her certainty about motherhood was suddenly replaced with doubt. Her doctor immediately tried to comfort her, saying, "I know this news is very hard to hear. As your doctor, it is my duty to give you my best advice. I would strongly encourage you to consider abortion as a viable option. All of my patients who have been faced with a similar situation have opted for abortion. Raising a child with Down's Syndrome is extremely difficult, especially for a single woman. You will have years of untold medical and emotional challenges facing you. And besides, you already have two healthy children. You are an attractive, intelligent and highly educated woman with your life ahead. Think of yourself." And then as a final note, he added, "Because of the rather advanced stage of your pregnancy, you have only a week to decide whether you want to terminate."

One week. Just seven days. Within that short span of time, she must make one of the most important decisions of her life! The easier course would probably be to take the very well-intentioned advice of her Country Mouse, her doctor. She would be quite justified with such a choice. Not only that, but the father of the child adamantly supported the doctor's position. It was painfully clear that a decision to keep the child would mean she, and she alone, would be the support of this child. A decision of this magnitude which involved the life of another could not be decided by logic alone. She wanted to listen to her deeper feelings, to the promptings of her heart.

Her High Mountain had always been the Dream World. Before going to bed that evening, she asked Great Spirit to come to her in a dream and grant her the wisdom to know with certainty what she should do. During the night, she had a very telling dream. In the dream, she saw her unborn son, a perfectly formed infant, but clearly a Mongoloid child. The dream dissipated any lingering hope that somehow a mistake had been made in the testing. But there was no mistake, either, in the tremendous love she felt for her unborn son. St. John of the Cross says, "Feelings are the language of God to the Soul." Theirs was a soul connection. No doubt now. This was indeed her child. Her son. The choice was no longer difficult. The next morning she announced her decision to her disbelieving doctor, her Country Mouse.

Trusting the Promptings of the Heart

A man from Norway, Ailo Gaup, had Country Mice of a different variety to confront, one that many indigenous people around the world have had to face. Ailo was born in the far north of Norway during World War II. With the war came the burning of houses and the destruction of roads. Ailo, along with many other children, was taken to a hospital for safety in the fall of 1944. His parents returned to

the tundra, and conditions prevented them from returning for a year. When his parents were finally
able to come and ask for him, the nurse at the
hospital refused to return him to them. The hospital
belonged to the Sami mission, and their unofficial
practice included, as Ailo describes it, "saving" some
children to send them south and make good Christian
Norwegians out of them. Ailo was separated from
his birthright—his family, his culture, his language,
and his land—and was sent to grow up as part of
a farm family in southern Norway. As if uprooting
a child were not enough, his new family brutalized
and terrorized him. In a sense he was their slave,
and until the age of nineteen he was so fearful of
consequences that he was afraid to leave, despite the
most deplorable circumstances.

All information about Ailo's original family and
culture was withheld. He was made to feel worthless
and was told that he would never be able to make
a life of his own. When we are severely shamed,
part of us knows that what we are told cannot be
true, but there is a part of us that is afraid that it
might be true.

Although his family discouraged education, Ailo's
one solace was reading. It was his one escape from
cruelty, his only safety from the "shadowland." In
literature he could touch feelings of love. He held
tight to the hope that if love can be written about
in books, then maybe it can exist somewhere in life.
He was determined to listen to and learn from the
promptings of his heart.

But by the time Ailo was nineteen, life had become
so unbearable for him that, after what was to be his
last beating, he lay in the barn at the point of suicide
with a knife to his own throat. Suddenly, a "spirit
of light" flew in though the wall, telling him not to
take his life. . .telling him about his path and his

destiny. That experience with light took away his sadness, his worry, and his hurt. He knew then with certainty what he must do. Ailo put his necessary belongings on his bicycle and left in the dark, in spite of the "brown spots that might reach down from the sky."

Years went by, and in time Ailo established a successful journalism career. But something deep inside him stirred. He longed to search for his biological mother and to explore his native roots. He was willing to give up all that he had, if need be, in order to satisfy this deeper calling. It would mean leaving his job and sacrificing his position on the paper. His journalism mentor, his Country Mouse, warned Ailo not to leave the security of his position for the impending uncertainty.

In spite of the admonishments and fears about what might lie ahead, that the "brown spots in the sky might swoop down," Ailo honored his commitment to himself and left for the far north. . .with no guarantees. So began the long hours of piecing together bits of information and going through the inevitable letdowns when hopes are kindled and then die sudden deaths.

In time, the painstaking research and patience were finally rewarded. The auspicious moment came when a elderly woman clothed in skins and hides entered a designated shelter in an isolated part of the icy tundra, where Ailo had been patiently waiting. The two sat across from each other in a pregnant silence; it was the long-awaited moment. Their eyes met and searched for a certainty that defies logic. Even amid the tears, he could clearly see his face in hers. There was no question, now. This woman was his mother.

She began to smoke a pipe and speak in a strange tongue which he did not understand but which stirred mysterious chords of memory. It was both the end and the beginning of a search. Although his search for his mother had ended, he would begin a lifetime quest to search the wisdom of the Lapps, also known as Sami. The journey would awaken a part of him heretofore asleep. In time, he would become a well-known shaman, a healer, and the author of numerous books and plays related to his native culture.

Of course, he could have stayed with Country Mouse.

And Jumping Mouse could have stayed with Country Mouse. For we can stop any place we want along the way. But even the fears and the doubts of Country Mouse were not strong enough to dissuade Jumping Mouse from following his own intuitive heart.

Even though Jumping Mouse listened as Country Mouse gave his fearful warnings, and even though in the sky there were still those brown spots. . .Jumping Mouse knew he must make his way to the Sacred Mountain. He stood still for a moment, took a deep breath, gathered his strength, and ran with all his might across the prairie.

CHAPTER FIVE

Opening the Intuitive Heart

*I*t was hard for Jumping Mouse to leave the comfortable life with Country Mouse. Out on the prairie was much to be afraid of. As Jumping Mouse gathered all his courage and ran as hard as he could, he could feel the brown spots flying high overhead. Would those brown spots really swoop down and catch him, just as Country Mouse had said? He shivered at the thought. He was truly in the unknown now.

All of a sudden, he ran into a stand of chokecherries. It was a wonderful place to explore. Why, there were things to gather, delicious seeds to eat, and many grasses for making nests. Jumping Mouse was busy investigating his new terrain when he saw an enormous, dark, furry thing lying motionless in the grass. He decided to climb up on it. There was a large mound to explore. There were even horns to climb on. That would be fun, thought Jumping Mouse. Immediately, he made his way on one of the horns, when all of a sudden he heard a sound. It sounded like a moan. It seemed to come from the dark furry thing! Quick as a wink, Jumping Mouse scurried down to the grass beneath. There was another moan, and the sound of deep breathing.

A voice said, "Hello, my brother."

"Who are you?" asked a curious Jumping Mouse.

"Why I am a buffalo!"

"A buffalo!" thought Jumping Mouse. Even in Mouse Village he had heard of the mighty buffalo!

Metaphor of the Buffalo

The buffalo appears at a time when it is difficult for Jumping Mouse to find his way on the unfamiliar terrain of the prairie. Mice are nearsighted. They tend to see only that which is close at hand. The old mouse way of seeing does not function well on the open prairie. If Jumping Mouse is to make his way through the challenges of this new landscape, he needs a broader perspective. He needs new inspiration. At the auspicious moment, Jumping Mouse meets Buffalo, the great giver of life.

Recently, I had the opportunity to observe a Buffalo Dance on a Pueblo reservation. The Buffalo Dance is a powerful ceremony which enacts the metaphor of how new ideas are planted in the psyche. For something new to enter, there must be an opening. We must first let go, either physically, mentally, emotionally, or spiritually. Either we willingly relinquish that which no longer serves us, or life creates situations which force us to let go. When we give up the ego, we create space for new thoughts to enter, for seeds to be planted in the psyche.

The Buffalo Dance begins when the dancers, males ranging in age from young to old, representing aspects of the masculine energy, climb out from the underground kiva. They dance first on an open space on one level and then move to a lower level, bringing to life the spiritual principle which says "As above, so below." As there is movement, or dance, which is the expansion of light in the upper world, that same movement is then brought into and expressed in the world of matter. Two men, representing the two worlds of spirit and matter, are dressed as buffalo. Their bodies are covered in buffalo skins and their heads are covered in magnificent buffalo headdresses. In their hands are long poles which they periodically poke in the earth, which is the metaphor for the self. As they poke their sticks in the earth, they symbolically plant new ideas in the earth/self. When there is an opening, or hole, in our psyche, we can receive insights from the higher dimensions. The dance dramatizes how ideas from the up-above world, or spiritual dimension, enter into the material realm.

While the buffalo poke holes in the earth, simultaneously another metaphor is being danced. At various intervals, some of the dancers, usually the younger boys, playfully run up to the buffalo, poke sticks at them, and then scurry away. The dancers want the buffalo to notice them. They want something from Spirit. They want new ideas, new inspiration, new thought. The old way of seeing life is no longer working. It has served its time. It is limited and outmoded. As soon as the dancers poke the buffalo, the buffalo, in turn, pursue and playfully poke the dancers. In a sense, the buffalo are saying, "You want something from us, but for you to receive anything, you must be open. You are blocked. You are closed off. Your ego is so strong that we will need to take our poles and poke holes in your psyche so you can give up your limited beliefs and perceptions. Once you let go of the ego, there is space. New insights can enter. We can give you new life. We can plant new ideas in your psyche."

Giving Up an Eye

Jumping Mouse had never before seen a buffalo. Certainly, no buffalo had ever lived in Mouse Village.

"What a magnificent being you are," Jumping Mouse said to Buffalo.

"Thank you, my little brother, for visiting me."

"You are lying down. What is wrong?" asked the little mouse."

"I am sick and I am dying," said Buffalo. "There is only one thing that can save me. That is the eye of a mouse. But there is no such thing as a mouse out here on the prairie!"

The eye of a mouse! Jumping Mouse was astonished! "You mean my tiny little eye could save this magnificent being?" He darted back to the chokecherries. He scurried back and forth. What to do, what to do. But he could hear the breathing of the buffalo. It was slowing down and becoming heavy.

"He will die," thought Jumping Mouse, "if I do not give him my eye. He is such a magnificent being. I cannot let him die."

Jumping Mouse knew that the only way to save the buffalo was to give up one of his tiny eyes. The only way to save the buffalo, who represents a higher, more inspired aspect himself, is to give up his mouse way of seeing. Yogis go to the Himalayas; shaman go to the desert; others enter the stillness in countless other ways. They go that they might give up limited sight and see instead with spiritual sight. Something is required; something is given.

With no time to waste, Jumping Mouse scurried back to the spot where Buffalo lay. "I am a mouse," he said with a shaky voice. "And you are such a magnificent being. I cannot let you die. I have two eyes. If my eye can save you, I will gladly give it to you."

The minute he spoke, Jumping Mouse's eye flew out of his head and Buffalo was made whole. The buffalo jumped to his feet, shaking Jumping Mouse's whole world.

What is the experience of giving up an eye? What does it mean to let go of our mouse way of perceiving?

Twenty years ago, I had a dream which indicated that 50 percent of the area in which I lived would go under water. At the time, I took the dream literally. Earth changes were quite the vogue. I was convinced the dream was an earth prophecy. The land referenced in the dream may literally one day go under water, but the more important message was the foretelling of an upcoming 50-percent change in my consciousness. I would definitely need to give up an eye. The Dream World was kind enough not to spell out the specifics of how that would unfold!

Sometimes, the "giving up of the eye" can occur only after a shock, a startling poke with the pole, which allows the space for new insight. A mother and daughter once came together for a retreat program I was conducting in England. There was a wide rift in their relationship. During the telling of their mutual stories, their psyches were poked. Disclosing previously untold parts of their individual histories allowed the possibility for a new kind of relationship to enter.

Until the program, neither the mother nor the daughter was aware of certain similarities in their childhood experiences. Ann, the mother, had been a child during World War II. Because London was so often under attack, the children of Londoners were parcelled out to relatives when possible, or to families in surrounding villages who could board children. Meanwhile, the parents stayed in the city to continue much-needed work and to maintain some sense of order and normality. The separations were painful for everyone. And visits to the country to see children were rare, since petrol was at a premium.

Ann recalled with anguish the initial, tense ride out to the countryside to her new family and the inevitable separation from her parents. What was to have been a temporary wartime situation extended into a three-year period, which was much longer than anyone had anticipated. It was an eternity for a child. The loneliness was eased, somewhat, because Ann was with her brother and they were placed with a couple who were very kind to them. Nevertheless, no matter how well-intended, her new family could never replace her real parents. She felt abandoned. An orphan child.

On one particular day, her new family announced happily, "Something wonderful is going to happen today," And, indeed it did; her mother and father came to visit! Childhood innocence returned. Ann was her real self again, happy and alive. The time with family was an enchanted interlude of warm cuddles, of walking hand-in-hand with Mom and Dad, of reading stories while sitting on comforting laps, of playing favorite games, of special talks and uproarious laughter. The magic was back!

Then, a few days later, it was over, just as suddenly as it had begun. Ann's parents announced abruptly that they had to return to London. Ann remembers being taken upstairs to her bedroom, tucked away for the night, and left alone in her room. At first, she cried silently. Then, she couldn't control the pain any longer. The sobbing became wails, deep primal moans, from a little girl with a broken heart.

Her mother rushed upstairs to her room. Ann will never forget the conversation. "I must go back to London," her mother said. "In order for me to go, you have to stop crying."

Ann's inner conflict was enormous. She wanted to please her mother she loved so dearly, and she needed to express her feelings. She made the only choice she could. She shut off her tears. Part of her died that day. She was only five.

Ironically, Katherine, Ann's daughter, had a similar trauma, also at the age of five. Katherine's father, a physician, occasionally traveled with his work. One day, when he was packing his car for a trip, something seemed different. It was unsettling and scary, an anxiety that children sense but seldom know how to articulate. Something uneasy was in the air. Something final about his departure.

No words were spoken. No explanation was given until minutes after her father had driven away. She remembers her mother sitting stoically in a rocking chair holding her baby brother, saying in a monotone voice, "Your father has left, and I don't know if he is coming back. You must be strong."

Be strong! That seemed impossible. He was the man she adored. How could she not feel? Not care? She made the only choice she could. To please her mother, she closed off her feelings. Something in her died that day, just as had happened with her mother years before.

Until that moment, neither mother nor daughter had realized that similar traumas at five caused them both to shut down emotionally. Unconscious childhood decisions had dictated their adult lives. As adults, both had issues with being able to express feelings. The mother decided that feelings are too painful. She learned to cover them up. Keep a stiff upper lip. Don't love too much. It will hurt. Katherine assumed she was responsible for her parents' separation. If she could have been nicer, if she could have been better, maybe this would not have happened. She stayed frozen in that childhood moment; part of her resisted growing up. If that is how it is to be grown up, she would simply not become an adult! Katherine became anorexic in a desperate attempt to resist maturity, to be in control in at least one area of her life.

The mother became the competent one; the daughter stayed the little girl. The mother had been irritated at her daughter for not being able to cope better; the daughter felt frustrated with the mother's demands and coldness.

Sharing the stories allowed mother and daughter to feel again. They embraced each other through heartfelt tears. A deep sisterhood began to emerge, a woman-to-woman understanding born of compassionate commonality. They both "gave up an eye." They let go of the misunderstandings about each other which had escalated through the years. The seeds of a much more genuine relationship had been firmly planted.

Then there is the story of Ellen, who had an eye of another kind to give up. During a retreat program, this time in Virginia Beach, participants were asked to spend their last afternoon in solitude. It was a time to be keenly aware of how directly the outer world reflects the inner world and to trust that what life brings to us is exactly what we need.

Ellen decided to spend her time walking barefooted on the beach and enjoying the surf of the Atlantic Ocean. She had not walked very far when she saw a multi-colored shell. Earlier in the week, it was noted in group feedback that Ellen's view of life was too polarized. She was stuck in either/or thinking. Things were either black or white, good or bad. The shell seemed to confirm her need to include more colors, more possibilities, to expand her perspective of herself and her life. She was pleased with her find.

As she continued walking, she was drawn to a lone feather lying in the sand. Not knowing why and not needing to know why, she picked up the feather and placed it in her pocket. Just as she had finished tucking away her newfound treasure, she noticed an adorable little girl, about three years old, totally absorbed in molding a figure in the sand. As she drew closer, she got a good look at the delightful fair-haired child. She had clear, sky-blue eyes, a slightly turned-up nose, and blond ringlets pulled high up on top of her head. She exuded an air of mischievousness, which made her all the more enchanting. The child, quite spontaneously, turned and smiled at the stranger. The obviously proud father sat close by, beaming, delighting in this magical child. Ellen said, "You have a beautiful little girl. Enjoy her." To which the father smiled in agreement and nodded.

Ellen flashed back to the vivid recollection of what had happened to her own little girl when she was three. Painful memories resurfaced. Like this father, Ellen had once been the adoring parent. But she had come from a severely abused childhood and was totally unprepared for parenthood. Unlike this seemingly stable father, she was an insecure, frightened mother who needed to be mothered herself.

When her daughter turned three, Ellen became afraid of her reactions to her daughter. In spite of good intentions, she found herself raging and hitting. She was repeating the same abusive behavior which she had endured. Terrified of where it might lead, she called her former husband, pleading with him to come and rescue their daughter before there was permanent damage. He took his child back. In the beginning, Ellen visited and had her daughter visit her. But circumstances changed rapidly. The father remarried and moved away and soon didn't want to share his daughter anymore with his former wife. She had, in essence, given her daughter to her husband. Legally, she had no grounds to get her daughter back. And emotionally, Ellen was too help-less to fight for visitation rights. She was too overcome with guilt and fear. Soon there was no contact at all with her daughter. The years raced. It had been fifteen years!

On her return walk on the beach, she again passed that little girl. This time the sand sculpture, which earlier had been in the beginning stages, was almost complete. With a little bit of imagination, she could clearly see the form of an angel. One of the hands was open and outstretched. Now Ellen knew what the feather was for. She gave it to the child, who smiled knowingly and promptly placed the feather in the angel's hand. It was through misty eyes that Ellen took one long last look at the little girl and waved goodbye.

As Ellen continued her walk, she saw a hotel key lodged in the sand. Intuitively, she knew exactly what the symbol was communicating. She had the key to something she had been missing for a long time!

When Ellen shared with the group that evening, she talked about the importance of the shell, the feather, the child on the beach, and the key to it all. Buffalo was asking for her eye. It was time to give up her mouse view which self-criticized and self-punished. With the new opening in her psyche, she had received new insights. She was ready, now, to do whatever it would take to be a mother and to reclaim her daughter.

By the time Ellen finished sharing her experience by the ocean, there wasn't a dry eye in the group. Some of us gave up our judgment about a mother who would abandon her child. We had eyes to give up as well.

Experiencing Synchronicity

Ellen's discoveries on the beach are examples of synchronicity, what Carl Jung calls "meaningful coincidences." It is those times when we feel a certainty that we are part of some deep oneness with the universe. At those times our outer world and our inner world unify, and the Greater Mystery lets us know when we are on track, and when we aren't! Synchronicity is a principle of the universe; thus it is always operating, even in Mouse Village. What is unique about this stage of the journey, in comparison to some earlier stage, is that by now our psyches have been "poked" somewhat. We are more able to see the Divine Play which is ever unfolding.

Sometimes the synchronistic events serve to give us confirmation that our prayers are indeed being answered. Several years ago, I suddenly developed a unexplainable longing for a rosary. Although I am not Roman Catholic, I love to pray the Rosary because of the closeness it brings to Mary. Since I was on my way to conduct a program at a Catholic convent in New York state, I decided I would purchase a rosary there. As it turned out, however, there were none for sale. When I returned home, there was a message on my answering machine from a California friend: "I have just returned from Medjugorje. The Mother told me she wants you to have a rosary. I am sending you one in the mail."

At other times, synchronistic events center around messages which Great Spirit sends in Nature. A woman on a retreat program in Hydra, Greece, had just finished processing a dream about reclaiming her feminine energy. During the break, she walked to the doorway in time to watch a giant tortoise, an ancient symbol of the feminine, cross the threshold. Nature was echoing her initiation into womanhood. What is so remarkable about the appearance of the sea turtle is that Zephra, the Retreat Center, is some 1,500 feet above sea level, and sea turtles are never seen on Hydra at that elevation!

During a retreat program in Norway, Nature brought a surprise gift to all of the participants. Originally, there was a specified limit of twelve persons for the retreat, because of the dynamics of this particular program. However, due to a mix-up in communication, thirteen persons were enrolled. Undoing the mishap would have created additional difficulties, so I agreed to include the extra person in the weekend.

The night before the retreat was to begin, I was awakened by the sounds of loud birds outside my bedroom window. I was curious as to what they were trying to communicate. The message became clear the next morning. My hostess stepped outside a moment on the balcony, which served as an extra refrigerator and which was adjacent to my bedroom. Much to her surprise, she discovered that in the early morning hours birds had broken into the cellophane package containing small loaves of bread and had meticulously taken thirteen loaves of bread, one for each participant, leaving five behind! In metaphor, birds, the messengers of Spirit, were eating bread, the beautiful light which comes from heaven. It was a clear sign that Great Spirit would be blessing each participant in a special way. Sometimes, shamans symbolically eat the shadow, or the dark negative energy, when they heal. In like manner, Great Spirit would be eating, thus transforming, each participant in the program.

The reason for thirteen participants now took on greater significance. Jesus, the thirteenth member at the Last Supper, broke bread and said, "This is my body. Eat this in remembrance of me." The number 13 also corresponds to the thirteenth path, a graduation or initiation. Once we overcome the twelve challenges, represented in the twelve houses in astrology, which are the horizontal paths in the great mandala of life, we enter the thirteenth path, the vertical path in the center of the Wheel. In Quabalistic gematria, the number 13 is the "I am" and also represents spiritual unification. It is when the Shahina is lifted, when the veil of illusion is rendered so we see God directly, face to face. The incident with the birds was Great Spirit's way of sending an affirming message to each person in the group. Each one would enter his/her sacred space, making it possible to see God more directly. That, of course, would mean coming face to face with one's own divinity.

> *Buffalo said to Jumping Mouse, "I know that you have been to the River. And I know of your quest to the Sacred Mountain. You have healed me. Because you have given so freely, I will be your brother forever. To cross the prairie, you must run under my belly. I will take you right to the foot of the Sacred Mountain. Have no fear for the spots in the sky. The eagles cannot see you while you run under me, for you will be safely hidden. All they will see is my back. I know the ways of the prairie. You are safe with me."*
>
> *Even with the confident words from Buffalo, it was frightening to be walking under a buffalo on an wide-open prairie. What about the brown spots? They were still in the sky. And the hooves were scary. What would happen if one landed on a little mouse? With only one eye, it was hard to see well enough to stay out of the way. Each time the buffalo took a step, it felt like the whole world shook. It seemed to take ever so long to walk across the prairie. But finally they stopped.*
>
> *"This is as far as I go," said Buffalo. "I am a being of the prairie. If I were to take you further, I would fall on you."*

Meetings with Buffalo

At this stage of the journey we encounter Buffalo. Buffalo are special persons who appear at auspicious moments and help take us across the prairie. They help us cross those barren places when we feel isolated and unprotected, afraid and alone.

Many years ago, when I first began my journey, I happened to quite "accidentally" come into the company of Brugh Joy, author and healer, who was in Virginia Beach for a conference. I was invited to join him in a threesome for lunch. During the course of the conversation, I had my left hand resting on the table when Brugh noticed a lapis ring I was wearing, one I had purchased in Egypt some years before. His comment about the ring triggered the spontaneous telling of a dream I had had the night before, involving the ring.

Brugh closed his eyes and went into his "Greater Brugh" self, an expanded state of awareness, which he distinguishes from his "Little Brugh," his ordinary self. From the "Greater Brugh" or Buffalo state, came some very needed insights about the dream which I had overlooked. They would help me cross my prairie. It was indeed an initiatory-level dream. How interesting that this Buffalo had appeared, just at the right moment! But then, that is the nature of Buffalo. Buffalo have impeccable timing. They know precisely how far across the prairie they should carry us and the exact place where they should stop. Though Brugh was careful to give some important clues about the dream, he was also careful not to reveal the whole symbology. The rest was for me to unravel. Unlocking the deeper levels of that dream would take several more years. But it was my task alone.

Afterwards, he said, "By the way, when you see [author and channel] David Spangler, tell him that I have been busy, so much so that I haven't been in touch, but I will write him soon."

As though there had been some mistake, I replied quickly, "Oh, I don't know David Spangler."

Nonchalantly he said, "Well, when you see him, pass this on."

It was only a week later that a friend asked me to go with him to pick up Peter Caddy, founder of Findhorn, who was speaking at a conference at the Association for Research and Enlightenment. To my astonishment, along with Peter Caddy came David Spangler, who ended up sitting next to me in the car. As Brugh requested, I passed on the message!

David smiled and said, "How like Brugh!"

We are connected in ways far beyond our knowing.

Sometimes a meeting with a Buffalo may occur without a physical meeting. We may simply hear about someone's story in a conversation and it can have impact, or we may "meet" someone in a book, or in an experience beyond this third-dimensional reality, such as in a dream or in meditation. What determines whether people are Buffalo in our lives is not whether we have seen them with our physical senses so much, but rather that they, or the energies they personify, help carry us across the prairie.

Monique had a most unusual encounter with a Buffalo. Monique is a beautiful, highly educated black woman, who lives a comfortable lifestyle. By contrast, her childhood in an inner city ghetto had been bleak. To fill the long hours when she was left alone in the apartment, Monique would sit with her face pressed against the barred window, looking out from an impoverished basement apartment, watching a strange world go by. Her mother was embarrassed by how this behavior might look to those who walked by and would scold her because she did not want her children to be seen as beggars!

Monique relished hot summer days. When the temperatures soared, the front window would stay open out of necessity, and the most aromatic smells and delectable fragrances would seep down from the apartment of a German lady two flights up. Monique would sit in the window and take deep inhalations, as though there were some unconscious, desperate hope that the smells could somehow help fill those empty places inside. The smells were goodness. It was sanity in an otherwise skewed reality. It meant somewhere there was warmth and caring and nurturing. Monique would be temporarily lifted out of her futility and the pervasive feeling of not wanting to be alive.

One imagines a blonde, stout, middle-aged *frau*, humming away, happily baking her strudel and sourdough bread in a second-floor flat. Three floors below, a dark, frail, little girl breathes as though her very life depended on it. The scintillating aroma was an umbilical cord which kept this frail child connected to life and, at the same time, lifted her spirit into another realm of possibility.

Strangely enough, Monique doesn't even remember what the German woman looked like, although she must have seen her coming in and out of the apartment. She certainly never talked to her. Nevertheless, the juncture of this nameless woman intersecting Monique's desolate existence was a foreshadowing of what would develop later as a major theme in her life. Today, as an adult, she is fascinated with food. Even the fragrances, subtleties, and delights of edible flowers have caught her fancy. It is not surprising that just as she was impacted by someone who gave her a sense of hope when there was none, Monique, now a child psychologist, offers hope to children in need. As was given to her, so she gives. Buffalo give us life that "we may have it more abundantly."

The Israeli Buffalo Woman

In my life, there have been several persons I would call Buffalo. One, whom I stumbled across on the prairie, had a major impact, even though the time spent with this person was relatively short.

Several years ago, I was in New York to give a presentation at a conference. As fate would have it, I became a last minute add-on for a dinner party in a penthouse apartment. It was a gathering where all the guests were writers or psychologists or artists, all involved, in some way, in cutting-edge thinking. The guests were expected to "sing for their supper" via meaningful conversation.

I spent the first part of the dinner talking to a psychologist who was seated on my right. Somewhere between the second and third courses, my attention turned to my left, to Dr. Jerry Epstein, author, psychiatrist, and guest of honor for the occasion. After exchanging some brief introductory remarks with Jerry, I was caught completely off guard as his tone of voice and focus of conversation completely switched. "You had a visionary experience when you were very young, didn't you?" he said, looking me right in the eye.

I almost dropped my fork. I had never met him before. He did not know me and certainly could not have had access to a very personal moment in my early life.

I was stunned. "Yes. How did you know?"

"I can read it in your face," he said. "I also had a life-changing experience, in my thirties." He referred to his teacher, a mystic, who had been extremely important in his spiritual development. When he started telling me about this eighty-year-old woman in Israel, I got a rush of energy from the top of my head to the tip of my toes. The body is the most ancient source of wisdom, one to be trusted, and that rush was a definite confirmation of a inner connection between this woman and me, one I could not ignore.

"You must go and see her," he said with authority.

I responded with an equal amount of certainty. "Yes, I will."

"January would be good."

"I can go then. I need to be in Germany the first of January. I will return home via Israel." (In retrospect, that travel route was hardly expedient, but it seemed perfectly reasonable at the time.)

"Send her your picture. Tell her I suggested you write and explain why you want to spend time with her."

I followed Jerry's suggestion and shortly thereafter received a reply from Israel and the go-ahead to continue with my plans.

Three months later, I arrived at Tel Aviv Airport. The ride from Tel Aviv to Jerusalem can be a sacred pilgrimage. As one travels the serpentine route between the two historical cities, simultaneously one winds through the delicate threads of a magnificent tapestry woven with the extraordinary colors of a rich and sacred heritage. It reflects a people with a deep faith and profound wisdom. On that particular day, however, any real appreciation of the journey was obscured by my own inner tension. Tension is a way of life in Israel. The constant threat of war keeps everyday life at a high pitch. This persuasive uneasiness, which is always in the air, as well as my travel weariness from the lengthy airplane flight culminating with the rather hostile atmosphere at the airport, combined to intensify my sudden doubts about the whole trip. There were the "could haves" to deal with. I could have stayed home and paid off my credit card. I could have researched this trip before plunging in. I could be home writing.

There were the "what ifs." What if she doesn't have much time to see me? What if my whole experience with her is a disappointment and I can't change my air ticket and leave early? What if. . .and on it went.

All concerns were born of Doubt. I was determined not to stay stuck in this state of mind. I began to dispel the doubt by going once again to the High Mountain and remembering the certainty I originally felt three months earlier in New York at the dinner party, when I first heard Collete's name. I needed to remember the universal principle that energy follows action, not the other way around. When we take a step in total trust, life responds. I reminded myself that every time I had trusted my inner feelings, life had responded. And that always, the greater the risk, the greater the benefit.

By the time the taxi arrived in Jerusalem, I was ready to enter the city and enter the experience which awaited me, whatever it might be. A quick phone call connected me with Collete. Within twenty-four hours I found myself knocking expectantly on her door and entering as the sound of a thick French Israeli accent warmly welcomed me with "Come in!"

I entered the house through an entrance hall filled with memorabilia and pictures of what appeared to be both this woman's biological family and her extended family which, no doubt, spanned the globe.

Waiting in the next room was the formidable Collete, gracefully perched on a chaise with bright Moroccan pillows plumped firmly behind her. Although she was a tiny woman, her erect posture, with her gray hair swept up high on her head and a shawl draped dramatically around her shoulders, gave her a commanding presence which defied her diminutive size. Her eyes beamed with a light that shines only in the eyes of the illumined. There sat an Israeli Buffalo woman, for sure!

"Come, sit," she said, wasting no time and pointing to a chair directly in front of her. Thus began what would be a sacred period of profound inner journeying and experiences in separate realities. Because Buffalo can dance in other realities, they are well-equipped to guide our journeys far beyond the confines of this third-dimensional world. They can dance in the fourth dimension, the psychic dimension where space as we know it does not exist and in the fifth dimension, where, mystics tell us, both space and time are transcended. And then beyond even that to the realms of archetypes and pure forms, and beyond the "beyond" to undivided wholeness. And then, in Buffalo style, they return to help us bring what comes from above so it can be planted solidly into our Earth.

It is a spiritual axiom that no one can take you deeper or higher than he has been himself. This eighty-one-year-old Jewish mystic gave unselfishly, but such is the nature of Buffalo. Country Mice, by contrast, do not have the courage to go beyond a certain point. They are restricted by their fear. But then, Collete was a Buffalo.

Despite my protests, Colette insisted there was no fee, at least on a monetary level; on the other hand, she demanded everything on a spiritual level. I am deeply grateful for her being in my life. Circumstances will perhaps preclude our meeting again. But perhaps she took me far enough.

> *"This is as far as I go, little brother," said the buffalo.*
> *"Thank you very much," said Jumping Mouse. "It was frightening crossing the prairie with only one eye. I was so afraid that one of your powerful hooves would land on me!"*
> *"You did not know, my little brother, that there was never any need for fear. For I am a Sundancer, and I*

*am always sure where my hooves land. My time with
you is over. I must go back to the prairie. You can
always find me there."*

With that, Buffalo turned and left.

Buffalo Dance Forever

When you have had a strong soul connection with
someone, the death of that person has a profound
effect. Such was my experience recently with the
passing of Paul Solomon, friend of many years, gifted
teacher, author, and channel. It was time for him to
leave and go back to the prairie. When I was informed
of Paul's death, I promptly lit a candle and kept a
flame burning for three days, as a ceremony to assist
Paul in making the transition from this life to the
next. The moment the three-day vigil was complete
and the last flickers went out from the candle, I left
Virginia Beach to present a seminar in New Orleans.
How ironic it was that this seminar was in New
Orleans, for my one visit to this magical and mysterious city had been many years before with Paul!
During that earlier trip, we were determined to experience New Orleans in grand style. There was the
late-night carriage ride through the French Quarter,
hot chocolate and beignets at the sidewalk cafe, walks
by the Mississippi River, dinner at all the best places,
jazz and more jazz, much laughter, and much joy.
We had truly celebrated life!

This trip to New Orleans was a second look at
the city, and perhaps a second look at a relationship
which had spanned some fifteen years. Just as New
Orleans is a city which contains great paradox, both
the divine and the temporal, my relationship with
Paul had included extremes, both peak experiences
and painful experiences. The relationship offered a

unique opportunity to walk through paradox and, in the end, embrace it all!

On this return visit to New Orleans I was sitting at the very sidewalk cafe where I had once been with Paul, once again enjoying hot chocolate and beignets, this time with my good friend Lynne. On this visit, rather than talking to Paul I was talking about him. Lynne had never known Paul, but as we sat and talked, it seemed appropriate that we would share in a final ceremony to honor this remarkable man. We agreed we would go together to St. Louis King of France Cathedral, which was nearby, and offer our prayers. What I wanted most was to ask the Mother to heal Paul's wounded child and to take away the pain of this man who had been the Good Shepherd to so many souls. No sooner had we agreed on the ceremony than an elementary school teacher, with students by her side, made her way to our table. There were no free tables and she wondered if we might share the extra chairs placed at our table with some of her children. Three little boys promptly took their seats with us. How appropriate that it be young boys in light of our conversation about Paul's inner child. One little boy rather dramatically propped his elbow on the table, positioned his head on his fist, and looked directly at me, as though to convey a message beyond words. "Do I know you?" he asked quizzically.

"Well," I said, smiling, "you do now!"

Hot chocolate and beignets consumed, Lynne and I crossed over to St. Louis' and entered the cathedral door. It was late afternoon, that numinous period when light gives way gently to the approaching mystery of the night, when what is known surrenders to what is unknown. We happened upon a quiet time in the church. A lone person, a man, sat by himself in a pew. I gave him only a momentary glance, noticing only the back of his head, for our attention was focused on the statue of Mary directly ahead. Once we made our way to the front of the church, we each lit a candle and knelt in prayer before the peaceful, welcoming arms of the Mother. After spending some time in a meditative mode, we walked back down the aisle and found the man still sitting in prayer. Only this time I managed to get a closer look at him. He was dressed in a red clerical collar with a large gold cross hung around his neck. What startled me was that he looked exactly as Paul did some fifteen years ago when we first met. I was stunned. It may have been an apparition. Or it may have been an amazing synchronistic event, that the one person sitting in the church when we were praying for Paul would resemble him so perfectly. Either way, the point was made. I knew that Paul, who had given me and others so much in life, was still giving, and would continue to give, this time from the higher realms.

Immediately after we stepped outside the church, a group of school boys ran up to us. They were happy children, laughing, playing, spontaneous, alive, vulnerable, trusting. I knew with certainty now that Paul was a happy child again, just as he had once been in New Orleans. No doubt, he was still celebrating life!

Buffalo continue to help others cross the prairie, even when they are in another dimension. This mighty Buffalo was still dancing. For Buffalo dance forever!

CHAPTER SIX

Inner Knowing

*J*umping Mouse was happy in his new surroundings. There were new things to investigate. There were plants in abundance and new seeds to enjoy. As he was busy exploring this new place, suddenly before him was a gray wolf. The wolf didn't seem to see the little mouse. In fact, he didn't seem to be seeing much of anything. He was just sitting there, doing nothing.

Jumping Mouse was pleased to find a new friend in the woods and spoke to him right away. "Hello, Brother Wolf."

Immediately, the wolf's ears sat up and he became alert. He looked directly at Jumping Mouse. "Am I a wolf? Yes, that is what I am. Wolf! Wolf! I am a wolf!" He seemed quite pleased with his new discovery. But then his mind dimmed again, and in a matter of minutes he had forgotten completely who he was!

Several times the same sequence occurred. The wolf would just sit, quietly staring out into nothingness, completely without memory as to who he was. Jumping Mouse would say, "But you are a mighty being. You are a wolf."

"Yes," would come the answer from the gray wolf. "I am a wolf! Yes, now I remember. That is what I am!" He would become excited once again, but soon would forget again.

"Such a great being," thought Jumping Mouse, "but he has no memory. He has forgotten who he is."

Meeting the Wise Innocent

The Wolf is the guardian of the threshold to the Sacred Mountain. He presents a paradox, for he is both an obstacle and the entry way to the mountain. The Wolf is akin to the Fool in the tarot. Within the tarot deck of cards is an ageless and ubiquitous representation of the archetypal journey. There are seventy-eight cards in all, with twenty-two major arcana cards, each with pictures which symbolically depict man's spiritual journey. The first card in the deck, and one of the major arcana, is one called the Fool, the Wise Innocent, who illustrates a reality beyond appearance.

In the tarot, the Fool is the most powerful of all the tarot trumps. He appears at the beginning of the journey and again at the end of the journey. He is both the Alpha and the Omega, the beginning and ending of manifestation. Unlike the other tarot cards, the Fool has no fixed number. Sallie Nichols explains, "The zero or 'nothing' is really something, and this 'nothing' occupies space and contains power." Because the Fool is the zero in the deck, he is free to travel at will, often in a way which creates havoc in the established order.

The Fool is most definitely an archetype to be reckoned with, one we meet in many guises. We must deal with him when he reveals himself in our inner world, and we must confront him when he appears in our outer world. In history and in literature, we learn of him in numerous portrayals. He is the Clown, the Court Jester, the Joker, the Kashari, the Trickster, and the Unexpected Messenger. He is Mishkin in Dostoevski's *The Idiot,* Parsifal in *The Holy Grail*, and Edgar, the alter ego, in Shakespeare's *King Lear.*

In *King Lear,* the central figure, rendered blind and helpless, must wander, aimlessly exposed to the wild rages of an untamed tempest from within and without. It takes Edgar, disguised as a fool, to guide Lear through a reconciliation of the extremes which in turn enables him to eventually assume a kingly clarity. Paradoxically, the way to true sanity is often through the safe passage between childishness and madness. The Fool can masterfully play the seductive devil, luring us to madness; at the same time, he is the potential Savior who helps us find our way to salvation. In the A.E. Waite tarot deck, the symbolical representation of the Fool reflects the opposites he embraces. On the one hand is the Innocent. His garments are flowered. There is a knapsack slung over his shoulder, and he carries a rose in his left hand. He is an androgenous being, a happy blend of both masculine and feminine qualities. Looming in front of him is a dangerous precipice, but in spite of the impending danger (the madness that he is one step away from) the young Fool prances along without a care. His head is tilted upwards, sheathed in cloudy dreams, oblivious to harm, with a heart which longs for romance and adventure. Like Parsifal in *The Holy Grail*, he is naive. He has no notion of what question to ask of life or even if one is required. By his side is a little dog, his instinctual self, the primal power of the Creator, who can both sense danger and help him avoid it. The Fool's redemption lies in his innate simplicity and trust. He fears nothing, for he knows that he is always guided and protected. He trusts God implicitly. And like all fools, he somehow survives, in spite of himself, for he has been touched by the Hand of God.

It is that very simplicity and trust which is required for one to be allowed entrance into the Sacred Mountain, the Heart of God within ourselves. When we meet the Wolf, our tendency might be to dismiss, negate, or avoid him altogether. After all, the Wolf has no memory. He is just a fool! But to dismiss the Wolf would mean that we would not find the Mountain and never fully discover our intuitive and compassionate selves.

The Magus of Strovolos, otherwise known as Daskalos, the amazing Cyprian healer, speaks of the three attributes of the Absolute: total wisdom, total power, and total goodness (what he also calls love). They are likewise the attributes within ourselves that must come into balance. In Nature, which is the macrocosm, the triangle is always balanced. In the microcosm within ourselves, however, the inner triangle is often an isosceles triangle, a triangle in the process of becoming isometric and balanced. At this stage of one's journey, it is quite possible that a person may have acquired both knowledge and power. But Daskalos warns about the necessity of acquiring the third quality, goodness (or love). He says that when an individual has only knowledge and power and lacks goodness (or love), a Satanic condition prevails. A demon is, after all, an "incomplete god." The closer one is to balancing his triangle, the closer one is to self-realization.

"Except Ye Become as a Little Child"

Jumping Mouse looked at the wolf and saw that he had no memory. But he also knew the wolf to be "a great being." Jumping Mouse looked at the wolf the way a child sees, with goodness, with pure innocence and an open heart. Jesus said, "Except ye become as a little child, ye shall not enter the kingdom of heaven."

I am reminded of Annie, a little girl who lives in Atlanta, Georgia, who, like Jumping Mouse, was able to see the Wolf when it crossed her path. Annie had that extraordinary quality of goodness which enabled her to see into the hearts of people and help them remember who they are. Why, Annie could even see inside stuffed animals! A conversation once overheard between Annie and her Mother went something like this:

"Oh, Annie, you have so many stuffed animals. Why, I can hardly find you in bed at night because of all your animals."

"Mom, to you they may just be stuffed animals. But to me, they have heart and soul."

With such a compassionate heart, it is not surprising that all of Annie's friends, including those stuffed with cotton, held important places in her life. But of her many friends, it was Jason to whom she was most loyal. For Jason was, according to Annie, her best friend and the "kindest person I know."

Seeing the two of them together was sheer delight. It was a magical blend, indeed! There would be Jason, smiling broadly, towering at least six inches over the head of his little Annie, who, in turn, would be looking up adoringly at her trusted friend. At times, you could catch glimpses of them playing their favorite game, He-Rah and She-Rah. They would spend endless hours chasing happily about, exuding joy and laughter, arrayed in homemade costumes, complete with flowing capes, wands, and sparkling headgear.

Jason and Annie attended the same school. There, however, the inseparable twosome were apart. In fact, they seldom saw one another, for Annie was placed in the gifted program for high-achievers while Jason was placed in a special education class for the mentally impaired.

In their neighborhood, there was predictable chatter about Jason. Parents were concerned about the effect

Jason might have on their "normal" children. Annie, however, like Parsifal, was not concerned about conventional good manners and the advice of elders. She was guided more by feelings, the "language of God to the soul." Annie could see inside Jason in a way that others could not. Just being around Annie somehow made it easier for others to see as well. When parents saw how much Annie cared for Jason and that being with him had not slowed her down, even one bit, they began to change their views. In time, Annie gave many people an appreciation of Jason.

And it was Annie who could help Jason "remember" who he was, especially during those times when he would get discouraged. "Come on, Jason, you can do it! I know you can." And somehow, assured by Annie's words, he would manage what, for him, had seemed the impossible.

When Annie was nine, Jason and his family moved away from the neighborhood. It was a sad farewell for two devoted friends. As a going-away gift, Jason gave Annie a "gold" ring. Of course, she would sometimes need to wash off the band of black which would appear on her finger underneath the ring. Nevertheless, for several years, that ring remained her most precious possession.

Mother Teresa was once asked, "There are so many people in India who are in need. What is it that one can give to them?"

Her response was, "Give them their dignity." I think Annie would understand.

Jumping Mouse would help the wolf remember who he was for a moment, but then he would forget again. Jumping mouse wanted to help his new friend. "If giving up an eye could help the buffalo, then maybe I could give up my eye to the wolf and he would be

well, too." This time there was no hurrying and scur-
rying around. And there was no need to ask anyone
else for advice. He knew how to find his own answer.
This time, he went to a peaceful spot and sat quietly.
In the silence, he listened to his heart. It told him
exactly what he must do.

To enter the Sacred Mountain, we first must see, or recognize, the Wolf, as did Annie, and then we must heal the Wolf. The Wolf is that aspect of ourselves who forgets who we are. We are gods and goddesses with amnesia. We momentarily forget our true nature. . .our divinity. As we see and heal our Wolf selves, we unleash our own instinctual selves. As with Parsifal, the Fool's connection with his instinctual side has the potential to save not only himself but all humankind.

I remember a story Elizabeth Kubler Ross shared. The story went something like this. . .She was travel-ing by herself somewhere in Europe, not as Elizabeth Kubler Ross, noted psychiatrist and authority on death and dying, but simply as a woman, traveling alone, like many others, with no special identity.

She arrived at the train station in plenty of time before departure and looked for a place to sit. Her attention was immediately drawn to a forlorn-looking boy, about thirteen years old, sitting slumped over on one end of a bench. He was overwhelmed with sadness. . .He had forgotten who he was.

So as not to disturb him, she sat down on the far end of the same bench. Her heart reached out to the young boy. Nothing was said; nothing needed to be said.

She sat for a long time in the silence, listening within. After a long, pregnant pause, she said simply, "Rough, huh?"

The youth nodded, mumbling a weak, "Yup."

They sat for some fifteen or more minutes, communicating nonverbally. She sat, as did Jumping Mouse, listening to her heart. It told her exactly what to do.

"That rough, huh?" she said.

"Yup."

With that, he slowly lifted his shirt up to expose a back with raised welts, still raw and red, evidence of a brutal beating from his father.

She sensed the moment and slid over on the bench, to sit closer to the boy. At least an hour remained before the train would come. She would know what to share. It would probably be the most important hour in this young boy's life. And perhaps it was a special hour for Elizabeth Kubler Ross, for all healing is self-healing.

Giving Up Another Eye

Wasting no time, Jumping Mouse hurried back to where the wolf was.

"Brother Wolf," he called out.

"Wolf? Wolf?" came the still-confused response.

"Brother Wolf, listen to me. I know now what will heal you. If I could give an eye to a buffalo and it would heal him, then I will gladly give you my eye."

No sooner had he said the words than the last eye of the little mouse flew out of his head. Now Jumping Mouse had no eyes. But that didn't seem to matter so much. What mattered was that the wolf was whole again. He could remember who he was.

Giving up the last eye requires us to surrender those remaining limited parts of self which prevent us from being able to totally trust within. Once we begin to listen with our hearts as did Jumping Mouse with the wolf, we must expect inner changes and, in all probability, outer changes as well. Most likely, the world we consider safe, familiar, and reliable may suddenly be shattered or be turned upside-down. And this shift can occur in the twinkling of an eye. The dramatic changes, the flip-flops, the sudden turn-arounds, the wrenching away from what we have thought was our security, all serve the greater purpose: to shift our focus from reliance on the outer to trust in the inner.

The story of the initiation of one man, Frederic Lionel, is told through a tale of espionage and true adventure in *Challenge: On Special Mission*. Frederic was living in France at the beginning of World War II when Germany suddenly invaded France. The world he relied on ceased to be. Frederic, a Frenchman who was fluent in German, offered his services to the British Government to initiate a rescue service for those wanting to escape from France to England. He was one of the first to develop a link between the Fifth Column and the Underground Movement in France. Thus began four years of high-level espionage work with the Underground Movement in France.

His book, at one level, is a gripping tale of adventure and intrigue. But at its most profound level, it is an account of the demanding training of an initiate. Frederic went through hair-raising adventures in order to make a breakthrough in consciousness. Through his experiences, he developed a highly sensitized intuition which eventually would enable him to instantly respond with total obedience to the promptings of the still, small voice within his own mind and heart. Not only his life, but the lives of many came to depend on his ability to trust solely in an invisible guidance which worked through the very center of his consciousness.

Seeing With No Eyes

Not everyone is required to experience war settings to learn total trust in the Higher Self. Experiences vary from person to person and seemingly are tailor-made to the precise needs of each individual. The circumstance in which one finds oneself are not what matters so much. What does matter is that one makes the shift from dependence on the limited sensory world of this third-dimensional reality to trust instead in the world of Spirit and the higher dimensions where we see with no eyes. It is here that we see with inner sight, a knowing born of compassion, intuition, and discernment. Like Jumping Mouse, we listen with our heart and know exactly what to do.

One who "sees with no eyes" is my dear friend, Ann Maria. When I worked as a cancer therapist many years ago, there were times when I felt that I needed more insight about certain patients in order to be of greater value. When I needed confirmation in pinpointing a deeply veiled core issue, or simply when I needed extra help with a patient, I would call on Ann Maria, who at that time lived in New York. I would set up a three-way phone conversation: Ann Maria, me, and an exceptional nine-year-old boy who also "sees with no eyes." When I gave them the name of a particular patient, they would then proceed to see that person, not with physical sight but with spiritual sight. They would describe the patient and illness, as well as the underlying cause of the illness, and suggest possible methods of helping the patient. In addition, they always offered prayers for the patient and his family. Ann Maria preferred being anonymous. The patients were never told about the unseen help they were receiving. But they were frequently puzzled by the sudden and often dramatic changes in their conditions.

Even as a child, Ann Maria could see in ways that others could not. One day, when Ann Maria was seven, she was spending time alone in the flower garden behind her house. A large white rose caught her attention. She picked the rose, being careful not to disturb its beauty, and then proceeded to sit on the grass and enjoy its exquisite form. She became aware of a soft, warm light from above which began to shine directly on the roses's fragile petals. The rose began to glow with an effervescent light. And the air was filled with the special ambiance of a pungent yet delicate scent.

Suddenly, in her peripheral vision,, she saw the sandaled feet of someone standing nearby. Although this stranger appeared unexpectedly, she was not frightened. He brought only peace. Her eyes moved from his sandals to the hem of his robe and then upwards. He was dressed as a Franciscan monk, in a long, dark-brown cloak, loosely belted at the waist with a knotted cord. A shawl collar framed a young man's face with eyes so compassionate that they could look deep inside, all the way to the soul. It was a look which never invaded, only loved.

She asked the stranger, in her childlike innocence, how he was able to be there. He just smiled. He took a step forward, took his hands out of his robe, pushed his right sleeve up slightly, and then placed his hand on the top of her head and blessed her. Her first communion would be in a few days. She wondered if he had come to celebrate this special event. When he was through blessing her, she offered him her rose. He smiled and graciously received her gift. With rose in hand, he disappeared, just as suddenly as he had first appeared.

Somehow she knew to "hide these things in her heart," in the Biblical sense. Only her father was privy to what had happened. He confirmed what she already knew: "Keep it to yourself!" As a young Catholic, Ann Maria knew the names and stories of many saints. She assumed the familiar stranger was St. Francis, even though the face of the man in the garden was not quite how she had pictured St. Francis. It was not until years later, when she took a pilgrimage to Capuchin Monastery in San Giovanni Rotondo at Foggia, Italy, that she knew the true identity of the person who had appeared years earlier in the garden. When she walked into the Rotondo of the monastery, there stood the same monk who had blessed her as a child. He was with the other monks, greeting the fifty or so persons who were gathered for Mass. His face was older, and he had grown a beard, but his eyes were unmistakably the same eyes she had seen as a child—kind, compassionate, and infinitely loving. She knew him, now, to be Padre Pia, a remarkable Italian monk. His words to her were, "I have been expecting you."

Ann Maria eventually learned that Padre Pia had accepted her and two other motherless children to be his Spiritual Children in 1918, the year Ann Maria's mother died. Unknown to Ann Maria, she had lost her mother and had been adopted at the same moment. Padre Pia recorded Ann Maria's name, her date of birth, and the name of her mother in a diary, which was a record of his revelations. (This information was documented and later sent to Ann Maria following Padre Pia's death.) Padre Pia had never been told anything about a little girl born in Brooklyn, New York. How could he possibly have known the needs of a child who lived all the way across a vast ocean? How little we know of the mysteries!

Padre Pia was said to have had many gifts, including bi-location, the ability to be in two locations simultaneously, which Ann Maria witnessed as a child, as well as the gifts of healing, prophecy, levitation, discernment, perfumes, and stigmata. Perhaps it is because of the blessing from Padre Pia, or perhaps for reasons quite unrelated to him, Ann Maria has many of these same gifts herself.

The term *hypertext* has been used to explain the process whereby you push one button and the entire range of information about a subject becomes available, as if it were a computer data base. Ann Maria describes her process of knowing in slightly different terms; she speaks of going "behind the veil" or going "into the silence." From that deep, still place of total trust within come the revelations, the positive knowings.

Not all of those who see with no eyes are mystics as are Padre Pia and Ann Maria. But there is a distinctive quality about people who are at this stage of the journey. They have a rare combination of both a highly developed intuitive sense and an enormous capacity for love.

Some years ago, when I was at a critical juncture in my life, my Aunt Nita, my father's sister, unexpectedly called from Washington, D.C. I hadn't heard from her in two years, so it was most auspicious that she would pick that particular night to call!

"Betty, I just had to call you tonight. Something told me to do so. I just want you to know how much you are loved. You are a part of our family and you always have a place in my home and in my heart." Tears ran down my face. Like the Wolf, I had been forgetting who I was. I needed a reminder. I could hear both my earthly father, deceased now for some years, and my Heavenly Father speaking through her. The timing was perfect. How like Aunt Nita to call at this moment. Even as a child, I was aware of her ability to know things others were not aware of.

As it turned out, I had an upcoming conference in Washington, and, even though I had already made reservations at a hotel, the synchronistic call signaled the need for an abrupt change of plans. I looked forward to this opportunity to stay with my aunt, for, as a child, staying with my aunts in the big city was a highlight of the summer. There was Chinatown, movies, restaurants, shopping, and amusement parks. It didn't seem to matter what we did; it was always fun! Aunt Nita was ninety-four now, and blind. She shared her home with her half-sister, my Aunt Alice Mae, who was now in her seventies. And I would be with them again, after all these years.

When I pulled in front of their house on Shepherd Street, I was stunned. Had it shrunk? Surely, the house was bigger than this. As a child I had thought this two-story, four-bedroom structure enormous. The yard had been a child's wonderland, with nooks and crannies that lent themselves as secret hiding places where one could go undetected during Hide and Seek. By contrast, now the yard looked quite manicured and the house certainly ample, but no way near the proportions I remembered.

Inside, very little had changed. Just as I had remembered, there was the rose-colored carpet, the marble fireplace, the same draperies, now slightly faded, and the carefully positioned furniture. In the bedroom where I used to sleep was the same rose-pink, floral wall paper and the tiny ballerina on the porcelain bed-side lamp, which when I was a child would dance me to sleep each night.

And Aunt Nita, a widow for some years now, was still as warm-hearted, outrageous, and funny as ever! Alice Mae, with incredible patience and dedication, tried to keep Aunt Nita in tow. They were a delightful "odd couple" indeed!

"How are you doing, Betty?" came the warm welcome from Aunt Nita. "It is so good to see you.

You are looking wonderful. Of course, I can't see a thing, but I know you are doing fine!" And out came one of her contagious belly laughs.

Although her spirit was intact, age had taken its toll. Aunt Nita's body was stooped, and she walked with the aid of a walker. What little hair she had left was concealed under a turban which she insisted Alice Mae place on her head. "Now, how do you like my hat? Isn't that something? I just wanted to dress up when I knew you were coming." Again, more warm-hearted laughter.

As we sat down in the living room to catch up on talk about her children, grandchildren, great-grandchildren and her church, as well as what was what was wrong in the White House (all her favorite subjects), the conversation was interrupted by a phone ringing.

"Alice Mae, get the phone!" came the direct orders of Aunt Nita.

Alice Mae responded in her gentle way, "Did the phone ring? I didn't hear it!"

To which Aunt Nita said, "Honestly, they think I am deaf and they think I am blind, but I have to tell them when the phone rings and what is going on!" And there would be more light-hearted laughter.

In the morning I said a hurried goodbye and rushed off to a full day of conference activities. When I returned that evening, I made a point to be early. Trying to be considerate of their advanced age, I turned the key at shortly after 10:00 PM, expecting to find the house quiet and everyone sound asleep. Instead, things were buzzing! Lights were on, Aunt Nita was on the phone, laughing and talking, and Alice Mae was busily engaged in some project of her own. "What are you doing home so early?" they asked.

"I thought you might be asleep. I didn't want to disturb you."

"Oh, for heaven's sake, no! We are just a bunch of gypsies around here. We are liable to go to bed almost anytime. We do what we want to do!" And reels of more laughter.

Aunt Nita and I had one last talk before I left Washington. "Now, Betty, your father told me many years ago that I would live to be ninety-five," she said. "Your father was right about most things, and I have known for some time he is right about this too. So, in case I don't see you again, on this side, I will see you on the other."

With that, I went up to Aunt Nita so I could pour my love into her with one last hug. I wanted to etch her clearly in my memory, the way one might do who has no physical eyes. I placed my fingers gently on her face and began to trace her high check bones, her marvelously smooth brow, the slight indentation in the center of the forehead, the noble, straight nose, and the firm jawline. So many feelings surfaced. Her head was almost identical to that of my father. And I had touched his head in similar fashion just before he died.

Aunt Nita's last words to me were, "It was wonderful seeing you again." Of course, she hadn't seen me with physical eyes, but then she had seen me. And she had given me an "eye." It was her love that helped me remember who I was.

> As soon as the eye of the mouse went into the wolf, he was healed.
>
> Tears started to flow down the wolf's face. Of course, Jumping Mouse could not see him because he had no eyes. He was blind. But even without eyes, he could see that the wolf was whole again. Now, the wolf could remember who he was.
>
> "Thank you, Jumping Mouse, for healing me."

CHAPTER SEVEN

With the Eyes of an Eagle

"*You have healed me,*" *said the wolf, as tears ran down his cheeks. "Thank you, my little friend. Now I can remember many things. I am the guide to the Sacred Mountain and to the Great Medicine Lake. And it is your time to go there. You are blind, so you must follow close beside me. But I know the way, and I will take you there.*"

The wolf, with his little friend close beside, slowly made his way through the tall pine trees to the edge of the Sacred Lake. Unlike the river which roared as it rushed over rocks, the lake sat in perfect stillness. "This lake," said the wolf, "is more powerful even than the mighty river. For this is a Medicine Lake. It reflects all the world, all the people of the world, the lodges of the people, and all the beings of the prairies and the skies. It is said that he who drinks of this Sacredness is given the wisdom to understand the mysteries of life."

Jumping Mouse leaned down and drank the cool, refreshing water from the Sacred Lake.

The wolf said, "This is where I must leave you, little friend, for I must return. There are others I must guide. But if you want, I will stay with you for a while."

"Thank you, my brother, but you must go, and it is my time to be alone." Even though Jumping Mouse was trembling with fear, he said goodbye to his friend.

Jumping Mouse stood alone and trembling, sensing what was to come. He knew, somehow, that an eagle would find him. All of a sudden he could feel a shadow on his back. Then he heard the noise of a giant eagle swooping down, coming closer. He braced himself for what was to come...the noise grew louder, an enormous swoosh...then, a thump on his back. Jumping Mouse fell into a deathlike sleep.

The Final Surrender

In many of the ancient traditions, in the myths and in the legends, the hero/heroine falls into an deathlike sleep just prior to the final initiation. In the myth *Eros and Psyche,* Psyche must descend into the underworld to complete her final challenges as a mortal. Her last task is to bring back an unopened vial of beauty ointment to Aphrodite, with a strict admonition not to open the vial. Psyche encounters the paradox: does she listen within or do as she is told? She follows her own promptings and opens the flask. Immediately she falls into a deathlike sleep. Alas, it appears that all is lost. Paradoxically, just the opposite is true. She passes her final initiation because she both demonstrated trust in her own inner authority above all other authority and demonstrated the discernment to know the right timing and the right action. If either action or timing were amiss, she would have failed the initiation. Psyche is subsequently lifted out of her deathlike sleep and taken to Mt. Olympus, where she, no longer a mortal, is transformed into a goddess.

In the Christian Mysteries, Jesus was placed in a tomb for three days, after which he overcame death and was resurrected into a new life. Likewise, in the Egyptian mysteries, the initiates lay in state, again for a three-day period, and demonstrated mastery over death and this third-dimensional reality by leaving their physical bodies and traveling into other dimensions. And mystics in many traditions describe a "dark night of the soul," a deathlike period of total isolation and desperation before their final illumination.

When don Juan pushes Carlos Castenada into another state of being, he hits him in the back between the shoulder blades with the palm of his hand. In a sense it is a death, death to the limited Carlos and the resurrection of the awakened Carlos. Likewise, when the eagle swooshes down and hits Jumping Mouse, the touch of the eagle induces him to fall asleep into the nether world.

"We make vessels of clay," observed Lao-tzu, "but their true nature is in the emptiness within." To contact this natural emptiness is the object of the spiritual practices in many traditions. We return to the place of the inexhaustible well of silence. It is from that still, primal silence that existed before the first word of creation that we replenish our spirit. To find a new creative word, we must plumb the primal silence and return to that point of light before thought.

T.S. Eliot, in *Four Quartets*, so poignantly expresses this state of total emptiness:

> I said to my soul, be still, and wait without hope
> For hope would be hope for the wrong thing; wait without love
> For love would be love of the wrong thing; there is yet faith
> But the faith and the love and the hope are all in the waiting;
> Wait without thought, for you are not ready for thought;
> So the darkness shall be the light, and the stillness the dancing.

Joseph Rael describes darkness as the "blowing breath that has eyes to see." Darkness is a profound teacher. One can learn something of her mysteries in the countries of the Far North. Norway, land of the midnight sun, has a compelling beauty, especially in the dead of winter when there are precious few hours of daylight. When we are unaccustomed to this more somber side of nature, the preponderance of darkness feels unfamiliar and hauntingly strange. It can be threatening, for we are conditioned with negative images about nighttime and darkness. Once we become accustomed to a world where nature is black and gray and diffuse, unformed and unknown, we gradually embrace the darkness. Within it we discover great peace. Black is the Deeper Self, the Breath, the Great Mystery, the Divine Feminine, the Infinite Void from which all comes. It teaches us to let go, to surrender, and to "give up our last eye." No need to know. No concern about past, no worry about the future. Only trust. Only the moment. The exquisite state of no thought. Silence. Being.

Entering the Stillness

"The Journey Into Silence" is a short story to tell but it can be a very long story to live. Like Jumping Mouse, one begins the journey in a rather bewildered state. It takes some time before one can trust the innermost stirrings of the heart and move through expectations, words, thoughts, and emotions to the silence which is at the center of the self. A favorite Zen story says it well.

A young man once approached a Master. "Master," he said, "I want to learn about wisdom. Would you teach me the way?"

"You may accompany me on my way, if you so choose," the Master replied.

"Oh, thank you, Master!" said the pleased disciple.

The two set out, walking together in silence. It wasn't very long before they entered a very dense forest. They continued walking. Again, no words were spoken.

The disciple began to lose his patience and become quite irritated. "The old man is walking so slowly," he thought to himself. "We will never get anywhere! Besides, he promised to teach me the way to wisdom. How can I learn anything like this? Days have gone by, and he has not said one word to me! What kind of a teacher is he?"

At that moment, the Master stopped abruptly and turned to the disciple. "What do you hear?" he asked.

"Hear?" replied a disgusted disciple. "I do not hear anything in this miserable forest!"

To that, the old man simply nodded. And continued on his way.

They walked on and on, without saying another word. Again, the Master stopped. "What do you hear now?" he asked.

"I hear something very beautiful! I hear the songs of a thousand birds and the wind making music in the trees!" the disciple exclaimed. "Why, this forest is full of life! Master, thank you for bringing me to this wonderful place. Let us stay here."

The old man simply nodded. And continued on his way.

They walked together, in silence. This time they walked for a very long time. At length, the Master stopped. "Now, what do you hear?" he asked.

"I hear the babbling of the brook. The sound comforts me," the disciple replied.

The old man nodded. And continued on his way.

They continued to walk together in silence, on and on, deeper and deeper into the forest. Then the Master paused again. "What do you hear now?" he asked.

This time the disciple whispered, "I hear the silence at the center of the forest. All is peace."

The old man said nothing, only nodded. And continued on his way.

They walked on in the silence together for what may have been many years. Then, one day, the Master stopped. He turned to the disciple and asked, "What do you hear now?"

The disciple turned toward the Master and smiled gently. This time he said nothing. Instead, he bowed to his Master.

And the Master then bowed to his disciple. "I will no longer have to accompany you on your way," he said.

The disciple nodded. And continued his way. Alone.

Becoming an Eagle

The metaphor of total surrender and the full awakening to the transcendent reality is beautifully enacted during the Picuris Pueblo Pole-Climbing Ceremony, in Northern New Mexico. This ceremony takes place annually on Feast Day, August 10. In the center of the pueblo stands an enormous wooden pole, towering at around fifty feet, which has been made from a fallen tree stripped of bark and limbs. Tied to the top of the pole is the carcass of a dead sheep (foundation of life), a watermelon (embracing betrayal), and loaves of bread (beautiful light). Every year, a *kashari* (*pa-wai-eh na* in Tiwa), also known as a clown, climbs the pole. In metaphor, the one who climbs the pole keeps the channels open to the Higher Realms. He is also the one who brings down abundance for the community and for the people.

As a preliminary to the pole-climbing ceremony, the *kashari,* with bodies and faces covered in black and white, entertain with their antics. The clown is the ubiquitous joker, the fool who is a combination of wisdom, madness, and folly. At every possible opportunity, the clowns embarrass and shock people. They make others both laugh at themselves and laugh at others. When the pole-climbing begins, everyone laughs at the clowns as they make their purposely foolish attempts to climb the pole and then fall down, over and over again. On one level, we can dismiss the clowns. They are just being silly. Maybe they have lost their memory, as did the wolf. They don't seem to know who they are.

But the clown teaches us that appearance and reality are not synonymous. See through the illusion. The world that we see is not what we perceive it to be! Just when we are convinced that what the clowns are doing is just buffoonery, one of the clowns begins to seriously climb the mammoth pole. He pulls with both arms, using his legs to brace himself and in that manner shimmies rhythmically up the pole. It is a breathtaking sight to see—ancient, primal, alive! As the clown ascends the pole, metaphorically he is going up the various levels of consciousness.

Each year it is the same ceremony and each year it is a different ceremony. During a recent Feast Day, one of the clowns made it halfway up the pole and then suddenly stopped climbing. It would seem that he had the physical prowess to go the rest of the way, yet he simply stopped. He placed his head against the pole, and his mouth was moving, as though he were speaking with Spirit for permission to continue the climb. He had reached an impasse. Like Jumping Mouse, he had entered a void, a darkness, an abyss which he could not cross. He came down and attempted the climb again. The same thing occurred. Again, he was blocked from going any higher. The portal of the gates of the higher dimensions was closed. It was not his time; he was not the one to complete the climb. He came down the pole and another *kashari* took his place. This time when the same spot in the pole was reached, the portals opened and he climbed effortlessly all the way through the impasse to the top, to the higher realms of consciousness, beyond form, to the state of emptiness. The *kashari,* the clown, the fool, both the alpha and the omega, takes us to Nothing, to zero, the perfect symbol of the state of undivided wholeness before the creation of things. This nothing is outside time and space. It is pure nature, pure being, the essence behind the veil.

When a *kashari* reaches the top, all eyes are fixed on the pole. Perched high on top, the *kashari* confidently unties the ropes (being watchful of thoughts) and lets down the sheep, the bread, and the watermelon to the people below. His majestic form is dramatically silhouetted against an open blue sky. He is fluid yet solid, graceful yet powerful. At this point in the ceremony, he no longer seems the clown; he has been transformed into another form. From that high place, he looks more like an eagle, a Great Being who is at home in the clouds, at home in the Mind of God!

> *Much to Jumping Mouse's surprise, he began to awaken. The surprise of being alive was great. And he could see! Even though everything was blurry, he could see colors and they were beautiful.*
>
> *"I can see! I can see!" said Jumping Mouse over again and again.*

A blurry shape started to move near Jumping Mouse. Jumping Mouse squinted hard, trying to see, but the shape remained a blur.

"Hello, brother," a familiar voice said. "Do you want some medicine?"

"Some medicine? Me? Yes! Yes!"

"Then," said the voice, "what you must do is crouch down as low as you can, and jump as high as you can."

Jumping Mouse did exactly what he was told. He crouched as low as he could and jumped as high as he could! Suddenly, a wind caught him and began to lift him higher and higher.

"Do not be afraid," the assuring voice called out. "Ride the wind. Hang on to it. It will carry you...TRUST!"

Jumping Mouse did as he was told. He closed his eyes and let go. The wind began to carry him. The wind, the breath of Great Spirit, lifted him higher and higher. This time, when Jumping Mouse opened his eyes, they were clear. The higher he went, the clearer they became. He could see with the eyes of an eagle. He could see through things and into things. He could see miles away. He could see in the Spirit Way.

As Jumping Mouse looked down, way below was his old familiar friend. There was the frog, sitting on a lily pad on the beautiful medicine lake.

"You have a new name," called the frog. "You are no longer Jumping Mouse. You are Eagle!"

So ends the story of Jumping Mouse. May you find yourself somewhere in this journey. May you see with new eyes.

May Your Heart be Opened and May your Spirit Soar like the Eagle!

The Story of Jumping Mouse

Once there was a mouse named Jeremy who, like all the other mice, lived in a little village hidden away in the woods. He was always busy, doing the things that mice do, running and jumping, looking and searching, hurrying and scurrying, to and fro. It seemed he was always in motion. In fact, he hardly ever stood still. And, like the other mice, he couldn't see very far. Nor was he able to see very clearly. For mice, as you may have noticed, usually have their whiskers in the ground.

One day Jeremy began to hear a new strange sound, one he had not heard before. It was a roar coming from somewhere out in the distance. Now, Jeremy was used to the sounds of the forest. He knew the different sounds of the two-legged and the four-legged and the winged and the hoofed. But this was unlike anything he had known.

Sometimes, he would stop everything and lift his head to the direction of the roar. He would strain to see what might be there, and he would wiggle his whiskers hoping to sense something in the air. What could it be, he wondered?

Jeremy scurried up to a fellow mouse and asked him, "Brother Mouse, do you hear a sound, a roaring in your ears?"

The other mouse didn't even bother to lift his whiskers out of the ground. He was too busy. "No, no, I don't hear anything. And besides, I don't have time to talk." And off he went before Jeremy had a chance to say anything more.

Not to be easily discouraged, Jeremy decided to ask another mouse the same question. Maybe this mouse had heard the sound.

The second mouse looked at him in a most peculiar way. "Sound? What sound?" And before Jeremy could stop him long enough to describe what he had heard, the second mouse scampered off, disappearing behind the pines.

When none of the other mice knew anything about the sound, Jeremy decided that the best thing he could do would be to forget about the whole thing and get busy. He knew how to be a busy little mouse. And so he started hurrying and scurrying to and fro once more.

But no matter how busy he was, he would still hear the sound. He tried to pretend that it had disappeared. But even when he tried not to hear it, he knew it was still there!

Jeremy became more and more curious about the sound. So one day, he decided to go off by himself and investigate. It was easy to scurry off from the other mice. They were too busy to notice he had gone anyway.

When he was off by himself, the sound was stronger and much clearer. Now he could sit quietly and listen hard.

Jeremy stood on the edge of Mouse Village and looked back at the only life he had ever known. He sat listening to the sound for a long time. But he knew he could no longer be content to just listen. It was time to discover more about this sound. He turned to face another direction. He looked out into the darkness of the vast unknown and boldly left Mouse Village.

Jeremy was listening hard to the sound in the distance, when suddenly he heard someone say, "Hello, Little Brother." Jeremy was so startled he almost ran away. "Hello," again said the voice. It sounded friendly enough.

"Who are you?" asked the timid little mouse.

"It is I, Brother Raccoon. You are all by yourself, Little Brother," said the raccoon. "What are you doing here all alone?"

Jeremy was embarrassed. He didn't want to have to talk to anybody about the sound. Especially not after what happened in Mouse Village.

"I heard a sound," he said timidly. "A roaring in my ears and I am investigating it."

"A roaring in your ears? You mean the River," said the raccoon, without any hesitation. "Come, walk with me. I will take you there."

"Once I find out about this River, I can go back to my work and my life in Mouse Village," thought Jeremy. "Why, I will even ask Raccoon to return with me. If the mice in the village don't believe me, they will surely believe a raccoon."

Little Mouse walked close behind the raccoon, so as to be sure not to lose his way. His heart was pounding. He had never known such excitement. They wound their way through a cathedral forest of tall evergreens. There was an intoxicating smell of pine and cedar. As they drew closer to the River, the sound became louder. The air became cooler, and there was a fine mist. There was a sense that something important was about to happen. Suddenly, they came to the River! The mighty River! It was so huge that Little Mouse could not see across it. And it roared, loudly, rushing swiftly on its course, coming from some other place, going to the great unknown.

"It's powerful!" the little mouse said, fumbling for words.

"Yes, the river is a great thing," answered Raccoon, "but here, let me introduce you to a friend."

In a smoother, shallower place was a lily pad,

bright and green. Sitting upon it was a frog, almost as green as the pad it sat on. The frog's white belly stood out clearly.

"Hello, Little Brother," said the frog. "Welcome to the river."

"I must leave you now," cut in Raccoon, "but do not fear, Little Brother, for Frog will care for you now."

"Who are you?" Jeremy asked.

"Why, I am a frog."

"A frog?" questioned Jeremy. He had never seen a frog before. "How is it possible to be so far out in the mighty river?"

"That is very easy," said the little frog. "I can go both on land and on water. And I can live both above the water and below in the water. I am the Keeper of the Water."

Jeremy was astonished! He tried to think of words. He had never met the Keeper of the Water. But no words came.

Without hesitating, the frog said, "Little Mouse, would you like some Medicine Power?"

"Medicine Power? Do you mean for me? Yes, of course. What do I do?" asked the eager little mouse.

"It is not that hard. All you need to do is crouch down real low and jump up as high as you can."

"That's all?" asked Jeremy.

"Yes. Crouch down as low as you can and jump up as high as you can! That will give you your medicine!"

Little Mouse did exactly what the frog told him to do. He crouched down as low as he could and jumped as high as he could. And when he did, his eyes saw something even more powerful than the mighty River. He saw the Sacred Mountain.

How long Jeremy gazed at the Sacred Mountain, we can't be sure. For such moments exist in a space somewhere beyond time. But suddenly, everything changed. Instead of landing on familiar ground, the little mouse splashed down in water. And mice, as you know, can't swim very well. Jeremy was terrified. He flailed his legs about, trying to keep head above water, choking and sputtering, struggling for his very life. He was frightened nearly to death. Finally, he managed to make his way to the river bank.

"You tricked me. . .you tricked me!" Little Mouse yelled at the frog.

Undisturbed by Jeremy's screaming, the frog said calmly, "Wait. No harm came to you. You saw the Sacred Mountain, didn't you? Let go of your anger and fear. It can blind you. What matters is what happened. What did you see?"

The little mouse, still shivering from the fear or landing in the water, could hardly speak. He stammered, "The. . .the Sacred Mountain!"

"You are no longer just a little mouse. You have a new name. You are Jumping Mouse."

"Oh, thank you," said a startled Jumping Mouse. "Thank you, thank you."

Jumping Mouse stood up and shook off the water. And he shook off the anger and fear. He thought instead about the beauty of the Sacred Mountain.

He thought, "I must go back and tell my people what has happened." He couldn't wait to share. Surely, they would be eager to hear his stories of the river and the mountain.

With great excitement, Jumping Mouse set off for Mouse Village. Everyone would be so pleased to see him. Why, there might even be a celebration in his honor!

When Jumping Mouse arrived, he was still wet. But it hadn't rained in Mouse Village and everyone else was dry! There was great discussion as to why Jumping Mouse was wet. Could it be that he had been swallowed by some horrible beast and then spit out again? That would mean there was something horribly wrong with this mouse. Fear took hold; who knew what could happen once you left Mouse Village? No one wanted to spend time with Jumping Mouse. His stories about the River and the Sacred Mountain fell on deaf ears.

Even though no one in Mouse Village believed Jumping Mouse, in time it didn't matter. He never forgot his vision of the Sacred Mountain. Jumping Mouse stayed in Mouse Village, but of course now life was different. But then, he was different.

Jumping Mouse settled quietly into life in Mouse Village. For a while, that is. But there came a day when he knew he must leave. The memory of the Sacred Mountain was not one he could forget. He knew that somehow he must find his way there.

Once again, Jumping Mouse went to the edge of Mouse Village and looked out onto the prairie. This time, there was no raccoon waiting. There was no path, even. He knew that now he must find his own way. He looked up in the sky for eagles. It was full of many brown spots, each one an eagle. At any moment, they could swoop down from the sky. Even though his heart was pounding with fear, Jumping Mouse was determined to go to the Sacred Mountain. And so, gathering all his courage, he ran just as fast as he could onto the prairie.

Jumping Mouse ran until he came to a mound of sage. He was safe now, out of view of those brown spots in the sky. He was resting and trying to catch his breath when he saw a kind old mouse, a country gentleman. This patch of sage, which was home for the old mouse, was a haven indeed. There were plentiful seeds, varieties which he had never seen, and material for making nests. So many things for a mouse to be busy with.

"Hello," said the kindly old mouse. "Welcome to my home."

Jumping Mouse was amazed. He had never seen such a place. Or such a mouse! "What a wonderful place you have. You have everything here. And you are even safe from the eagles. I have never seen such a place like this before."

"Yes," smiled the kindly old mouse, "it is safe here. And from here, you can see all the beings of the prairie. Why, there are buffalo and rabbit and coyote and fox and. . ."

Jumping Mouse listened in amazement as the old mouse named every animal of the prairie. Why, he knew all their names by heart!

"Sir, what about the river and the mountains? Can you also see them?"

"Well, little friend, you can certainly see the river. I know of the river. But as to the mountain, I am afraid that does not exist. It is just a myth, a story that people enjoy telling. Young man, take my advice and forget about the mountain. Everything you could want is here. You can stay with me for as long as you like. And besides, this is the best place to be."

For a moment, Jumping Mouse questioned his decision to go to the Sacred Mountain. He was tempted to stay put and make a life here with Country Mouse. It was such a comfortable place. And certainly it was far greater than the life he had known in Mouse Village.

Jumping Mouse listened carefully to the words of Country Mouse, especially what he had to say about the Sacred Mountain.

"How can you say that the Great Mountain is only a myth?" challenged Jumping Mouse. "Once I saw the Sacred Mountain, and it is not something one can ever forget."

Jumping Mouse had his own answer. He knew he must go. He thanked Country Mouse for making him feel so welcome and for sharing his home. "I cannot stay longer. I must go now, to seek the Mountain."

"You are a foolish mouse, indeed, if you leave here. The prairie is a dangerous place, especially for a little mouse! Why, just look up in the sky. The old mouse pointed dramatically to the sky. See up there? Those spots are eagles, just waiting for a little mouse. They can see for miles. And they will catch you!"

Even though Jumping Mouse listened as Country Mouse gave his fearful warnings, and even though in the sky there were still those brown spots. . .Jumping Mouse knew he must make his way to the Sacred Mountain. He stood still for a moment, took a deep breath, gathered his strength, and once again ran with all his might across the prairie.

It was hard for Jumping Mouse to leave the comfortable life with Country Mouse. Out on the prairie was much to be afraid of. As Jumping Mouse gathered all his courage and ran as hard as he could, he could feel the brown spots flying high overhead. Would those brown spots really swoop down and catch him, just as Country Mouse had said? He shivered at the thought. He was truly in the unknown now.

All of a sudden, he ran into a stand of chokecherries. It was a wonderful place to explore. Why, there were things to gather, delicious seeds to eat, and many grasses for making nests. Jumping Mouse was busy investigating his new terrain when he saw an enormous, dark, furry thing lying motionless in the grass. He decided to climb up on it. There was a large mound to explore. There were even horns to climb on. That would be fun, thought Jumping Mouse.

Immediately, he made his way on one of the horns, when all of a sudden he heard a sound. It sounded like a moan. It seemed to come from the dark furry thing! Quick as a wink, Jumping Mouse scurried down to the grass beneath. There was another moan, and the sound of deep breathing.

A voice said, "Hello, my brother."

"Who are you?" asked a curious Jumping Mouse.

"Why I am Buffalo!"

"A buffalo!" thought Jumping Mouse. Even in Mouse Village he had heard of the mighty buffalo!

Jumping Mouse had never before seen a buffalo. Certainly, no buffalo had ever lived in Mouse Village.

"What a magnificent being you are," Jumping Mouse said to Buffalo.

"Thank you, my little brother, for visiting me."

"You are lying down. What is wrong?" asked the little mouse."

"I am sick and I am dying," said Buffalo. "There is only one thing that can save me. That is the eye of a mouse. But there is no such thing as a mouse out here on the prairie!"

The eye of a mouse! Jumping Mouse was astonished! "You mean my tiny little eye could save this magnificent being?" He darted back to the chokecherries. He scurried back and forth. What to do, what to do. But he could hear the breathing of the buffalo. It was slowing down and becoming heavy.

"He will die," thought Jumping Mouse, "if I do not give him my eye. He is such a magnificent being. I cannot let him die."

With no time to waste, Jumping Mouse scurried back to the spot where Buffalo lay. "I am a mouse," he said with a shaky voice. "And you are such a magnificent being. I cannot let you die. I have two eyes. If my eye can save you, I will gladly give it to you."

The minute he spoke, Jumping Mouse's eye flew out of his head and Buffalo was made whole. The buffalo jumped to his feet, shaking Jumping Mouse's whole world.

Buffalo said to Jumping Mouse, "I know that you have been to the River. And I know of your quest to the Sacred Mountain. You have healed me. Because you have given so freely, I will be your brother forever. To cross the prairie, you must run under my belly. I will take you right to the foot of the Sacred Mountain. Have no fear for the spots in the sky. The eagles cannot see you while you run under me, for you will be safely hidden. All they will see is my back. I know the ways of the prairie. You are safe with me."

Even with the confident words from Buffalo, it was frightening to be walking under a buffalo on an wide-open prairie. What about the brown spots? They were still in the sky. And the hooves were scary. What would happen if one landed on a little mouse? With only one eye, it was hard to see well enough to stay out of the way. Each time the buffalo took a step, it felt like the whole world shook. It seemed to take ever so long to walk across the prairie. But finally they stopped.

"This is as far as I go," said Buffalo. "I am a being of the prairie. If I were to take you further, I would fall on you."

"Thank you very much," said Jumping Mouse. "It was frightening crossing the prairie with only one eye. I was so afraid that one of your powerful hooves would land on me!"

"You did not know, my little brother, that there was never any need for fear. For I am a Sundancer, and I am always sure where my hooves land. My time with you is over. I must go back to the prairie. You can always find me there."

With that, Buffalo turned and left.

Jumping Mouse was happy in his new surroundings. There were new things to investigate. There were plants in abundance and new seeds to enjoy. As he was busy exploring this new place, suddenly before him was a gray wolf. The wolf didn't seem to see the little mouse. In fact, he didn't seem to be seeing much of anything. He was just sitting there, doing nothing.

Jumping Mouse was pleased to find a new friend in the woods and spoke to him right away. "Hello, Brother Wolf."

Immediately, the wolf's ears sat up and he became alert. He looked directly at Jumping Mouse. "Am I a wolf? Yes, that is what I am. Wolf! Wolf! I am a wolf!" He seemed quite pleased with his new discovery. But then his mind dimmed again, and in a matter of minutes he had forgotten completely who he was!

Several times the same sequence occurred. The wolf would just sit, quietly staring out into nothingness, completely without memory as to who he was. Jumping Mouse would say, "But you are a mighty being. You are a wolf."

"Yes," would come the answer from the gray wolf. "I am a wolf! Yes, now I remember. That is what I am!" He would become excited once again, but soon would forget again.

"Such a great being," thought Jumping Mouse, "but he has no memory. He has forgotten who he is."

Jumping Mouse would help the wolf remember who he was for a moment, but then he would forget again. Jumping mouse wanted to help his new friend. "If giving up an eye could help the buffalo, then maybe I could give up my eye to the wolf and he would be well, too." This time there was no hurrying and scurrying around. And there was no need to ask anyone else for advice. He knew how to find his own answer. This time, he went to a peaceful spot and sat quietly. In the silence, he listened to his heart. It told him exactly what he must do.

Wasting no time, Jumping Mouse hurried back to where the wolf was.

"Brother Wolf," he called out.

"Wolf? Wolf?" came the still-confused response.

"Brother Wolf, listen to me. I know now what will heal you. If I could give an eye to a buffalo and it would heal him, then I will gladly give you my eye."

No sooner had he said the words than the last eye of the little mouse flew out of his head. Now Jumping Mouse had no eyes. But that didn't seem to matter so much. What mattered was that the wolf was whole again. He could remember who he was.

As soon as the eye of the mouse went into the wolf, he was healed.

Tears started to flow down the wolf's face. Of course, Jumping Mouse could not see him because he had no eyes. He was blind. But even without eyes, he could see that the wolf was whole again. Now, the wolf could remember who he was.

"Thank you, Jumping Mouse. You have healed me," said the wolf, as tears ran down his cheeks. "Thank you, my little friend. Now I can remember many things. I am the guide to the Sacred Mountain and to the Great Medicine Lake. And it is your time to go there. You are blind, so you must follow close beside me. But I know the way, and I will take you there."

The wolf, with his little friend close by, slowly made his way through the tall pine trees to the edge of the Sacred Lake. Unlike the river which roared as it rushed over rocks, the lake sat in perfect stillness. "This lake," said the wolf, "is more powerful even than the mighty river. For this is a Medicine Lake. It reflects all the world, all the people of the world, the lodges of the people, and all the beings of the prairies and the skies. It is said that he who drinks of this Sacredness is given the wisdom to understand the mysteries of life."

Jumping Mouse leaned down and drank the cool, refreshing water from the Sacred Lake.

The wolf said, "This is where I must leave you, little friend, for I must return. There are others I must guide. But if you want, I will stay with you for a while."

"Thank you, my brother, but you must go, and it is my time to be alone." Even though Jumping Mouse was trembling with fear, he said goodbye to his friend.

Jumping Mouse stood alone and trembling, sensing what was to come. He knew, somehow, that an eagle would find him. All of a sudden he could feel a shadow on his back. Then he heard the noise of a giant eagle swooping down, coming closer. He braced himself for what was to come. . .the noise grew louder, an enormous swoosh. . .then, a thump on his back. Jumping Mouse fell into a deathlike sleep.

After a while—we have no way of knowing how long, since time in such experiences has no mean-ing—Jumping Mouse began to awaken. The surprise of being alive was great. And he could see! Even though everything was blurry, he could see colors and they were beautiful.

"I can see! I can see!" said Jumping Mouse again and again.

A blurry shape started to move near Jumping Mouse. Jumping Mouse squinted hard, trying to see, but the shape remained a blur.

"Hello, brother," a familiar voice said. "Do you want some medicine?"

"Some medicine? Me? Yes! Yes!"

"Then," said the voice, "what you must do is crouch down as low as you can, and jump as high as you can."

Jumping Mouse did exactly what he was told. He crouched as low as he could and jumped as high as he could! Suddenly, a wind caught him and began to lift him higher and higher.

"Do not be afraid!" the assuring voice called out. "Ride the wind. Hang on to it. It will carry you. . .TRUST!"

Jumping Mouse did as he was told. He closed his eyes and let go. The wind began to carry him. The wind, the breath of Great Spirit, lifted him higher and higher. This time, when Jumping Mouse opened his eyes, they were clear. The higher he went, the clearer they became. He could see with the eyes of an eagle. He could see through things and into things. He could see miles away. He could see in the Spirit Way.

As Jumping Mouse looked down, way below was his old familiar friend. There was the frog, sitting on a lily pad on the beautiful Medicine Lake.

"You have a new name," called the frog. "You are no longer Jumping Mouse. You are Eagle!"

Appendix

EXPERIENTIAL GUIDE

*Rituals, Ceremonies, Exercises,
and Reveries to Accompany*
Jumping Mouse

*The experiential guide is designed for persons who
have read* Jumping Mouse *and would like to go
deeper in the exploration of their own journey. The
rituals, ceremonies, exercises, and reveries are created
for individuals, couples, and groups.*

CHAPTER ONE: MOUSE VILLAGE

Journal the following questions and/or share in a
group.

1. *What activities keep you "hurrying and scurrying"
   in your Mouse Village?*
2. *Which of these activities could you eliminate?*
3. *What family "rules" still govern you but no longer
   serve? Identify separately Mother "rules" and
   Father "rules." Name one or two rules for each
   parent.*
4. *What "rules" by society, community, church, or
   organizations govern you but no longer serve?
   Choose one or two.*
5. *When I am in Mouse Village I _____.
   Describe yourself. Be honest and be amused.*

Medicine Shield
(Individual and/or Group)

Draw a large circle on a piece of paper or on a cloth. Make eight equal-size segments. You will be asked to draw, paint, or sew a symbol for each segment of the story. In so doing, you create your own unique Medicine Shield, a symbolic representation of sacred images that depict your journey and serve to empower you.

In the first segment of the circle, draw a symbol that represents your life in Mouse Village. If you are sharing this ritual with a group, allow enough space and time for everyone to share their symbol.

Saying Good-bye to Mouse Village:
Father Loss/Mother Loss

Journal the following questions by yourself; share the questions with a partner or with a group. The group pairs off in twos. Think of your father when he was a child. Both partners journal his positive and negative traits. Place an empty chair in front of you. One partner holds sacred space; the other talks out loud to the "father." There is power in giving voice to feelings and thoughts. The roles are then reversed.

Complete the following sentences:

1. *I think I still blame you for* _____.
2. *What I resent about you is* _____.
3. *The losses that resulted from you not meeting my needs are* _____.
4. *It has made it hard for me as a man/woman to* _____.

5. *I have been stuck in (bargaining, blaming, anger, sadness, etc.) while grieving the father loss I experienced.*

6. *I am not yet ready to let go of _____ and I accept that I have to do more work on this.*

7. *I know now as an adult that things in your life made it hard for you to give me what I needed. I am ready to release my feelings about _____.*

8. *What I thank you for and appreciate about you is _____.*

Release your father and say good-bye in such a way that will let him go and will set you free.

Repeat the same process, this time with your mother.

When the process is complete, partners share their experiences and insights with each other.

Rite of Passage Ceremony

This powerful ceremony helps a person at any age complete his/her initiation into manhood or womanhood. The intent of the ceremony is a shift in consciousness, from outer authority to inner authority.

Six people are needed to perform the ceremony: the candidate for initiation and people to role-play the Shaman, Mother Earth, Father Sky, the candidate's mother, and the candidate's father. Persons play either sex. Several groups with six persons can perform this ceremony simultaneously. If there are more than six people, but not enough for a second full group, then start with six people and allow others to come in and change places with the original six as the ritual proceeds.

Each person in the group has a turn to be a candidate for initiation. For the first ceremony, people choose who they want to role-play. For each subsequent ceremony, roles are rotated automatically, as each person moves to the role on their left. There is no set script for any role. Participants speak what they feel guided to say. (This ceremony also serves as a wonderful experience in trust. People are often amazed at the insights they are given as they take on various roles.)

Diagram for Rite of Passage Ceremony

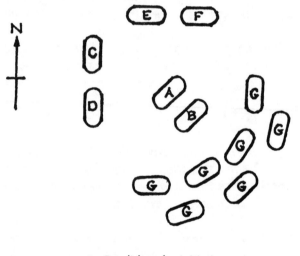

A. Candidate for Initiation
B. Shaman
C. Mother
D. Father
E. Mother Earth
F. Father Sky
G. Group

Mother Earth and Father Sky stand side by side in the direction of the North, facing southward. The parents stand side by side in the direction of the West, facing east, toward the group. The Shaman introduces the candidate for initiation. He speaks to the "people," to the seen and unseen presences who have gathered to witness and participate in this rite of passage. All have gathered to enable (name candidate) to shift from outer authority, symbolized by the parents, to inner authority, symbolized by Mother Earth and Father Sky.

The Shaman takes the arm of the candidate and escorts them to a position standing and facing their parents. The Shaman says that he brings their son or daughter to share some final words as he/she prepares to make this important step into full womanhood or manhood. The Shaman then steps back and becomes a witness.

The candidate speaks to each parent individually. He/she states what they will no longer carry and want to give back and what they appreciate and want to take from each parent.

Example: *I want to acknowledge the positive things I learned from you about what it means to be a woman. You taught me softness and nurturing. You were always there to support me. I knew I mattered. That is the greatest gift a mother can give her child. You knew how to comfort me, how to make me feel safe. I always had a place with you. That has made it possible for me to know how to nurture myself and how to nurture others. I thank you for that.*

I give back the confusing messages about male-female relationships. I learned that women endure and suffer. That belief has caused me a lot of pain. That is your truth. I give it back to you. I am no longer willing to believe that I must sacrifice myself to get love. I want to experience relationships that are balanced and supportive. And I am learning how to create that in my life.

Suggestions for what to keep:

strong faith
joy in the little things of life
fairness with all family members
model of a healthy spousal relationship
clear guidance
healthy sexuality
the trust you had in me
the courage to risk
how to laugh at myself and at life
willingness to listen
commitment, responsibility

Suggestions for what to give back:

responsibility for living a parent's unlived life
guilt for being the child who lived (when a sibling died)
secrecy and uncertainty, which has made me create and expect chaos
distrust of the opposite sex
overconcern about other people's opinions
overcontrol and manipulation as a way of relating
harsh judgment of others
mother's or father's unresolved pain

Each parent speaks after the candidate has spoken to them. They will sense what needs to be said. When the parents finish, they sit down together, symbolizing that they have completed their parenting task.

The Shaman escorts the candidate to Mother Earth and Father Sky: "I bring you (name), who has learned what is needed from his/her parents and has dropped all blame. He/she comes seeking your guidance and wisdom. The Shaman steps back. The candidate stands and listens attentively as Mother

Earth and then Father Sky speak. The candidate makes no response, only listens.

Mother Earth and Father Sky speak according to the promptings of their heart. The messages are personal and relevant to the individual candidate. Below are suggestions of how to begin.

Mother Earth, the feminine aspect of God, speaks first.

Welcome, my daughter. I have been watching you, (give name), for many years and have been waiting for the time when you would turn to Mother Earth for your wisdom and nurturing. Now is that time. I will. . .

Mother Earth is associated with receptivity, nurturing, intuition, interrelatedness of all things, softness, timing, understanding the cycles of things, stillness, quiet strength, fierce mother love, inner knowing, abundance, giving, etc.

Father Sky is the masculine aspect of God.

I welcome (name of the candidate). There is much that I want to give you, my daughter. When you need strength, when you need inspiration. . .look up in the sky. I am there. When you are confused, be open to my clarity. I am always there to. . .

Father Sky is associated with clarity, strength, awareness, focus, commitment, inspiration, insight, etc.

When both Mother Earth and Father Sky have finished blessing the candidate, they sit down, symbolizing that there is no longer any need for dependence on outer form. The candidate closes his/her eyes, puts his hand on his heart, turns clockwise saying several times: "Tah Chee Who" (I walk with God).

Hearing "The Call": Guided Reverie
(A group leader is needed to facilitate this experience. Have the group sit in a circle.)

Close your eyes. Take several deep breaths. . .letting go completely. Play soft flute music in the background (Suggested music: Side 1 of "Nikai Canyon Trilogy").

Begin to breathe deeply. . .listen to the flute music. In metaphor, the flute is a hollow tube through which Great Spirit descends. As you hear the lyrical sounds, become open, receptive, like a hollow tube. . .allow the Divine Feminine, the descending light, to totally fill your body. . .Become more and more relaxed. Very quiet. Very still. Go deep inside. . .ask Spirit to help you hear and know your "call." Be open to insights, deep knowings, feelings, thoughts, images, metaphors, etc. Continue to breathe.

What is it that stirs you at this time in your life? What moves you? What are your deepest feelings? Where does your energy want to be? What matters? What pulls you? What is important? Spend several minutes allowing yourself to experience whatever surfaces.

Begin to come back. Slowly move your hands and feet; slowly move your head from side to side. Open your eyes.

The group leader asks the following questions, pausing after each one. Each person answers in the quiet of their own inner selves. They may want to journal their answers.

1. *What feelings did you experience? Be aware of contradictory or opposing feelings. Be willing to hold opposite feelings without needing to choose one feeling over another.*

2. *Title your "call" as you would title a chapter in a book. For example:*

> *Going Home to See Where I Am*
> *Bold New Beginnings*
> *Reunion*
> *Putting My House in Order*
> *Transition*
> *"Nesting" Time*
> *Sedona, Here I Come!*

3. *Was anyone in your reverie? What aspects of self do they represent?*

4. *Were there any metaphors or symbols? What meaning do they hold for you?*

5. *Is this call one that emerged only recently? Is it something you have felt for a long time?*

Re-enter the guided reverie. Play the same music as before.

Close your eyes. . .breathe deeply. Revisit the scene from the earlier experience. What quality do you need to awaken in order to answer this call?. . .patience, boldness, openness, daring, etc. Breathe in those qualities. What action steps, if any, do you need to take? See yourself effectively doing those tasks. What, if anything, do you need to accept? What, if anything, do you need to release?

When you are ready, begin to come back. Open your eyes.

Medicine Shield

Draw, paint, or sew a symbolic representation of "the call" in the second segment of the Medicine Shield. Allow time for group sharing.

Prayer Mound

If you are outside, create a small prayer mound, an earth circle twelve to eighteen inches around and twelve or so inches high. If you are inside, make a sacred circle, which will be a prayer mound. At the end of each chapter, a group leader, or a member of the group, goes to the prayer mound and reads an appropriate selection from the corresponding chapter. He/she says a few words about the significance of the animal archetype. The mouse is *(say a few words about the meaning of the mouse archetype)*. I place this mouse on the mound. It is a metaphor that signifies that as a group, we have met and acknowledged our mouse and are ready to continue on our journey.

CHAPTER TWO: LEAP OF FAITH

Identifying Raccoons

The Raccoon is a guide, a way-shower, the midwife who helps with the birth of new consciousness. Journal the following questions and/or share in a group.

> 1. *Who was your first Raccoon? (high school coach, music teacher, neighbor, precipitous meeting, book, etc.)*
> 2. *What insight did the Raccoon bring?*
> 3. *What change, or shift, did you make as a result of meeting this Raccoon?*
> 4. *Who, or what, is the most recent Raccoon in your life?*
> 5. *What has been the effect on your life?*

Medicine Shield

Draw, paint, or sew a symbolic representation of a significant Raccoon in the third segment of your Medicine Shield. Share.

Leap of Faith

At some time in our journey, we are asked to "jump as high as we can" with no certainties of how, or even if, things might turn out. The more daring the leap, the more the reward. Journal and/or share with a partner or in a group the following questions:

1. *What, thus far, has been your biggest "leap of faith"?*
2. *What have been the rewards of making this leap?*
3. *In what area of your current life (self-identity, career, relationships, creativity, etc.) do you need to "jump as high as you can" in order to: move from one condition to another, move from one stage to another, or begin or end something decisively?*

Leap of Faith Ceremony

Make a bonfire or build a fire in a fireplace or build a small fire in a ceremonial bowl. Place one candle for each person in front of the fire, to be lit at the end of the ceremony. Fire is a metaphor for courage, inspiration, passion, commitment, will, desire, intent. The fire you make on the outside is the fire you want to ignite on the inside. Clarify your intent. What inner qualities do you need in order to make a leap of faith in a particular area of your life?

Hold the focus on that intent during the ceremony. Dance "for" something.

Begin the ceremony by dancing. You can dance by yourself, with a partner, or in a group. Drum, chant, or use any music you find inspiring—music that opens you to new possibilities. Suggestions are: the music of Gabriel Roth, "Ancient Voices" by Denise Hysom, or "Woman Spirit" by Marina Ray. When we dance, we expand the psyche. We are never in the same place at the end of the dance that we were before we danced. Dance for an hour, several hours, all night even.

When the dancing is over, each person picks up a candle and lights their candle from the fire. The group takes their lighted candles and sits together in a circle. Each person, in turn, holds up their candle claiming the energy, or attribute, which will enable them to make their "leap of faith."

Prayer Mound

A group member goes to the prayer mound and reads an appropriate selection from chapter two. A raccoon is *(say a few words about the archetype of the raccoon)*. I place this Raccoon on the mound as a metaphor to signify that, as a group, we have met and acknowledged our Raccoon. We are ready to continue on our journey.

CHAPTER THREE: DEATH OF TRUST

Betrayal is the death of trust. Journal or share with a friend or in a group answers to the following questions:

1. *What has been your biggest betrayal? What happened? How did you feel?*
2. *Who was the Frog, or the betrayer? In what way were you tricked? Identify the energy of the Frog (deceptive, confusing, abusive, withholding, unavailable, controlling, vague, erratic).*
3. *Frogs are often mirrors. They reflect our same, or opposite, energy. SAME: If the Frog is a withholder, we may withhold feelings, fun, money, etc., from ourselves. OPPOSITE: If the Frog is a withholder, it might mirror how we overdo and sacrifice.*
4. *We know we have completed a betrayal pattern when what we learned from the experience equals the pain we had invested in the experience. What did you learn from this betrayal?*
5. *What qualities are you developing as a result of being betrayed? (Example: clear communication, honesty, clarity)*
6. *In what other experiences, if any, have you been betrayed? Is there a similar theme that runs throughout these experiences?*

Medicine Shield

Draw, paint, or sew a symbol of a Frog, or a person who tricked you or betrayed you. Put this in the fourth segment. Share with a friend or the group.

Betrayal Ceremony

The purpose of this ceremony is to identify and release a betrayal pattern.

Form a large circle with eight to ten persons. Each person, in turn, goes to the center of the circle and asks someone from the group to symbolically stand in for the person(s) who they feel betrayed them. Both persons stand facing each other with arms across their chests, as a metaphor to protect their hearts. The person whose turn it is uses their crossed arms to push the betrayer out of the circle. Meanwhile, he/she shares his story and the feelings about his betrayal. If betrayal has been a repeating pattern, they might reference other similar experiences. For example, a similar experience may have happened with someone else too.

Make sure the circle is large enough so that the betrayed person can feel the power of pushing the betrayer. The betrayer accepts the pushes and shoves. The betrayer must resist somewhat so that the person who was betrayed feels the power of meeting resistance and finally "pushing" the betrayal experience out of his/her life. In the past, we could not choose. Now we can. Now, he/she can choose not to call this pattern back. And if this pattern should ever return, he/she will not be a victim but will immediately notice the pattern and deal with it confidently.

Once the betrayer has been pushed out of the circle, the person who was betrayed can uncross his arms and go back in the center of the circle. He then extends his arms, reaching up to Great Spirit, who, out of kindness, kept his heart in safekeeping when he was being betrayed, so his heart would not be harmed. Take your heart, symbolically, from Great Spirit and place it inside your body. Place your hand over your heart. Turn clockwise, repeating the prayerful words: "Ta Chi Who" (I walk with God). Then, walk anywhere in the circle. Feel your new sense of freedom, symbolized by the open space in the circle.

What was your experience with this ceremony?

Prayer Mound

A group member goes to the prayer mound and reads an appropriate selection from chapter three. A Frog is (*say a few words about the meaning of the frog archetype*). I place this Frog on the mound as a metaphor to signify that, as a group, we have met and acknowledged our Frog. We are ready to continue on our journey.

CHAPTER FOUR: FACING DOUBT

Discern Between Wishing, Wanting, Hoping, and Trusting

Pair off in small groups of three to five persons. Each person, in turn, begins a statement with: My idea of wishing is one time when I was four. . . Go around the entire circle and then continue the same statement, with each of the following words: "wanting," "hoping," and "trusting." After everyone has shared, the group discusses the subtle differences between these intentions. If no group is available, then journal or share with one other person.

Confronting Country Mouse

The Country Mouse is a metaphor of your own inner doubt.

1. *Who in the outer world has been your Country Mouse? Who has made you doubt, question, or second-guess your inner direction?*
2. *What was your response to your Country Mouse? Were you discouraged, agreeable, defeated, self-righteous, passive, confused, angry?*

3. *Was the Country Mouse able to convince you to change your mind? Did you stay longer than intended in a situation? Give up your own vision?*
4. *Did you continue on your way? How difficult was the decision? What were the results of your decision?*
5. *If there is no outer Country Mouse, are you your own Country Mouse? Explain.*

Medicine Shield

Draw, paint, or sew a symbol that represents an important Country Mouse in the fifth segment of your Medicine Shield. Share with the group.

Ancient Method of Precipitation: Dispelling Doubt

When you have done everything you know to do and still have doubt about what direction to take, you may want to use an ancient method of precipitating an answer. This is done ONLY after you have done everything within your power to find an answer and ONLY if you are willing to follow your guidance. Otherwise, the exercise is better left undone.

Journal a letter to your inner teacher with a twenty-four-hour mandate for a response.

Dear Inner Teacher,
I have done all l know to do to gather the information and the energy needed to make a decision. I am still in considerable doubt. It seems the best choice, decision, direction, etc. for me is _____. Unless I hear DIFFERENTLY from you within the next twenty-four hours, that is what I plan to do.

Pay close attention to signs, symbols, and metaphors for the next twenty-four hours. If there is a contrary sign, shift immediately. If there is no contrary sign, put your full energy into the decision stated in your letter.

At an agreed-upon later time, journal, or share with a partner or with a group the results of using this ancient prayer.

Prayer Mound

A group member goes to the prayer mound and reads an appropriate selection from Chapter Four. The Country Mouse is *(say a few words about the meaning of this archetype)*. I place the Country Mouse on the prayer mound as a metaphor to signify that as a group we have met and acknowledged our Country Mouse and are ready to continue on our journey.

CHAPTER FIVE: OPENING THE INTUITIVE HEART

1. *Reflect on a time in your life when you were challenged by new and unfamiliar situations. Because of old patterns you found yourself faltering instead of opening to the moment.*
2. *What quality did you need then and now to push ahead: courage, faith, resilience? This is your Buffalo.*

Ceremony of Shattering: Giving Up an "Eye"

This ceremony can be done by yourself, with a friend or partner, or in a group.

Shattering is a metaphor for breaking up old patterns. As we let go, we open to the intuitive heart. Find a large rock that is suitable for this ceremony. Use a clay pot to represent your old limited way of seeing things.

Stand above the rock, holding the pot at least five feet above the ground. Prayerfully ask Great Spirit to break a particular pattern. Then drop the pot and shatter the old way of experiencing life. Take the time to feel the sound of shattering. When you are ready, gather the pieces of clay and bury them in the earth. Give them to the Great Mother. She can easily absorb them.

What was your experience with this ceremony?

Meetings with Buffaloes

Recall an experience when you had a "remarkable" meeting with a Buffalo. What did you have to give up? What new thought was planted in your psyche? Journal and/or share with a friend or in a group.

Medicine Shield

Draw, paint, or sew a symbol that represents the Buffalo in your journey. Place this in segment six. Share with the group.

Prayer Mound

Someone from the group goes to the prayer mound and reads an appropriate selection from chapter five. The Buffalo is *(say a few words about the meaning of this archetype).* I place this Buffalo on the mound, as a metaphor to signify that as a group, we have met and acknowledged our Buffalo. We are ready to continue to the next stage of our journey.

CHAPTER SIX: INNER KNOWING

1. *Remember situations when you "forgot" who you were? When you acted inappropriately, when you were seduced by the illusion of the ego, when you were the Wolf who forgot the majesty of the Self?*
2. *By contrast, recall when you acted in childlike innocence, when you trusted totally in your innate nature.*

Confronting the Wolf

Journal with your Wolf or dialogue with a partner who represents your Wolf, your Higher Self. The partner says nothing, only holds sacred space. Talk to your Higher Self about how you sometimes forget your real Self. Explore those times of darkness, those desolate and often desperate interior spaces that seem without hope. Then change position and be the metaphor for the Higher Self for your partner.

Medicine Shield

In the seventh quadrant of your Medicine Shield, draw, paint, or sew an image of a Wolf.

Prayer Mound

A group member goes to the prayer mound, or sacred circle, and reads an appropriate section from chapter six. The Wolf is *(share briefly about the meaning of the wolf archetype)*. I place this Wolf on the prayer mound as a metaphor to indicate that as a group, we have met our Wolf and are ready to continue on our journey.

CHAPTER SEVEN: WITH THE EYES OF AN EAGLE

Journal the following questions and/or share in a group.

1. *Reflect on a time in your life when you entered a dark period, when you thought everything was hopeless, when you were swished up by the Eagle grabbing the blind Jumping Mouse, and were taken down a dark tunnel.*
2. *Who or what was the Eagle who took you into that dark period? Describe that period in detail. What did you feel? What occurred during that period? How long did you stay in that period?*
3. *Who or what was the Eagle who brought you out of the dark tunnel, who showed you the broader perspective?*

Ceremony to Clear Darkness

This ceremony can be performed with a partner or in a group setting.

Sometimes we become overwhelmed in our darkness and cannot see our way through. When we get stuck in darkness, we are stuck in our head. The breath clears darkness.

For this ceremony, the group sits in a circle. The group leader goes to each person and blows four breaths on the top of their head. The four breaths clear the mental, emotional, physical, and spiritual body.

Eagle Reverie

This guided reverie can be done with or without music. (A musical suggestion is Vangellis' "Chariots of Fire.") A group leader guides the process.

Close your eyes. Take a few deep breaths. Allow yourself to become completely relaxed.

Like Jumping Mouse, you stand all alone. A familiar voice begins to speak, "Hey, little mouse, do you want some power?" Crouch down as low as you can. Jump as high as you can. . .keep going.

As you begin to jump, extraordinary changes occur in your body.

Huge feathers begin to appear on the backs of your arms. Your arms suddenly become wings. A great tail feather extends from the base of your spine.

And on your chest are soft, downy feathers.

The shape and structure of your legs suddenly change. . .and your feet are transformed. They are no longer feet. They are the claws of a bird.

Your face is changed instantly. Your nose becomes a hard beak. And your eyes become sharp. You can see farther than a human. . .past what a human can see.

You hear a familiar voice, "You are no longer a mouse. You are an Eagle!"

Feel yourself being lifted. . .let the wind carry you. . . soar. . .go higher. . .feel the breeze rushing past. Let the great bird that is within you fly. . .tuck your claws against your body. Stretch your body out.

Leave your wings outstretched resting on the currents. . .FLY. . .SOAR.

Hear a sound from deep within. . .the sound of the renewal of your life. . . .See with sharp eyes. . .with eagle vision. Look out beyond the human horizon. With one glance you view an entire panorama. Enjoy the expansive vista of a mountain range, rolling hills, and a valley below. . .you can even see the clear silhouette of a single blade of grass miles below.

Feel the wind hitting your wings from underneath your torso. Tuck your claws against your body. Stretch your body out. Leave your wings outstretched resting on the current. Flap your wings. With every movement you are lifted. Listen to the flap of the wings. . .Feel the air vibrating, fluttering the edge of your feathers. Feel the mists from the clouds touch your wings as you soar yet higher.

See in the Eagle Way, in the way of Spirit. Fly in the clouds. . .and beyond the clouds. Become one with the mind of God. You can go forward or backward in time. . .to the place where all is known. . .You can see into. . .through. . .and beyond. . .you see with an all-knowing, all-loving, compassionate heart.

Look down on the earth. . .How tiny, how minuscule it is. All that has occurred on earth is available to you. . .fly back in time or fly forward to the destiny of the earth. . .From here, all the events you have considered great events are tiny little happenings you can embrace with your body, as though it were a little egg in your nest. . . .How different all life seems. . .how different your life appears. . . .From this perspective all is known. . .is understood. . .is accepted. The meaning behind things is unveiled. Pure essence. . .Truth. . .Light. . .Love.

Begin to return to earth. . .let the earth be an

egg to be kept warm by your great feathers. The earth is also yourself, your life, all that has been and will be, the essence of who you are. . .Now you can embrace much more, hold much more. . .love much more. . .trust much more. . .

Fold your wings across your breast and tuck your head down inside your chest. The feathers disappear. The wings and the beak form human arms and legs. . .Sense your skin, your arms, your legs. . .You are human once again. . .and inside you is an Eagle who sees in the Spirit Way.

Slowly open your eyes.

What was your experience with this reverie? Journal or share with the group.

Medicine Shield

Leave the eighth quadrant of your Medicine Shield blank as a reminder to always trust, knowing that everything you need will be given to you.

Prayer Mound

Someone from the group goes to the prayer mound and reads an appropriate selection from chapter seven. The Eagle is *(say a few words about the metaphor of the Eagle)*. I place this Eagle on the mound to represent that, as a group, we open to trust. May we always see in the Spirit Way, with the eyes of an Eagle. And may we soar like an Eagle!

References

Bolen, Jean Shinoda. *The Tao of Psychology.* San Francisco: Harper & Row, 1982.

Bradshaw, John. *Creating Love: The Next Stage of Growth.* New York: Bantam, 1992.

Campbell, Joseph. *The Hero With a Thousand Faces.* Princeton: Bollingen Series, 1989.

Campbell, Joseph. *The Masks of God: Creative Mythology.* New York: Viking, 1968.

Cooper, David A. "Invitation to the Soul." *Parabola, XIX*, no. 1 (February 1994):#7-11.

Course in Miracles: Workbook for Students. Huntington Station, New York: Coleman Graphics, 1975.

Dorff, Francis. *The Art of Passing Over.* New York: Integration Books, 1988.

Eliot, T.S. *Four Quartets.* Byrnt Norton, New York: Harcourt Brace Jovanovich, 1943.

Eliot, T.S. *The Love Song of J. Alfred Prufrock.* In *Modern American & Modern British Poetry* by Louis Untermeyer. New York: Harcourt, Brace and Company.

Hesse, Herman. *Siddhartha*. Translated by Hilda Rosner. New York: New Directions Publishing Company, 1951.

The I Ching. The Richard Wilhelm translation rendered into English by Cary F. Baynes. Bollingen Series XIX, Princeton University Press, 1950.

Jongeward, David. *Weaver of Worlds*. Rochester, Vermont: Destiny Books, 1990.

Lionel, Frederic. *Challenge: On Special Mission*. Great Britain: Biddles, Ltd., Guildford and King's Lynn, 1980.

Markides, Kyriacos C. *Homage to the Sun*. London: Arkana, 1987.

Nichols, Sallie. *Jung and Tarot: An Archetypal Journey*. York Beach, Maine: Samuel Weiser, Inc., 1980.

Storm, Hyemeyohsts. *Seven Arrows*. New York: Ballentine Books, 1972.

Sugrue, Thomas. *There is a River*. New York: Henry Holt & Company, 1942.

About the Author

Mary Elizabeth Marlow is a transpersonal teacher, author, intuitive counselor, international speaker, and seminar leader. She is the author of *Handbook for the Emerging Woman* and co-author, with Joseph Rael, of *Being and Vibration.* She has spoken to a wide variety of audiences and has been featured in a number of international magazines, including *New Woman, Livs Lyst, Human Potential, Onkruid, Human Potential Resources, Hjemmet,* and *Libelle.*

Mary Elizabeth draws from a rich and eclectic background that provides the basis for both her writing and her teaching. Her academic background includes a degree in English with a minor in religion and fine arts, graduate work in counseling, and certification with Dr. Carl Simonton and Stephanie Simonton as a cancer therapist.

Her primary education, however, has been from life itself. What was once a childhood interest in exploring the unifying Spirit behind all traditions deepened to become a lifetime quest. Her many journeys, which have included visits to Europe, India, Egypt, and the Middle East, have allowed her to interface with the mysteries and metaphors of a variety of traditions and cultures.

Recognized as a gifted storyteller and ritualist, Mary Elizabeth brings a unique approach to the transformational process. She has the ability to absorb the inner meanings of the great ancient stories and to juxtapose them with experiences from her own life and with stories of those she has encountered along the way.

She invites her readers to pause and sense their own inner alliance with the collective wisdom of the great stories, to be inspired through the experiences of others, and to awaken to their own truth.

Mary Elizabeth serves as a guide to many in the seminars and retreats she conducts worldwide. In Europe she teaches in Greece, Norway, Holland, and England. In the United States she offers programs in Virginia Beach, Virginia, where she lives, and in a number of other locations.

Noted for her innovative and creative approaches to inner healing, Mary Elizabeth has developed a number of original in-depth processes that she uses with individuals, with groups, and in one-day family sessions. She is uniquely gifted in being able to identify and facilitate the healing of core patterns and issues and to empower others with a new sense of their authentic selves.

For information on schedules,
books, or tapes, contact:
Mary Elizabeth Marlow
903 Goldsboro Avenue
Virginia Beach, VA 23451
(757) 425-7452

Hampton Roads Publishing Company
publishes and distributes books on a variety of subjects,
including metaphysical, health, complementary medicine,
visionary fiction, and other related topics.
To order books or receive a copy of our latest catalog, call
toll-free, (800)766-8009, or send your name and address to:

Hampton Roads Publishing Company, Inc.
134 Burgess Lane
Charlottesville, VA 22902

Visit our website at www.hrpub.com
e-mail: hrpc@hrpub.com

A MINISTRY
ANYONE COULD TRUST
A STUDY OF 2 CORINTHIANS 1–7

BIBLE STUDY GUIDE

From the Bible-teaching ministry of

Charles R. Swindoll

INSIGHT FOR LIVING

Charles R. Swindoll is a graduate of Dallas Theological Seminary and has served in pastorates since 1964, including churches in Texas, New England, and California. Since 1971 he has served as senior pastor of the First Evangelical Free Church of Fullerton, California. Chuck's radio program, "Insight for Living," began in 1979. In addition to his church and radio ministries, Chuck enjoys writing. He has authored numerous books and booklets on a variety of subjects.

Based on the outlines and transcripts of Chuck's sermons, the study guide text is coauthored by Ken Gire, a graduate of Texas Christian University and Dallas Theological Seminary. The Living Insights are written by Bill Butterworth, a graduate of Florida Bible College, Dallas Theological Seminary, and Florida Atlantic University.

Editor in Chief: Cynthia Swindoll	**Director, Communications Division:** Carla Beck
Coauthor of Text: Ken Gire	**Project Manager:** Alene Cooper
Author of Living Insights: Bill Butterworth	**Project Supervisor:** Cassandra Clark
Assistant Editor: Karene Wells	**Art Director:** Don Pierce
Copy Manager: Jac La Tour	**Production Artist:** Gary Lett
Copyediting Supervisor: Marty Anderson	**Typographer:** Bob Haskins
Copy Editor: Kevin Moritz	**Print Production Manager:** Deedee Snyder

Unless otherwise identified, all Scripture references are from the New American Standard Bible, © The Lockman Foundation 1960, 1962, 1963, 1968, 1971, 1972, 1973, 1975, 1977. Used by permission.

An effort has been made to locate sources and obtain permission where necessary for the quotations used in this book. In the event of any unintentional omission, a modification will gladly be incorporated in future printings.

ISBN 0-8499-8403-3

Printed in the United States of America.

COVER PHOTOGRAPH: SuperStock International Inc.

CONTENTS

A MINISTRY ANYONE COULD TRUST

A STUDY OF 2 CORINTHIANS 1–7

In a time of disappointment and disillusionment, it is refreshing to return to the Word of God and find the model of a ministry anyone could trust. In the first seven chapters of 2 Corinthians, such an example appears. Here we find the ingredients that all of us admire: integrity, compassion, dedication, servanthood, realism, hope, and a half dozen other qualities worth emulating.

My desire in providing the following material is to bring our attention back to the trustworthy truths of the Scriptures, from which we can glean a renewed perspective regarding ministry. It is easy to become jaded and cynical if our focus stays too long on ministries today where the consequences of doctrinal error and personal failure have taken their toll. It is time to lift our sights!

I invite you to take this journey with me as we walk through one scene after another where the underlying secrets of an effective ministry are unveiled. One warning: Be ready for a few surprises!

Chuck Swindoll

PUTTING TRUTH INTO ACTION

K nowledge apart from application falls short of God's desire for His children. He wants us to apply what we learn so that we will change and grow. This study guide was prepared with these goals in mind. As you go through the following pages, we hope your desire to discover biblical truth will grow as your understanding of God's Word increases, and that you will be encouraged to apply what you've learned.

To assist you in your study, we've included a section called Living Insights at the end of each lesson. These exercises will challenge you to study further and to think of specific ways to put your discoveries into action.

There are many ways to use this guide—in personal devotions, group studies, discussions with friends and family, and Sunday school classes. And, of course, it's an ideal study aid when you're listening to its corresponding "Insight for Living" radio series.

To benefit most from this study guide, we would encourage you to consider it a spiritual journal. That's why we've included space in the Living Insights for recording your thoughts and discoveries. We hope you'll return to those sections often for review and encouragement as you continue to grow in your walk with Christ.

Ken Gire
Coauthor of Text

Bill Butterworth
Author of Living Insights

ͣMINISTRY
ANYONE COULD TRUST

A Study of 2 Corinthians 1–7

Chapter 1

TELLING IT LIKE IT IS

A *Survey of 2 Corinthians*

S ome people are so admired, they loom larger than life. One such man is the late Albert Schweitzer. In his biography of that famous physician, Norman Cousins writes about his visit with Schweitzer at Lambaréné, in French Equatorial Africa.

> Albert Schweitzer is not above criticism. Few men of our century have come closer to attaining the Greek idea of the whole man—the thinker, the leader, the man of action, the scientist, the artist. But like all great figures in history, he becomes real not despite his frailties but because of them. . . .
>
> History is willing to overlook almost anything—errors, paradoxes, personal weaknesses or faults—if only a man will give enough of himself to others. The greater the ability to identify and serve; the more genuine the response. In the case of Schweitzer, later generations will not clutter their minds with petty reflections about his possible faults or inconsistencies. In his life and work will be found energy for moral imagination. This is all that will matter. . . .
>
> Returning home, I felt happy that my two specific purposes in going to Lambaréné had been met. But even more important was the fact that the image of Albert Schweitzer I carried away with me was intact—fortified, if anything, by a direct view. For at Lambaréné I learned that a man does not have to be an angel to be a saint. [1]

1. Norman Cousins, *Albert Schweitzer's Mission* (New York, N.Y.: W. W. Norton and Co., 1985), pp. 137, 138, 140.

1

Those last thirteen words form a perfect introduction to the apostle Paul—to his life in general, and to his second letter to the Corinthians in particular—"a man does not have to be an angel to be a saint."

Some General Information

About Paul

Except for that of Jesus, no New Testament life looms larger than Paul's. Take a look at his impressive resume: born in Tarsus . . .

> circumcised the eighth day, of the nation of Israel, of the tribe of Benjamin, a Hebrew of Hebrews; as to the Law, a Pharisee; as to zeal, a persecutor of the church; as to the righteousness which is in the Law, found blameless. (Phil. 3:5–6)

And all of this *before* his conversion on the Damascus road (see Acts 9:1–31). God used that road to strike Paul down by blinding him, and then to lift him to incredible heights—as an apostle, evangelist, pastor, missionary, and finally, martyr. No one was more committed to the cause of Christ than Saint Paul.

A saint? Without question. But an angel? No. Not according to his own testimony: "For I am the least of the apostles . . . the very least of all saints . . . foremost of all [sinners]" (1 Cor. 15:9, Eph. 3:8, 1 Tim. 1:15).

About Second Corinthians

Aside from his impressive resume, Paul penned thirteen New Testament letters. He traveled extensively, plowing new mission fields and planting a number of churches in the furrows of the once-fallow Roman Empire. The letters he wrote grew out of his travels and became accepted as the basic theology of the Christian faith.

Second Corinthians, however, is different from Paul's other letters. It reads more like a journal, chronicling the man's personal life and struggles and showing him at his most transparent. Chapter 1 gives us a sample of this self-disclosure.

> For we do not want you to be unaware, brethren, of our affliction which came to us in Asia, that we were burdened excessively, beyond our strength, so that we despaired even of life; indeed, we had the sentence of death within ourselves in order that we should not trust in ourselves, but in God who raises the dead. (vv. 8–9)

2

In 4:8–11, he shares more of the struggles he experienced.

> We are afflicted in every way, but not crushed; perplexed, but not despairing; persecuted, but not forsaken; struck down, but not destroyed; always carrying about in the body the dying of Jesus, that the life of Jesus also may be manifested in our body. For we who live are constantly being delivered over to death for Jesus' sake, that the life of Jesus also may be manifested in our mortal flesh.

The word *perplexed* in verse 8 means "without a way" in the original Greek. That's how Paul felt. His life looked like a confusing array of crossroads and intersections and flashing red, green, and yellow lights.

If you've felt like that at times—and who hasn't?—you'll feel right at home as you study Paul's struggles.

Some Biblical Observations

As we turn to open the cabinet to the book's themes, we see that 2 Corinthians provides a well-stocked cupboard of food for thought. Let's bring a few of its principles down from the shelf and take a cursory look at the labels.

Great people are not immune to difficult times.

Even though Paul was a great man with a great ministry, even though God's hand was obviously on his life, and even though his ministry was centered in God's perfect will, life was difficult for him.

Hard times bring tensions that are easily interpreted as unfair contradictions.

Paul's driving desire was that his life would blossom as a fragrant aroma of Christ, regardless of how strong the stench of the fertilizer that was mixed into it.

> Giving no cause for offense in anything, in order that the ministry be not discredited, but in everything commending ourselves as servants of God, in much endurance, in afflictions, in hardships, in distresses, in beatings, in imprisonments, in tumults, in labors, in sleeplessness, in hunger, in purity, in knowledge, in patience, in kindness, in the Holy Spirit, in genuine love, in the word of truth, in the power of God; by the weapons of righteousness for the right hand and the left, by glory and dishonor, by evil report and good

report; regarded as deceivers and yet true; as unknown yet well-known, as dying yet behold, we live; as punished yet not put to death, as sorrowful yet always rejoicing, as poor yet making many rich, as having nothing yet possessing all things. (6:3–10)

Afflictions, hardships, distress. He's talking about real life, isn't he? And that's where the tension is . . . between reality and our wants.

We want comfort. We want success. We want money. We want to look good. We want to make a good impression. But reality is that life will often be merciless (vv. 4–5), and we will often be misunderstood (v. 8: "evil report"), as well as maligned (v. 8: "regarded as deceivers").

In 11:23–27, Paul presents yet another not-so-inviting travel brochure of the Christian life:

Are they servants of Christ? (I speak as if insane) I more so; in far more labors, in far more imprisonments, beaten times without number, often in danger of death. Five times I received from the Jews thirty-nine lashes. Three times I was beaten with rods, once I was stoned, three times I was shipwrecked, a night and a day I have spent in the deep. I have been on frequent journeys, in dangers from rivers, dangers from robbers, dangers from my countrymen, dangers from the Gentiles, dangers in the city, dangers in the wilderness, dangers on the sea, dangers among false brethren; I have been in labor and hardship, through many sleepless nights, in hunger and thirst, often without food, in cold and exposure.

Not exactly Club-Med Christianity, is it?

Such tensions are needed reminders of our own weakness, forcing us to draw upon God's power.

God took Paul from the darkest of valleys to the brightest of mountaintops—from prison up to Paradise (compare 11:23 with 12:1–4). But after giving Paul a heavenly revelation, God gave the apostle a humbling reminder.

And because of the surpassing greatness of the revelations, for this reason, to keep me from exalting myself,

4

there was given me a thorn in the flesh,[2] a messenger of Satan to buffet me—to keep me from exalting myself! (12:7)

In spite of Paul's fervent, repeated prayers (v. 8), God said no. For Paul's thorn in the flesh was like a string tied around his finger—reminding him of an all-important truth.

And He has said to me, "My grace is sufficient for you, for power is perfected in weakness." Most gladly, therefore, I will rather boast about my weaknesses, that the power of Christ may dwell in me. Therefore I am well content with weaknesses, with insults, with distresses, with persecutions, with difficulties, for Christ's sake; for when I am weak, then I am strong. (vv. 9–10)

Like Paul, George Matheson had his thorn in the flesh. Born in Glasgow, Scotland, in 1842, Matheson had eye trouble all of his childhood. By the time he went into the ministry, he was blind. Yet for forty years he preached all across Scotland. His journal, *Thoughts for Life's Journey,* tells of the lessons he learned.

My soul, reject not the place of thy prostration! It has ever been the robing room for royalty. Ask the great ones of the past what has been the spot of their prosperity; they will say, "It was the cold ground on which I once was lying." Ask Abraham; he will point you to the sacrifice of Moriah. Ask Joseph; he will direct you to his dungeon. Ask Moses; he will date his fortune from his danger in the Nile. Ask Ruth; she will bid you build her monument in the field of her toil. Ask David; he will tell you that his songs came from the night. Ask Job; he will remind you that God answered him out of the whirlwind. Ask Peter; he will extol his submission in the sea. Ask John; he will give the palm to Patmos. Ask Paul; he will attribute his inspiration to the light that struck him blind. Ask one more—the Son of Man. Ask Him whence has come His rule over the world. He will answer, "From the cold ground

---

2. Paul's "thorn in the flesh" has been the subject of much debate. Tertullian thought it was a pain in the ear or head. Chrysostom thought it was troublesome adversaries, such as Hymenaeus and Alexander. Other suggestions range from epilepsy to ophthalmia to malaria to attacks of depression. Paul, however, does not provide enough of a description to pinpoint the malady. For a further discussion, see Philip E. Hughes' *Commentary on the Second Epistle to the Corinthians* (Grand Rapids, Mich.: William B. Eerdmans Publishing Co., 1962), pp. 442–48.

on which I was lying—the Gethsemane ground; I received my sceptre there."[3]

Matheson, along with Paul, recognized that God's power is perfected in weakness. Not in degrees or in diplomas. Not in accomplishments or in accolades. Not in wealth or in wisdom. But in weakness. It is the leg that limps which leans on something other than itself for support. And so God may touch our leg so we might learn to lean on Him.

Humanity plus difficulty brings humility and maturity, not inferiority.

If you're limping along, feeling depressed because you can't keep up with the footmen, let alone run with the horses, Paul has some encouraging words about how God can use a nobody to accomplish the miraculous.

> I have become foolish; you yourselves compelled me. Actually I should have been commended by you, for in no respect was I inferior to the most eminent apostles, even though I am a nobody. The signs of a true apostle were performed among you with all perseverance, by signs and wonders and miracles. (vv. 11–12)

The Christian life is a life of paradox. Giving, we receive. Losing, we find. Dying, we live. Consider some of the paradoxes found in 2 Corinthians that we will study in this series:

- Brokenness gives wholeness to our ministry.
- Meekness brings strength into our lives.
- Weakness puts power on display.

Some Practical Suggestions

Jesus has been the Word of God from all eternity. But only when the Word was incarnate in the flesh could we see and touch the truth. Here are three suggestions to help you incarnate some of the truths of 2 Corinthians into *your* life so others may see and touch the truth of God.

1. Let's not hide our humanity; it is directly linked to authenticity.

2. Let's not deny our weakness and inadequacies; they open doors to God's strength.

---

3. George Matheson, as quoted by V. Raymond Edman, in *The Disciplines of Life* (Minneapolis, Minn.: World Wide Publications, 1948), p. 126.

3. Let's not hesitate to call for help; for our hope is in the Lord.

Some Closing Comments

After conducting Beethoven's magnificent *Ninth Symphony,* Arturo Toscanini brought down his baton to a burst of applause. The audience roared its approval. Toscanini and his orchestra took repeated bows. When the cheering finally subsided, Toscanini turned back to his musicians and leaned over the podium. Voicing his words in staccato whispers, he said to the men: "Gentlemen, I am nothing. . . . Gentlemen, you are nothing. . . . But Beethoven . . . Beethoven is everything, everything, everything!"

Whether it's Schweitzer or Toscanini or the apostle Paul, whether it's a mentor or a parent or some historic hero, these people are nothing. We are nothing. But Christ is everything. When that gets cemented in our minds, we won't even try to be an angel. We'll just be satisfied to be the least of saints, the foremost of sinners, used in the hands of God.

 *Living Insights* STUDY ONE

When we think of the apostle Paul, we tend to picture a man larger than life. His story is admirable indeed. A better understanding of his life will help us appreciate even more the intimate book of 2 Corinthians.

- Use this time to go back to the book of Acts and study the life of Paul. Begin in Acts 9 and read through chapter 19. Record your observations in the space that follows.

The Life of Paul
Acts 9–19

Reference _____

Observations _____

_____

_____

Reference _____

Observations _____

_____

_____

Reference _____

Observations _____

_____

_____

Reference _____

Observations _____

_____

_____

Reference _____

Observations _____

_____

_____

Reference _____

Observations _____

_____

_____

Reference _____

Observations _____

_____

_____

Reference _____

Observations _____

_____

_____

Reference _____

Observations _____

_____

_____

Reference _____

Observations _____

_____

_____

 Living Insights

Paul's life was so full, we still haven't finished his biographical study. Let's continue that study to gain further insight into the life of this great man of God.

- Continue your trek through the book of Acts, marking your observations as you go.

The Life of Paul
Acts 20–28

Reference _____

Observations _____

_____

_____

Reference _____

Observations _____

_____

_____

Reference _____

Observations _____

_____

_____

Reference _____

Observations _____

_____

_____

Reference _____

Observations _____

_____

_____

Reference _____

Observations _____

_____

_____

Reference _____

Observations _____

_____

_____

Reference _____

Observations _____

_____

_____

Reference _____

Observations _____

_____

_____

Reference _____

Observations _____

_____

_____

2 Corinthians: A Man and His Ministry

Writer: Paul
Date: A.D. 54–55
Style: Personal, Bold, Defensive

Uniqueness: It is almost impossible to analyze this letter. It seems to be the least systematic of Paul's writing—almost like a journal. These are the words of a man who freely expresses his feelings about himself and his ministry.

Introduction and Salutation	Crucial Concerns Suffering and God's Sufficiency Ministry and Our Involvement Godliness and Its Impact	Grace Giving Example of Macedonians Command to Corinthians	Apostolic Authority Reply to Critics Justification of Ministry False Teachers Visions, Revelations, Credentials, Warnings	Conclusion and Farewell
1:1–2	1:3–7:16	8:1–9:15	10:1–13:10	13:11–14
Scope:	Past	Present	Future	
Issues:	Misunderstandings, Concerns, Explanations	Financial Project	Vindication of Paul's Ministry	
Tone:	Forgiving, Grateful, Bold	Confident	Defensive, Strong	
Key verses:	"For we do not preach ourselves but Christ Jesus as Lord." (4:5a)	"God loves a cheerful giver." (9:7b)	"I shall not be put to shame." (10:8b)	

11

Chapter 2

UNRAVELING THE MYSTERY OF SUFFERING

2 Corinthians 1:1–11

T he sun pours luxuriantly through the stained glass window, bathing the padded pews of a Sunday service. Distended chords of organ music hang in the air and mingle with the streams of mid-morning light. With one accord the choir sings:

> Come, ye disconsolate, where'er ye languish;
> Come to the Mercyseat, fervently kneel.
> Here bring your wounded hearts, here tell your an-
> guish;
> Earth has no sorrow that Heav'n cannot heal.[1]

But despite the angelic harmony of the choir, a discordant note plucks at the heartstrings of those in the audience who suffer. The pain may be physical, marital, financial, or emotional . . . afflicting a friend, a relative, an immediate family member, or themselves.

Whatever the circumstances, those who suffer carry in their hearts a tangle of emotions, entwined with all kinds of questions, both personal and theological.

"Why? Why this? Why me? Why now?"

Unraveling the mystery of suffering is no easy task. But that's the purpose of this lesson. Hopefully, it will nimble up your mental fingers so you can sort out all the winding threads that have tied your life in knots.

Suffering: Understanding Its Reality

In his book *The View from a Hearse,* the late Joseph Bayly wrote:

> Death is the supreme enigma. We cannot explain its
> mystery and the unknown makes us fear. This mystery
> is greatest in a generation whose stance toward death
> is denial.[2]

1. Thomas Moore, "Come, Ye Disconsolate," *The Lutheran Hymnal* (St. Louis, Mo.: Concordia Publishing House, 1941), no. 531.

2. Joseph Bayly, *The View from a Hearse* (Elgin, Ill.: David C. Cook Publishing Co., 1969), p. 16.

One thing knits us all together into the same tapestry—suffering. Its muted threads are woven throughout our lives: death, divorce, bankruptcy, cancer, heart disease, scandal, kidnapping, rape. From our earthly perspective, all we see are twisted knots. No wonder we look up, straining to see some design, some purposeful pattern, and ask why.

Suffering: Unraveling Its Mystery

The Bible gives us a glimpse of the heavenward side of that tapestry in the first eleven verses of 2 Corinthians. This passage faces the mystery of suffering head-on and begins to untangle it strand by strand.

Warm Words of Introduction

Written by a man whose authority had often been undermined, 2 Corinthians begins by verifying Paul's credentials.

> Paul, an apostle of Christ Jesus by the will of God,
> and Timothy our brother, to the church of God which
> is at Corinth with all the saints who are throughout
> Achaia. (1:1)

Paul calls himself "an apostle of Christ Jesus." The word *apostolos* literally means "one sent forth." It was used to describe that unique first-century individual who was gifted with the miraculous ability to speak as an oracle of God. There were only twelve apostles in the technical sense of the word—the eleven disciples plus Judas' replacement.

Paul was an apostle not because he inherited the role, not because he was selected by the people or appointed by some commission, and not because he appointed himself. He was an apostle "by the will of God." In contrast, Paul describes Timothy affectionately as a brother. The young pastor is not an apostle but rather an apostolic delegate.

The letter is addressed to the church at Corinth and was meant to be forwarded from that commercial center to the concentric circle of believers radiating throughout the region of Achaia.[3]

With the formalities aside, Paul greets them warmly.

> Grace to you and peace from God our Father and the
> Lord Jesus Christ. (v. 2)

3. Achaia was the Roman province comprising all the territory of Greece south of Macedonia. Presumably, copies of the letter would be made at Corinth and then circulated throughout the province.

Grace is a key word for Paul. It is what God does for us which we don't deserve and which we cannot repay. And in its wake comes peace. Peace is a freedom from inner distraction, an inner rest. Grace and peace don't come from ourselves—no matter how positive our thoughts; or from others—no matter how assuring their counsel. They come only from God.

Wise Words of Explanation

Since so much of his letter focuses on pain, suffering, and heartache, it's not surprising that Paul explains some of the reasons behind these trials.

> Blessed be the God and Father of our Lord Jesus Christ, the Father of mercies and God of all comfort; who comforts us in all our affliction so that we may be able to comfort those who are in any affliction with the comfort with which we ourselves are comforted by God. (vv. 3–4)

The word *comfort* almost leaps off the page and is key to Paul's explanation. In verses 3–7, the same root word is used ten times. It comes from the Greek word *paraklētos*, which is formed from the prefix *para*, meaning "alongside," and the root *kaleō*, meaning "to call." Comfort is given by someone called alongside to help—like a nurse called to a patient's bedside. The word is used as another name for the Holy Spirit in John 14:16—"And I will ask the Father, and He will give you another Helper [Comforter], that He may be with you forever."

When tragedy strikes, collapsing our life like a house of cards, that's when we cry out to God. That's when we need comfort. That's when we need someone to come alongside and put an arm around us, to be there, to listen, to help. Though God is often silent during those times, He's always there . . . as the *Parakletos*, the Father of mercies and the God of all comfort.

In explaining why we suffer, Paul lists three reasons in 2 Corinthians 1:4–11. The first is found in verse 4.

> Who comforts us in all our affliction so that we may be able to comfort those who are in any affliction with the comfort with which we ourselves are comforted by God.

That we might be prepared to comfort others. It's like a chain reaction: when we go through suffering, God comforts us. And when His comfort has done its work in our lives, then we, in turn, can comfort others. A perfect example of this is Joni Eareckson Tada. God has comforted her in her affliction, and she, in turn, has comforted thousands of other people with physical disabilities.

The person who has suffered the shattering effects of a divorce can best comfort a divorcée. The person who has lost a child can best comfort another parent who has lost a child. The businessman who once was bankrupt can best comfort another person in the throes of financial disaster. Therefore, one reason God allows suffering is so we might have a well of experiences deep enough to draw from it compassion and counsel to comfort others.

> For just as the sufferings of Christ are ours in abundance,
> so also our comfort is abundant through Christ. (v. 5)

God's salve is dispensed in proportion to the extent of our wounds. And that salve is stored in us so at the appropriate time we might dispense it to others.

> But if we are afflicted, it is for your comfort and salvation; or if we are comforted, it is for your comfort, which is effective in the patient enduring of the same sufferings which we also suffer; and our hope for you is firmly grounded, knowing that as you are sharers of our sufferings, so also you are sharers of our comfort. (vv. 6–7)

Lest we think Paul's advice is only theoretical, he shares a dark chapter from his life to show us that these principles come straight from the textbook of real life.

> For we do not want you to be unaware, brethren, of our affliction which came to us in Asia, that we were burdened excessively, beyond our strength, so that we despaired even of life; indeed, we had the sentence of death within ourselves. (vv. 8–9a)

Whatever his affliction in Asia, it was more than he could bear and pushed him to the brink of death's abyss.[4] But while teetering on that brink, Paul discovers a second reason for suffering.

> Indeed, we had the sentence of death within ourselves
> in order that we should not trust in ourselves, but in
> God who raises the dead. (v. 9)

4. With his back against the wall, Paul sees himself wedged in a crushing situation from which there is no escape. "The rare word *exaporēthēnai* ('despaired') implies the total unavailability of an exit." *The Expositor's Bible Commentary,* ed. Frank E. Gaebelein (Grand Rapids, Mich.: Zondervan Publishing House, 1976), vol. 10, p. 321.

That we might not trust in ourselves. Intense suffering is designed to remind us of our utter helplessness. For it is when we are most helpless that we are most dependent. Since our understanding is finite and feeble, we should acknowledge that handicap and seek support that is infinitely stronger.

> Trust in the Lord with all your heart,
> And do not lean on your own understanding.
> In all your ways acknowledge Him,
> And He will make your paths straight. (Prov. 3:5–6)

The reason why we don't depend on God more is because the world's wisdom is diametrically opposed to the wisdom of Proverbs. We are indoctrinated by a pull-yourself-up-by-your-own-bootstraps philosophy. In a country whose most prized document is *The Declaration of Independence*, it's easy to see why we have such a hard time leaning, trusting, and depending.

Turning to another document highly prized, we come to the book of Jeremiah. Through the impassioned pen of the weeping prophet—himself well-acquainted with grief—God gives one of the grandest promises in all the Bible.

> "'For I know the plans that I have for you,'" declares the Lord, "'plans for welfare and not for calamity to give you a future and a hope.'" (29:11)

Signed, "God." Isn't that a tremendous love note? Doesn't that help you endure your present suffering so you can see the outcome, the future, the hope? You may think there's no rhyme or reason to the doggerel verse of pain you're experiencing. But in God's eyes, your pain is just the first draft of a poem in the making.

Paul concludes his introduction with a thank-you note that provides the third reason why we suffer.

> Who delivered us from so great a peril of death, and will deliver us, He on whom we have set our hope. And He will yet deliver us, you also joining in helping us through your prayers, that thanks may be given by many persons on our behalf for the favor bestowed upon us through the prayers of many. (2 Cor. 1:10–11)

That we might learn to give thanks in everything. Not until we can say "Thank You, Lord," have we fully accepted suffering's yoke. A whole new dimension of the tapestry comes into view when we learn to shoulder the yoke with thanksgiving (compare Lam. 3:27–32 with 1 Thess. 5:18).

Suffering: Handling Its Perplexities

> That we might be prepared to comfort others.
> That we might not trust in ourselves.
> That we might learn to give thanks in everything.

Almost sounds like a stanza out of an old hymn, doesn't it? Suffering *can* be transformed into a song. Here are three suggestions to turn your discordant notes of pain into beautiful music.

1. Instead of focusing only on yourself now, think of how you can help others later. This will sound a note of hope.

2. Rather than fighting, surrender; rather than resisting, release. This will produce a note of faith.

3. Although getting even seems to come more naturally, try giving thanks. This will bring a note of peace.

Hope. Faith. Peace. Hear the melody? Hear the harmony? Let Christ turn your suffering into a symphony. And where there was only the whining of instruments warming up, let Him orchestrate a musical score that would make even Beethoven stand up and applaud.

Living Insights STUDY ONE

It's easy to wax eloquent on the benefits of suffering when your life is relatively pain-free. But finding good in heartache is much more difficult when you are in the midst of it.

• As you review the first eleven verses of 2 Corinthians, use the space that follows to record ten or twelve key words. These words should stand out to you due to their significance to the overall text. See if you can define each word from the context. If you can't, consult a Bible dictionary. Finally, write a statement as to why you think the word is significant.

2 Corinthians 1:1–11

Key Word _____

Definition _____

_____

17

Significance _____

_____

Key Word _____

Definition _____

_____

Significance _____

_____

Key Word _____

Definition _____

_____

Significance _____

_____

Key Word _____

Definition _____

_____

Significance _____

_____

Key Word _____

Definition _____

_____

Significance _____

_____

Key Word _____

Definition _____

_____

Significance _____

_____

Key Word _____

Definition _____

_____

Significance _____

_____

Key Word _____

Definition _____

_____

Significance _____

_____

Key Word _____

Definition _____

_____

Significance _____

_____

Key Word _____

Definition _____

_____

Significance _____

_____

Key Word _____

Definition _____

_____

Significance _____

_____

Key Word _____

Definition _____

_____

Significance _____

_____

🍇 *Living Insights* STUDY TWO

No stranger to suffering, the apostle Paul brings out some helpful strategies for coping in a time of crisis. These strategies are well worth reviewing.

- If you're going through a tough time right now, write down ways to apply these three statements. Or tell how these principles helped you through a past crisis.

    Instead of focusing only on yourself now, think of how you can help others later.

    _____

    _____

    _____

    _____

    _____

    Rather than fighting, surrender; rather than resisting, release.

    _____

    _____

    _____

    _____

    _____

    Although getting even seems to come more naturally, try giving thanks.

    _____

    _____

    _____

    _____

    _____

Chapter 3

IN DEFENSE
OF INTEGRITY

2 Corinthians 1:12–2:4

O ne of the smallest muscles in the human body is also the most destructive. In seconds it can cut and slash, leaving its victim in emotional shreds. This muscle is the tongue. Concerning it, Washington Irving wrote:

> A sharp tongue is the only edge tool that grows keener
> with constant use. [1]

The tongue can ruin a reputation, malign a motive, and destroy one's dignity. This lethal weapon may be wielded publicly without shame. But more often it is a dagger cloaked in stealth, stabbing its victim in the back.

Surprisingly, the fingerprints on this dagger do not point to a hardened criminal but to some haloed saint who only minutes before might have sung the sweetest song, uttered the most beautiful prayer, or spoken the most encouraging words.

James mentions this incongruity in the third chapter of his book.

> No one can tame the tongue; it is a restless evil and
> full of deadly poison. With it we bless our Lord and
> Father; and with it we curse men, who have been
> made in the likeness of God; from the same mouth
> come both blessing and cursing. My brethren, these
> things ought not to be this way. (vv. 8–10)

If you've felt the thrust of this dagger between your shoulder blades, you're not alone. David also knew the piercing pain of an assassinated character, and his cry for vindication is recorded in Psalm 7.

> O Lord my God, in Thee I have taken refuge;
> Save me from all those who pursue me, and deliver me,
> Lest he tear my soul like a lion,
> Dragging me away, while there is none to deliver.

---

1. *Bartlett's Familiar Quotations*, 14th ed., rev. and enl., ed. Emily Morison Beck (Boston, Mass.: Little, Brown and Co., 1968), p. 550.

O Lord my God, if I have done this,
If there is injustice in my hands,
If I have rewarded evil to my friend,
Or have plundered him who without cause was my
adversary,
Let the enemy pursue my soul and overtake it;
And let him trample my life down to the ground,
And lay my glory in the dust.
Arise, O Lord, in Thine anger;
Lift up Thyself against the rage of my adversaries,
And arouse Thyself for me; Thou hast appointed
judgment.
And let the assembly of the peoples encompass Thee;
And over them return Thou on high.
The Lord judges the peoples;
Vindicate me, O Lord, according to my righteousness
and my integrity that is in me. (vv. 1–8)

In the final analysis, all we have is our reputation. You can take away my business, my money, and my possessions. But take a stab at my integrity and you've attacked the very core of my life. That is what's so precious to David, and that is why he prays so fervently.

Vindicate me, O Lord, for I have walked in my integ-
rity;
And I have trusted in the Lord without wavering.
Examine me, O Lord, and try me;
Test my mind and my heart.
For Thy lovingkindness is before my eyes,
And I have walked in Thy truth. . . .
As for me, I shall walk in my integrity;
Redeem me, and be gracious to me. (Ps. 26:1–3, 11)

The Pain of Enduring False Accusation

We all chanted it when we were young: "Sticks and stones may break my bones, but words will never hurt me." The truth is, though, that words do hurt. Those hard, verbal attacks inflict wounds as damaging as any bodily wounds.

Among the many trials we face, few are more devastating than statements made against us. They may be made against our *conduct*—things we didn't do; against our *words*—things we didn't say; or against our *motives*—things we didn't mean.

That's what happened to Paul in 2 Corinthians 1. In fact, those were the three areas the Corinthians used to falsely accuse the apostle.

First accusation: carnal conduct. Berating Paul's actions, they said he was shrewd, manipulative, and insincere.

Second accusation: fickle vacillation. Attacking his words, they rumored that he made promises he couldn't keep.

Third accusation: dominating dictator. Finally, maligning his motives, they said that underneath the sheepskin of servanthood he really wanted to "lord it over" them (see v. 24).

In Defense of True Character

The two most common reactions to false accusations are passivity—saying nothing; or aggression—vindictively lashing out. The former leaves the lie unanswered. The latter only complicates the problem.

Paul does neither. Rather, with wisdom and truth as his only defense, he faces the accusations one at a time.

Carnal Conduct

Paul responds to this accusation in verse 12:

> For our proud confidence is this, the testimony of our conscience, that in holiness and godly sincerity, not in fleshly wisdom but in the grace of God, we have conducted ourselves in the world, and especially toward you.

Holiness and sincerity. These are the character witnesses for the defense. For further proof of the purity of his conduct, Paul exhibits before the jury both his letters and his life. His plea is that the jurors understand what he writes and how he lives.

> For we write nothing else to you than what you read and understand, and I hope you will understand until the end; just as you also partially did understand us, that we are your reason to be proud as you also are ours, in the day of our Lord Jesus. (vv. 13–14)

Fickle Vacillation

Paul answers this charge in verses 15–16:

> And in this confidence I intended at first to come to you, that you might twice receive a blessing; that is, to pass your way into Macedonia, and again from Macedonia to come to you, and by you to be helped on my journey to Judea.

At the end of his first letter to the Corinthians, Paul had expressed his desire to visit them. But notice in 1 Corinthians 16:5–7 how he guarded himself with the words "perhaps . . . I hope . . . if the Lord permits."

> But I shall come to you after I go through Macedonia, for I am going through Macedonia; and perhaps I shall stay with you, or even spend the winter, that you may send me on my way wherever I may go. For I do not wish to see you now just in passing; for I hope to remain with you for some time, if the Lord permits.

The Corinthians mistook his full intentions for a firm promise. And when he didn't come, they concluded: "If you can't trust a man to keep a promise, how can you respect his authority as an apostle?"

In self-defense, he argues that his change in plans was not capricious. He had every intention of visiting them, but circumstances postponed his travel plans.

> Therefore, I was not vacillating when I intended to do this, was I?[2] Or that which I purpose, do I purpose according to the flesh, that with me there should be yes, yes and no, no at the same time? (2 Cor. 1:17)

Paul tries to convince the Corinthians that he is not sending double messages. He doesn't say yes and no in the same breath. When he says yes, he means yes. When he says no, he means no. In the following verses, Paul ties his argument to the Godhead.

> But as God is faithful, our word to you is not yes and no. For the Son of God, Christ Jesus, who was preached among you by us—by me and Silvanus and Timothy—was not yes and no, but is yes in Him. For as many as may be the promises of God, in Him they are yes; wherefore also by Him is our Amen to the glory of God through us. Now He who establishes us with you in Christ and anointed us is God, who also sealed[3] us and gave us the Spirit in our hearts as a pledge. (vv. 18–22)

Just as God is faithful, so Paul's words are faithful. Just as the preaching about Christ was without vacillation, so Paul's words are

---

2. In the original Greek, this question is introduced by the negative word *mēti*, which expects no for an answer.

3. The Greek word is *sphragizō*. The middle voice of the verb carries the sense that the Holy Spirit sealed us for Himself. "The seal, given and preserved intact, was a

without vacillation. Just as we can count on the Holy Spirit's seal on our lives, so we can trust that Paul's words bear the marks of integrity and truth. Paul's point is this: it would be inconsistent for a person who trafficked in the truth about Jesus Christ to be fickle with the truth in his personal life. He doesn't speak out of both sides of his mouth when he publicly proclaims Christ to them, and he doesn't do so in his private life either.

Dominating Dictator

In response to this third charge, Paul again calls God to the witness stand.

> But I call God as witness to my soul, that to spare you
> I came no more to Corinth. Not that we lord it over
> your faith, but are workers with you for your joy; for
> in your faith you are standing firm. (vv. 23–24)

The Corinthians had charged Paul with wanting to throw his spiritual weight around, trying to be some sort of guru for people to obsequiously follow. But that is not the case. Paul stands before them as a fellow worker (v. 24) and as a sincere bond servant (2:17, 4:5). Thus his example should be emulated rather than attacked.

Is your example one that people want to emulate—or attack? Servanthood is a rare quality today, mainly because there are so few examples of it. In the church, pastors, teachers, elders, and deacons often lord it over the flock. In the workplace, employers often lord it over their employees. In the home, husbands often lord it over their wives, and parents often lord it over their children. Maybe the problem stems from the fact that we don't have our eyes on the ultimate servant—Jesus, who came not to be served but to serve (Mark 10:45). How about you? Do you lord it over others? Or do you look to the Lord and use Him as your example for leadership?

Looking back now to our text, Paul says he didn't go to Corinth because he wanted to spare them (2 Cor. 1:23). The question that comes immediately to mind is: Spare them what? Chapter 2 reveals the answer:

> But I determined this for my own sake, that I would
> not come to you in sorrow again. For if I cause you

---

proof that a document had not been falsified, or goods tampered with in transit. It was also a mark of ownership; and the Christian, sealed . . . with the Spirit, was both visibly marked out as God's property, and secured ready to meet examination at the day of judgement." C. K. Barrett, *A Commentary on the Second Epistle to the Corinthians* (New York, N.Y.: Harper and Row, Publishers, 1973), p. 79.

sorrow, who then makes me glad but the one whom I made sorrowful? And this is the very thing I wrote you, lest, when I came, I should have sorrow from those who ought to make me rejoice; having confidence in you all, that my joy would be the joy of you all. For out of much affliction and anguish of heart I wrote to you with many tears; not that you should be made sorrowful, but that you might know the love which I have especially for you. (vv. 1–4)

Paul wanted to spare them sorrow. Apparently he had written them an additional letter after 1 Corinthians. And apparently, too, it was a blistering one, perhaps relating to the incestuous relationship denounced in 1 Corinthians 5:1–8. On the heels of that letter, Paul didn't want to come and stir up the sorrow his letter had created. He wanted to wait until the matter was resolved and the church was joyful again. His words are those of a loving shepherd, not of a self-serving tyrant.

Some Principles Worth Remembering When Accused

How nice it would be if all false accusations had stopped in the first century. What a relief it would be if Paul had silenced all those critical tongues. Unfortunately, the tongues are as sharp as ever . . . and their attacks, as relentless today as in the first century. To help defend yourself, here are three suggestions.

There are times when defending one's integrity calls for strong action.

At such times, confront the accuser. Don't talk with a lot of other people—just go directly to the person holding the knife. For until you take the knife away, the back stabbing will only continue.

There are other times when the best response is silence.

You may not hear the accusation until much later, when the accuser has disappeared. Or maybe the more you defend yourself, the more you appear guilty. In those cases, silence is the best defense. Instead of speaking out, go immediately to God, plead for vindication, and then step out of the way and let Him fight the battle (see Psalm 26).

Whether with assertiveness or silence, never take revenge.

Never! "Vengeance is Mine," says the Lord (Deut. 32:35). Wait in the wings and let God stage His own deliverance (Ps. 40:1–3). Trust in Him as your help and your deliverer (vv. 13–17).

Before we can defend integrity, we need to define it. Psalm 15 gives an excellent definition of integrity. Let's check it out.

- As you peruse Psalm 15, look for descriptions of integrity (every verse is loaded!). Write them down in the left column of the following chart. Then determine what each phrase means. Don't hurry—take time to discover how God views integrity.

Integrity: Psalm 15	
What It Says	What It Means

In our last exercise, you should have come up with a concise list that defines integrity. The question now is . . . how do *you* measure up?

- Under the heading Traits of Integrity, condense your discoveries from Psalm 15. Then take some time to answer the question, How do I measure up? In some traits you'll score well; in others, you may need to improve. Use this as a time to learn more about yourself.

Psalm 15	
Traits of Integrity	How Do I Measure Up?

Chapter 4

WHEN FORGIVENESS REALLY MEANS PROBATION

2 Corinthians 2:5–11

T here is nothing quite as liberating as the assurance of being forgiven. A pardon wipes the slate clean. Probation, on the other hand, keeps you feeling unsettled, distrusted, and watched. Webster defines *probation* as the

> subjection of an individual to a period of testing and trial to ascertain fitness . . . the action of suspending the sentence of a convicted offender and giving him freedom during good behavior under the supervision of a probation officer. [1]

Have you ever been placed on probation? Ever been told, "I forgive you"; but what you really heard was, "I'm putting you on probation"? At best, probation is half-forgiveness, dangling you somewhere between suspicion and supervision. You feel more like a criminal out on bail than a Christian accepted in the family.

Today we're going to examine a situation in the Corinthian church where a man had committed a serious offense, later repented, but was not fully forgiven.

Christ's Guidelines on Forgiveness

Matthew's Gospel contains a magnificent section on the subject of forgiveness in 18:21–35. Here Jesus answers three questions: How often should I forgive someone? Why not stop at a certain limit? What if I choose not to do as You have said?

How often?

In verse 21, Peter raises the question.

> Then Peter came and said to Him, "Lord, how often shall my brother sin against me and I forgive him? Up to seven times?"

Peter is looking for some kind of easy formula to calculate forgiveness, but Jesus gives him an equation that boggles his mind.

---

1. *Webster's New Collegiate Dictionary,* see "probation."

Jesus said to him, "I do not say to you, up to seven times, but up to seventy times seven." (v. 22)

Religious leaders of the day thought the number should be three. Most likely, Peter is feeling rather generous in upping it to seven. But those feelings deflate when Jesus factors the number by seventy. He isn't putting the limit at 490; He's using a colloquialism for infinity.

Why not?

Jesus anticipates this second question, "Why not stop at a certain limit?" and meets it with a parable (see vv. 23–35). It revolves around a king whose slave owed him an astronomical sum, equivalent to ten million dollars. Since the slave couldn't repay the money, he and his family were sentenced to be sold. But the slave fell on his face and begged for more time. The response of the king was extravagantly benevolent.

"And the lord of that slave felt compassion and released him and forgave him the debt." (v. 27)

By comparison, the Lord has forgiven us an infinite debt—our sin. That is why we should forgive others an infinite amount. As Paul says in Ephesians 4:32, "forgiving each other, just as God in Christ also has forgiven you."

There's another reason why we should forgive without limit: to do anything less for another is a gross act of hypocrisy.

The pardoned slave left the king's presence and met one of his fellow slaves who owed him a small amount of money. Rather than forgiving as he had been forgiven, he mercilessly insisted on payment, and then threw the man into prison when he couldn't pay (Matt. 18:28–30). When the king heard news of his servant's hypocrisy, he confronted him.

"Then summoning him, his lord said to him, 'You wicked slave, I forgave you all that debt because you entreated me. Should you not also have had mercy on your fellow slave, even as I had mercy on you?'" (vv. 32–33)

What if?

Forgiving an infinite number of times doesn't sound like good business to us. After all, a person could take advantage of us. What if we choose not to forgive and substitute probation instead? Jesus answers that question in verses 34–35.

"And his lord, moved with anger, handed him over to the torturers until he should repay all that was owed him. So shall My heavenly Father also do to you, if each of you does not forgive his brother from your heart."

Jesus is saying that the person who places another on probation instead of forgiving suffers greater consequences than the one not fully forgiven.

The Corinthians' Failure to Forgive

The Problem

The background to the Corinthians' failure to forgive can be found in 1 Corinthians 5. Paul had confronted the church on an immoral incident they were condoning—one of their members was living in an incestuous relationship with his stepmother (v. 1). This scandal would have shocked the Gentile community, but it hardly raised an eyebrow in the church. In fact, the church was even arrogant about it, apparently feeling very progressive and sophisticated (v. 2). In no uncertain terms, Paul told them to clean up their act. Just as the Jews cleaned out the leaven from their house during Passover (vv. 6–7), so the Corinthians should remove the immoral man from their midst (vv. 11–13).

The Punishment

Somewhere between Paul's first and second letters to the Corinthians, the church must have brought the gavel down hard on this man's life (2 Cor. 2:6–7). The incident isn't mentioned specifically, but it seems plausible that this is what Paul has in mind when he says:

> But if any has caused sorrow, he has caused sorrow not to me, but in some degree—in order not to say too much—to all of you. Sufficient for such a one is this punishment which was inflicted by the majority. (vv. 5–6)

The Pardon

Apparently, the man had repented but was held distanced by the congregation instead of welcomed with open arms. And so, rather than pardoning him, they put him on probation. Paul urges the Corinthians to fully pardon the man because he has suffered enough.

> So that on the contrary you should rather forgive and comfort him, lest somehow such a one be overwhelmed by excessive sorrow. Wherefore I urge you to reaffirm your love to him. For to this end also I wrote that I

31

might put you to the test, whether you are obedient in all things. (vv. 7–9)

The man no longer needs discipline; he needs forgiveness. Notice the process: There is punishment (v. 6), which leads to repentance; there is forgiveness (v. 7a), which prevents despair; there is comfort (v. 7b), which rebuilds esteem and dignity; and there is a reaffirmation of love (v. 8), which gives purpose and direction to life.

Paul then shows that he struggles side by side with them in this process; he's not lording it over them.

But whom you forgive anything, I forgive also; for indeed what I have forgiven, if I have forgiven anything, I did it for your sakes in the presence of Christ. (v. 10)

As Paul concludes his case, he warns them of the consequences of choosing probation over pardon, of shunning the man instead of embracing him. They are warned to forgive.

In order that no advantage be taken of us by Satan; for we are not ignorant of his schemes. (v. 11)

This verse states the ultimate purpose of forgiveness: "that no advantage be taken of us by Satan." The construction of the phrase *by Satan* suggests direct, personal involvement. The word *advantage* means "overreaching, getting more than is due." When we don't fully forgive a person who has fully repented, we invite the involvement of Satan. He then steps in and grabs more than his due, benefiting not only from the fall but from the failure to forgive. The word *scheme* comes from the Greek word for "the mind." Satan's schemes are mind games in which he distorts our thinking.

The goal of discipline is not removal; it's restoration and reconciliation. When we lose sight of that, we go too far. And when we go too far, Satan gets too much.

The parable of the prodigal son illustrates how we should respond to the repentant believer who wants to return to the fellowship of the church. Remember what happened when the wayward son came to his senses and returned home?

"Okay, stay in your room for the next three months, and remember, I'll be watching you."

Was that the response of the father? No.

"But while he was still a long way off, his father saw him, and felt compassion for him, and ran and embraced him, and kissed him. . . . The father said to his slaves, 'Quickly bring out the best robe and put it on him, and put a ring on his hand and sandals on his feet; and bring the fattened calf, kill it, and let us eat and be merry; for this son of mine was . . . lost, and has been found.'" (Luke 15:20b, 22–24)

Is that how you respond when one of your errant children comes home? Are you there waiting with open arms or are you keeping that child at arm's distance? Do you fully pardon your mate or do you put that person on probation when wronged?

Remember: *Our forgiveness should be as swift as our discipline is severe.*

Christian Principles for Today

True repentance calls for immediate and full forgiveness.

Even if the sinner feels unworthy, the forgiver should take the initiative toward restoration. Most people who repent come with a make-me-one-of-your-slaves speeches like the one the prodigal son had rehearsed (Luke 15:18–19). But remember, his father stopped him before he had a chance to get his speech out (vv. 20–22). God, like the prodigal's father, wants to restore sons, not recruit slaves. And so should we.

Full forgiveness is demonstrative, not theoretical.

It's not simply something we say; it's something we do. Remember the commands in verses 7 and 8 of 2 Corinthians 2? They're all action words: "forgive . . . comfort . . . reaffirm."

To hold back invites trouble from the adversary.

When you refuse to forgive someone who has genuinely repented, that person becomes confused and unproductive, wondering: What else must I do? How else can I prove myself? Will I ever be used again by God? Ultimately, bitterness sets in and Satan claims another victory.

Are you holding others in bondage who deserve to be free? Are you still keeping tally of their wrongs though they've confessed them and repented?

If so, ask yourself one question: Why?

If you're the one who's fallen and is living an unproductive life, distant from your family and distant from God, here's some good news.

If we confess our sins, He is faithful and righteous to forgive us our sins and to cleanse us from all unrighteousness. (1 John 1:9)

Come back to Christ, won't you? Confess the sin. Be cleansed. And let Him throw His arms around you and welcome you back.

🍇 *Living Insights* STUDY ONE

So which quality governs your life—forgiveness or probation? Today we learned some key teachings concerning forgiveness. Let's look now at these passages from another perspective.

- Reread Matthew 18:21–35, 1 Corinthians 5:1–13, and 2 Corinthians 2:5–11 in a version other than your usual one. You may want to try a translation such as the King James Bible, the New American Standard Bible, the New International Version, or the Revised Standard Version. Or you may wish to read a paraphrase like Phillips' or the Living Bible. This exercise will show you the passages in a fresh light, helping you glean insights you could overlook in a more familiar version.

🍇 *Living Insights* STUDY TWO

This lesson concluded with a penetrating probe: Do you still hold in bondage people who have repented? If so, let's deal with this issue.

- Are any of your relationships stressful because you have been unwilling to forgive? The answer is clear, though not necessarily easy. Go to that person and make peace. Remember the key is forgiveness, not probation. God will give you the strength, friend. Settle your accounts . . . and do it now!

Chapter 5

WHAT IS THAT FRAGRANCE?

2 Corinthians 2:12–17

G ood communication—communication that is clear, honest, and vulnerable—is hard work. And the deeper the level of communication, the harder the work. According to John Powell, there are five levels of communication, each increasing in difficulty. [1]

> *Level one: clichés.* This is the most superficial level. It's a hi-how-are-you type of conversation that is entirely social in nature.
>
> *Level two: facts and reports.* This level exchanges only external information. It is safe conversation that ranges from the weather to who-won-the-game to the nightly news.
>
> *Level three: opinions and judgments.* This is the first level to scratch below the surface and reveal something of ourselves. On this level, words like "ought" and "should" and "like" and "dislike" come out of hiding to reveal our convictions.
>
> *Level four: feelings.* This is the level that reveals our emotions, a level most people seldom penetrate. "I feel sad" or "I'm afraid" or "I am angry" are all examples of level four communication.
>
> *Level five: maximum truth.* This deepest level speaks truth in its most open and candid form. Maximum truth includes affirmation, confrontation, confession, forgiveness, the sharing of dreams and disillusions, and the telling and keeping of secrets.

When we can communicate on all five levels, we are healthier and happier people. Paul shows us his mastery of healthy communication in the passage we'll be studying today: 2 Corinthians 2:12–17.

---

1. Based on information in *Why Am I Afraid to Tell You Who I Am?* by John Powell (Niles, Ill.: Argus Communications, 1969), pp. 54–58.

Paul's Life: An Open Book

In this immensely personal book, Paul opens his life to us. We cannot help but admire the man and appreciate his openness—an openness he demonstrates throughout the letter. In chapter 1 he immediately expresses himself on levels four and five.

> For we do not want you to be unaware, brethren, of our affliction which came to us in Asia, that we were burdened excessively, beyond our strength, so that we despaired even of life. (v. 8)

In 2:4 he continues to open up.

> For out of much affliction and anguish of heart I wrote to you with many tears; not that you should be made sorrowful, but that you might know the love which I have especially for you.

Two things stand out in that verse. First, here is a grown man who cries; and second, he uses the word *love*. Pretty rare qualities for a man, especially a man in authority.

Another example of level five communication can be found in Paul's rebuke (vv. 6–8).

> Sufficient for such a one is this punishment which was inflicted by the majority, so that on the contrary you should rather forgive and comfort him, lest somehow such a one be overwhelmed by excessive sorrow. Wherefore I urge you to reaffirm your love for him.

Finally, he makes himself extremely vulnerable in 7:2–4.

> Make room for us in your hearts; we wronged no one, we corrupted no one, we took advantage of no one. I do not speak to condemn you; for I have said before that you are in our hearts to die together and to live together. Great is my confidence in you, great is my boasting on your behalf; I am filled with comfort. I am overflowing with joy in all our affliction.

Between the lines of theology, inklings of Paul's humanity bleed through, endearing himself to the Corinthians as well as us.

A Personal Struggle at Troas

In 2:12–13, the apostle becomes more transparent by discussing a personal struggle he experienced at Troas.

Now when I came to Troas for the gospel of Christ and when a door was opened for me in the Lord, I had no rest for my spirit, not finding Titus my brother; but taking my leave of them, I went on to Macedonia.

Troas was the northwesternmost city in Asia Minor, or Turkey, as it is known now. Paul had traveled all the way from Ephesus to this coastal city and, once there, found that God had opened a door of ministry. In fact, so wide was the door opened, he found little time to rest, physically or emotionally.

The word translated "rest" is an old term for *relaxing*. It's the same word used for "freedom" in Acts 24:23, and for "ease" in 2 Corinthians 8:13. Paul had an absence of inner peace. In spite of God's work in the city, Paul was restless and uneasy, churning inside.

The reason? He couldn't find Titus. Paul trusted this brother in the Lord and held him in high regard. He not only had given Titus the responsibility of collecting the famine relief money for the Christians in Jerusalem (8:6), but he had also picked him to send this letter to the Corinthian church (vv. 16–17). Not having Titus by his side so unnerved Paul that he left this great ministry opportunity and sailed to Macedonia to find him.

At first Paul's actions seem irresponsible, in light of the opportunity God has given him in Troas. But merely an open door does not automatically mean that we should walk through it. To be most effective, we must have an accompanying assurance from the Lord. A need, in itself, does not constitute a call to ministry. Apparently, Paul feels more compelled to find Titus than he feels called to minister in Troas.

Paul, however, doesn't wallow in his depression over not finding Titus. Instead he changes the subject. Beginning in 2:14 and continuing through 6:10, he discusses ministry in greater depth than he does anywhere else in the New Testament.

A General Statement of Ministry

Instead of being downcast with pity, Paul overflows in an outburst of praise. As A. T. Robertson writes,

> we can be grateful for this emotional outburst . . . for it has given the world the finest exposition of all sides of the Christian ministry in existence, one that reveals

the wealth of Paul's nature and his mature grasp of the
great things in service for Christ.[2]

In this section of praise in 2:14–17, we find three marks of an
effective ministry.

Ministry is following the Leader, not taking the lead.

But thanks be to God, who always leads us in His
triumph in Christ. (v. 14a)

Our ministry becomes effective when we follow the Leader instead of jumping ahead of God and taking the lead ourselves. Few
have been called to minister who are more gifted than the apostle
Paul. Few have had brighter minds, more determination, or greater
vision. And yet this most gifted man openly declares that God is
the Leader, not him.

Commenting on verses 14–16, William Barclay notes:

In [Paul's] mind is the picture of a Roman *Triumph* and
of Christ as a universal conqueror. . . . In a Triumph
the procession of the victorious general marched
through the streets of Rome to the Capitol in the
following order. First came the state officials and the
senate. Then came the trumpeters. Then were carried
the spoils taken from the conquered land. . . . Then
came pictures of the conquered land and models of
conquered citadels and ships. . . . Then there walked
the captive princes, leaders and generals in chains,
shortly to be flung into prison and in all probability
almost immediately to be executed. Then came the
lictors bearing their rods, followed by the musicians
with their lyres; then the priests swinging their cen-
sers with the sweet-smelling incense burning in them.
After that came the general himself. He stood in a
chariot drawn by four horses. . . . After him rode his
family; and finally came the army wearing all their dec-
orations and shouting *Io triumphe!* their cry of triumph.[3]

Christ, our conqueror, is in the lead, and we, His chosen war-
riors, follow behind Him, enjoying the benefits of His triumph. For
at the cross, Christ undertook a battle that was not rightly His so
that we might share in a triumph that is not rightly ours.

2. A. T. Robertson, *Word Pictures in the New Testament* (Nashville, Tenn.: Broadman
Press, 1931), vol. 4, p. 218.

3. William Barclay, *The Letters to the Corinthians*, rev. ed., The Daily Study Bible
Series (Philadelphia, Pa.: The Westminster Press, 1975), pp. 183–84.

Ministry is emitting a pleasing fragrance to God, not being overly concerned with the response of others.

> [God] manifests through us the sweet aroma of the knowledge of Him in every place. For we are a fragrance of Christ to God among those who are being saved and among those who are perishing; to the one an aroma from death to death, to the other an aroma from life to life. (vv. 14b–16a)

In the ancient processional that Barclay describes, an aroma was emitted along the way by the priests swinging giant jars of smoking incense. The smell would flow equally over those exulting in triumph and those hanging their heads in defeat. To the former, it was the sweet scent of a victorious life; to the latter, an acrid reminder of their imminent death.

Ministry is modeling the truth though inadequate, not corrupting the message while appearing adequate.

What an honor to accompany the triumphant conqueror in that victory parade! That is why Paul proclaims:

> And who is adequate for these things? For we are not like many, peddling the word of God, but as from sincerity, but as from God, we speak in Christ in the sight of God. (vv. 16b–17)

Peddling the Word of God. The image is one of street salesmen, hawking their wares, interested only in making the sale—not in serving the customer. Just as there were money changers in the temple courtyard, there will always be street salesmen in the church. Peddling prophetic pills . . . cure-all tonics . . . positive thinking . . . health and wealth . . . legalism and negativism. In short, peddling whatever the public is gullible enough to purchase.

But Paul assures the Corinthians that he represents the real thing—"from God"—and that he represents Him with pure motives—"from sincerity."

Our Lives . . . An Honest Evaluation

Now that we've looked into the open book of Paul's life, it's time to read a page or two from our own. Let's take a closer look by examining four crucial categories.

First: *Are you really depending upon God?* Are you really waiting on Him? Or do you take advantage of every opportunity that comes your way and plow right into it? Are you really sensitive to God's leading? Remember, a need doesn't constitute a call. Nor does an open door necessarily mean you are the one to walk through it.

Second: *Is your life truly triumphant in Christ?* Is your focus truly on Christ's conquering power? Remember, He "always leads us in His triumph" (v. 14, italics added).

Third: *How's your fragrance?* Are you wearing My Sin or My Savior these days? Christ has an unmistakable fragrance, and you can smell it on someone who is genuinely Christlike. Unfortunately, there's a fragrance of the flesh that's just as obvious.

Fourth: *Do you sincerely model authenticity?* Is being real one of your goals? Authenticity is coming to grips with who you are and being transparent about what your life is like beneath its polished exterior. It's painful to be real, but that's the way we impact others most deeply.[4]

If you answered no to any of these questions, maybe your relationship with the Lord is stuck at a superficial level. Fortunately, just as God always leads in triumph, so He always leads His children into a deeper relationship with Him. He's always drawing us into more meaningful levels of openness with Him, always encouraging us to communicate on level five. If you want to have a deeper, more meaningful spiritual life, take some time now to pray about that. And when you pray, don't worry about making King James proud. God is pleased with your stutters if only you are sincere.

Living Insights

Effective ministry is emitting a pleasing fragrance to God, not being overly concerned with the response of others. Isn't that a vivid word picture? This is a rich passage, worthy of further study.

- A valuable method for digging deep into a Bible passage is paraphrasing. On the next page, write out 2 Corinthians 2:12–17 in your own words. As you do, explore the feelings and emotions Paul communicates, and try to capture them on paper.

---

4. "We wish we were better than we are, but we're not. And that realization brings shame, a desire to hide, to avoid real contact, to present to others only that part of us we think will be well received. We want to hide the rest—not because we desire to avoid offending others with our ugly side, but because we fear their rejection. We live for the purpose of self-protection, clinging to whatever brings us happiness and security. The effect is a discouraging distance between ourself and the people we long to be close to. The quality of our life diminishes." Larry Crabb, *Inside Out* (Colorado Springs, Colo.: NavPress, 1988), p. 30.

Our approach to ministry needs an honest evaluation. Use the following questions to honestly evaluate your ministry effectiveness, circling your answers. If you need to improve in any of these areas, jot down a little strategy for how you will accomplish this.

- Are you really depending on God?

  Not Much   Only Sometimes   Definitely

- Is your life truly triumphant in Christ?

  Not Much   Only Sometimes   Definitely

- How's your fragrance?

  Offensive   Nonexistent   Pleasing

- Do you sincerely model authenticity?

  Not Much   Only Sometimes   Definitely

- What are your strategies for improvement?

  _____

  _____

  _____

  _____

  _____

  _____

  _____

  _____

  _____

  _____

  _____

  _____

  _____

Chapter 6

WHAT'S A NEW COVENANT MINISTRY?

2 Corinthians 3

S uccess. We dream about it. We dress for it. We die for it. From *Fortune 500* to the *Lifestyles of the Rich and Famous*, success is a front-page, prime-time item.

Businesses that are profitable are considered successful. Teams that win are considered successful. People who move quickly up the corporate ladder are considered successful.

Most would agree that success has three primary ingredients: achievement, confidence, and promotion. Successful people are those who have accomplished something, who are confident in their expertise, and who have been publicized. At least, this is how our culture measures success.

As hard as it may be to accept, these are not the things that add up to success in God's eyes. His scales are weighted to much different values. But, if we're not careful, we can easily tip the scales to favor the world's view of success. By focusing on human accomplishment, we can lose sight of divine enablement; by emphasizing self-confidence, we fall into the trap of pride; and by relying on advertising, we depend on fleshly means to obtain spiritual ends.

A Popular Yet Incorrect Concept of Success

If anyone was ever dressed for success, it was Paul.

> Although I myself might have confidence even in the flesh. If anyone else has a mind to put confidence in the flesh, I far more: circumcised the eighth day, of the nation of Israel, of the tribe of Benjamin, a Hebrew of Hebrews; as to the Law, a Pharisee; as to zeal, a persecutor of the church; as to the righteousness which is in the Law, found blameless. (Phil. 3:4–6)

From head to toe, Paul was a power dresser. His ancestry was impressive (v. 5a); his orthodoxy, impeccable (v. 5b); his activity, incredible (v. 6a); his morality, immaculate (v. 6b). No doubt, his graduating class would have voted him "Most Likely to Succeed."

By the world's tape measure, Paul's success was staggering. But by God's standards, it didn't amount to much.

> But whatever things were gain to me, those things I have counted as loss for the sake of Christ. More than that, I count all things to be loss in view of the surpassing value of knowing Christ Jesus my Lord, for whom I have suffered the loss of all things, and count them but rubbish in order that I may gain Christ, and may be found in Him, not having a righteousness of my own derived from the Law, but that which is through faith in Christ, the righteousness which comes from God on the basis of faith. (vv. 7–9)

These are not the words of a modest man; these are the words of a transformed man—transformed by Jesus Christ, where the old things have passed away, and all things have become new (2 Cor. 5:17).

An Unpopular Yet Correct View of Service

A Statement of Clarification

In Philippians 3, Paul shows the inadequacy of human accomplishment. But in 2 Corinthians 3, he completes the picture. Here we are shown where our adequacy for service really comes from.

In the last paragraph of 2 Corinthians 2, Paul says that he comes in triumph, in the fragrance of Christ, and in sincerity.

A skeptic could read those words and conclude that Paul was bragging, attempting to present himself as the one who is to be commended. But in 3:1 Paul addresses that skepticism.

> Are we beginning to commend ourselves again? Or do we need, as some, letters of commendation to you or from you?

In those days itinerant evangelists would often travel with letters of endorsement and recommendation. This functioned as a seal of approval upon their ministry. But Paul says his credentials are different.

> You are our letter, written in our hearts, known and read by all men; being manifested that you are a letter of Christ, cared for by us, written not with ink, but with the Spirit of the living God, not on tablets of stone, but on tablets of human hearts. (vv. 2–3)

No longer is Paul interested in impressing people. No longer does he draw on himself for inner strength. And no longer is his confidence in credentials—it's in Christ.

> And such confidence we have through Christ toward God. Not that we are adequate in ourselves to consider anything as coming from ourselves, but our adequacy is from God. (vv. 4–5)

So often we work overtime to get people to notice us, to show them how adequate we are, how competent, how gifted, how important. But it's not important that they see us, only Him. And our impressive qualifications and accomplishments only obscure the view.

A Series of Contrasts

Verses 5–11 delineate several contrasts that help us sort out our motives for serving God. They fall into two broad categories: the old arrangement, of the flesh; and the new arrangement, of the Spirit.

> Not that we are adequate in ourselves to consider anything as coming from ourselves, but our adequacy is from God, who also made us adequate as servants of a new covenant, not of the letter, but of the Spirit; for the letter kills, but the Spirit gives life. But if the ministry of death, in letters engraved on stones, came with glory, so that the sons of Israel could not look intently at the face of Moses because of the glory of his face, fading as it was, how shall the ministry of the Spirit fail to be even more with glory? For if the ministry of condemnation has glory, much more does the ministry of righteousness abound in glory. For indeed what had glory, in this case has no glory on account of the glory that surpasses it. For if that which fades away was with glory, much more that which remains is in glory.

Let's go back over the verses and fill in the contrasts in the following table.

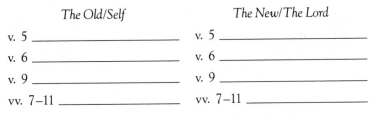

The Old/Self	The New/The Lord
v. 5 _____	v. 5 _____
v. 6 _____	v. 6 _____
v. 9 _____	v. 9 _____
vv. 7–11 _____	vv. 7–11 _____

Under the Old Covenant or arrangement, known as the Mosaic Law, God's truth was external—etched in tablets of stone. As such, it had only the power to condemn, not to give life.

After Jesus died, however, fulfilling every iota of the Law, His life-giving Spirit was placed in our hearts. Since then, truth has been internal, not external. Where the Law only produced guilt and conflict and death, the Spirit now produces peace, life, light, help, joy, and purpose.

This means we are not to approach the Law to fulfill it but to come to Christ and let Him live His life through us. That's the glory of it all!

For sake of illustration, think of glory as light. There is a certain glory of the moon and stars that shine at night. But when the sun comes up in the morning, these stellar luminaries pale. Why? Because the glory of the sun outshines that of the moon and stars.

Similarly, the Old Covenant, with all its glory, paled with the dawn of Christ. Consequently, this age ushered in a fresh and radiant confidence.

> Having therefore such a hope, we use great boldness
> in our speech. (v. 12)

Turning our attention from the dawn of this new age to the fading darkness of that old era, we come upon an obscure incident in Moses' life. When he received the stone tablets from God on Mount Sinai, his face glowed from being in the presence of deity. After he came down from the mountain, Moses veiled his face. He did this, at least initially, because the people were afraid (Exod. 34:29–35). But verse 13 of 2 Corinthians 3 indicates that he kept it on to cover up the fact that the glory was fading, to veil his own inadequacy.

> And [we] are not as Moses, who used to put a veil over
> his face that the sons of Israel might not look intently
> at the end of what was fading away.

Regarding Moses, the veil represents an attempt to protect and preserve one's reputation—something we all do from time to time, though needlessly, now that our adequacy is in Christ. Regarding the Jews, the veil represents a hardened blindness to the realities the Old Covenant foreshadowed.

> But their minds were hardened; for until this very day
> at the reading of the old covenant the same veil re-
> mains unlifted, because it is removed in Christ. But

to this day whenever Moses is read, a veil lies over their heart; but whenever a man turns to the Lord, the veil is taken away. (vv. 14–16)

The Secret of Confidence

When we come to Jesus, our lives are transformed. We come to the cross, confessing our own inadequacy; we go away, claiming only His adequacy. Like the hymnist says, "Nothing in my hand I bring, Simply to Thy cross I cling."[1]

If we strip away the veil, the truth is that our glory is ephemeral, fleeting, fading. Then what is the secret of our confidence? Look at verses 17–18.

Now the Lord is the Spirit; and where the Spirit of the Lord is, there is liberty. But we all, with unveiled face beholding as in a mirror the glory of the Lord, are being transformed into the same image from glory to glory, just as from the Lord, the Spirit.

The source of confidence is no longer in ourselves, but in His Spirit. No longer do we need to live imprisoned in fear, because we are free to live by His power. No longer do we need to be concerned about transforming ourselves, but rather in *being* transformed by the power of His Spirit.

Two Essential Yet Overlooked Ingredients

This recipe for a transformed life will fall flat if two essential ingredients are overlooked.

First: *True spirituality comes from God; it doesn't come from us.* We can make ourselves available. We can take away the veil of false piety. We can choose to walk by the Spirit instead of by the flesh. But, in the final analysis, only He has the power to energize that walk. As Paul says in Galatians 2:20, "I have been crucified with Christ; and it is no longer I who live, but Christ lives in me."

Second: *True spirituality takes time to develop; it doesn't happen overnight.* From quick-stop convenience stores to cosmetic make-overs, we're used to instant results. It's easy to assume that God, especially a God of miracles, specializes in instant discipleship. But that is not the case. Heaven never hangs out the sign: Overnight Transformations. Inquire Within.

---

1. Augustus M. Toplady, "Rock of Ages, Cleft for Me," *Worship and Service Hymnal for Church, School, and Home* (Chicago, Ill.: Hope Publishing Co., 1957), no. 223.

God's specialty is not while-you-wait make-overs but over-a-lifetime transformations.

🍇 *Living Insights*

STUDY ONE

Paul often uses contrasts in his writing to help his readers understand his message. We studied one example of contrasting in our lesson today. Now let's take a look at another one.

- The book after Second Corinthians in your New Testament is the letter to the Galatians. Turn there, begin reading, and use the space that follows to record the many contrasts found in this brief epistle.

Contrasts in Galatians

Verse _*1:1*_

Contrast _*not sent through agency of man but through Christ*_

Verse _*1:10*_

Contrast _*Seeking favor of men instead of favor of God*_

Verse _____

Contrast _____
_____

Verse _____

Contrast _____
_____

Verse _____

Contrast _____
_____

Verse _____

Contrast _____
_____

Verse _____

Contrast _____
_____

Verse _____

Contrast _____
_____

Verse _____

Contrast _____
_____

Verse _____

Contrast _____
_____

🍇 *Living Insights*   STUDY TWO

True spirituality comes from God, not us. And it takes time to develop—it doesn't happen overnight.

- Spend some time talking to God about your current spiritual condition. Pour out your struggles, asking for His forgiveness and the strength to press on. Reflect on how far you've come and set your sights on where you want to go. Thank Him for the journey He's taking you on and for His help along the way.

Chapter 7

CHECKLIST FOR AN EFFECTIVE MINISTRY

2 Corinthians 4:1–6

I f the apostle Paul had fallen asleep in the first century and then awakened in the twentieth, like Rip Van Winkle, imagine his shock. Can't you see him stumbling from one church to another, rubbing his eyes in utter disbelief? How disillusioning it would be for him, how depressing to see so many churches so ineffective.

Paul, who had seen the baby pictures of the church and who had cared for it in its infancy, would be horrified to see it now in its adult state. How could the church have gotten off to such a good start and arrived at such a dead end? Where did it go off course? When did it take a wrong turn?

In our study, we will take a look at ministry today and then at ministry as God intended it. In doing so, maybe we will be able to steer our respective ministries back on the right track of serving Christ.

Ministry Today: A Study in Confusion

Three salient reasons contribute to today's confusion in Christian ministry. First: *There is a rarity of biblical instruction.* This doesn't mean that the Bible is not referred to or used; merely that its truths are often not explained nor its principles followed. And inevitably, this lack of substance results in the absence of a standard. Can you imagine a carpenter without a tape measure? In the same way, the Bible is our standard against which all of life is measured.

Second: *There is an overemphasis on emotional persuasion.* Some ministries exploit and manipulate people, using slick, Madison Avenue pressure tactics to appeal to their emotions and to prompt desired responses.

Third: *There is a breakdown of personal integrity.* Sadly, when we look behind the scenes, when we turn off the lights, cameras, and microphone, we will often find an offscreen 70-mm ego. And if we look hard enough, we will also find dishonesty and hypocrisy lurking in the shadows.

Like supermarket cereal, when Christianity is brightly packaged and sugarcoated and enticingly offers free prizes on the inside, we fail to see the fine print on the side of the box. And so we never know about all the empty calories we've eaten . . . or realize how malnourished we've become.

That is hardly what God intended ministry to be.

Ministry As God Intended It

To lead correctly, to keep its motives pure, and to maintain proper integrity, a ministry must have three qualities: a correct mentality, an inspired methodology, and an authentic model.

A Correct Mentality

Second Corinthians 4:1 is our reference point.

> Therefore, since we have this ministry, as we received mercy, we do not lose heart.

The words "this ministry" have chapter 3 as their antecedent. Anyone hoping to sustain an effective ministry that glorifies God must begin with the right mentality. First: *An effective ministry requires a right philosophy.* It must be a ministry with the openness, liberty, and authenticity that chapter 3 sets forth. A ministry without veils—without anything to hide, and without anything to prove.

Second: *An effective ministry includes an abundance of mercy.* Underscore the word "mercy" in verse 1. Mercy, as someone once said, is God's ministry to the miserable. And having received mercy, we reach out to others with open arms and extended hands.

Third: *An effective ministry provides consistent stability.* A ministry as God intended isn't one that makes us lose heart. It doesn't drag us down; it lifts us up. It doesn't depress us; it motivates us (see v. 16).

An Inspired Methodology

Paul becomes more specific about this ministry in verses 2–4.

> We have renounced the things hidden because of shame, not walking in craftiness or adulterating the word of God, but by the manifestation of truth commending ourselves to every man's conscience in the sight of God. And even if our gospel is veiled, it is veiled to those who are perishing, in whose case the god of this world has blinded the minds of the unbelieving, that they might not see the light of the gospel of the glory of Christ, who is the image of God.

In this passage, Paul leaves us with five specifics that form an inspired methodology. First: *There is a rejection of deceit.* Paul has renounced "things hidden," referring to that which is secretive and underhanded. Paul was open and unguarded. What you saw in him was what you got. And what others see in us should be what they get too.

Second: *There is an unwillingness to rely on cleverness.* Paul was committed to "not walking in craftiness." He didn't rely on gimmicks to get results. He didn't play on people's emotions. He didn't use high-powered, promotional campaigns to get the job done.

Third: *There is a refusal to mishandle Scripture.* Paul dedicated himself to not "adulterating the word of God." He didn't tamper with its meaning, or read into the text something that wasn't there in order to prove his point, or use it for his own selfish purposes.

Fourth: *There is a reaching out to touch everyone's conscience.* Paul stated that by setting forth the truth plainly they were commending themselves "to every man's conscience." That is all the Holy Spirit needs to do surgery—just the clean, sharp knife of the Word.

> For the word of God is living and active and sharper than any two-edged sword, and piercing as far as the division of soul and spirit, of both joints and marrow, and able to judge the thoughts and intentions of the heart. And there is no creature hidden from His sight, but all things are open and laid bare to the eyes of Him with whom we have to do. (Heb. 4:12–13)

Truth cuts through the hypocrisy in our lives and goes straight to the heart. Before God, that heart is like an open book. He can see every word of wickedness, every line of lust, every page of pride, every chapter of corruption. And that's when the knife starts its incisive, healing work.

Fifth: *There is a realization that some will not believe.* In verses 3–4 of 2 Corinthians 4, there is a clear explanation of why the same truth is exciting to one person and boring to another, why some people get turned on and others get turned off. The average person would rather live in an illusion than have the veil lifted to reveal the reality of biblical truth.

Scripture powerfully shatters the illusions in people's lives. That's why being a minister can be such a heady experience. And that's why, all the more, power should be wielded only by an exemplary person.

An Authentic Model

In verses 5 and 6 Paul states four characteristics of the person who best exemplifies a minister of God.

> For we do not preach ourselves but Christ Jesus as Lord, and ourselves as your bond-servants for Jesus' sake. For God, who said, "Light shall shine out of darkness," is the One who has shone in our hearts to give the light of the knowledge of the glory of God in the face of Christ.

First: *That person does not proclaim himself or herself "as Lord."* It's easy in a job of such power and prestige to become filled with pride. How can you tell when that's happened? When the person makes frequent references to self. When the person expects special treatment and favors. When the lordship of Christ is personally resisted. When there is a desire to be seen, known, and promoted. When that person requires the blind and complete submission of others. And finally, when there is a refusal to be accountable and vulnerable.

Second: *That person lifts up Christ as Lord.* The model minister of God promotes Christ and has a deep, sincere love of His Word. This individual takes God seriously, fearing Him and holding Him in the highest esteem.

Third: *That person is a servant.* We can see this principle incarnated in the lives of Paul and Barnabas in Acts 14. When the pagan people of Lystra saw Paul heal a lame man, they exalted him and Barnabas: "The gods have become like men and have come down to us" (v. 11). They called Barnabas, Zeus, and they called Paul, Hermes, wanting to offer sacrifices to them (vv. 12–13). But their response was that of servants, refusing the temptation to be exalted.

> But when the apostles, Barnabas and Paul, heard of it, they tore their robes and rushed out into the crowd, crying out and saying, "Men, why are you doing these things? We are also men of the same nature as you, and preach the gospel to you in order that you should turn from these vain things to a living God, who made the heaven and the earth and the sea, and all that is in them. (vv. 14–15)

Fourth: *That person gives God the glory and points others to Christ.* Only God can cause light to shine out of darkness, both in the creation of the world and in the creation of a believer's heart. Consequently, only He deserves the credit. We may carry the lamp that shows Christ to others, but the flame is from the Lord.

Ministry Questions That Must Be Asked

As we conclude this study, it might be helpful to personalize this by letting a few questions linger in your mind. Have you come to terms with deception in your life? Are you open to the same truth you proclaim? Is servanthood the model you follow? If you have a chance to promote someone else, do you do it, or do you become jealous? And finally, does Christ really reign as Lord in your life? If you can answer yes with all honesty, you're well on your way to having an effective ministry that will honor God.

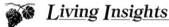 *Living Insights* STUDY ONE

What a powerful passage on ministry as God intended it. This stuff is too good to pass over in haste. Let's linger a little longer at this great text.

- Perhaps you'll want to commit these verses to memory. If all of 2 Corinthians 4:1–6 is too much, reduce it to a more manageable size. Try writing out the passage and then reading it aloud. Soon you'll discover that you're depending less on the page and reciting more from the heart.

Living Insights STUDY TWO

Your thoughts probably centered on your pastor as we took this look at effective ministry. This might be a good time to let him know just how much you appreciate him.

- Write a note of encouragement to your pastor. Thank him for all that he's doing to provide leadership to your local body of believers. Be as specific as possible, pointing out the little things he does, things that others tend to overlook.

Chapter 8

POWER IN POTS . . .
LIFE IN DEATH

2 Corinthians 4:7–12

P ower does not consist of missiles and tanks any more than it consists of muscles in tank tops. No matter how powerful the bombs or how pumped-up the biceps, true power is not found there.

True power exists in paradox, the most significant of which occurred two thousand years ago when God in the flesh died. When omnipotence surrendered to impotence.

Jesus, who had the power to call angels down from heaven to destroy His enemies, didn't. Instead, He endured the shame of the cross, "and while being reviled, He did not revile in return; while suffering, He uttered no threats" (1 Pet. 2:23).

And as if the rejection from man wasn't painful enough, Jesus also faced the silence of His Father during those dark hours before death: "My God, My God, why hast Thou forsaken Me?" (Mark 15:34). Isaiah even tells us that "the Lord was pleased / To crush Him" (Isa. 53:10).

A loving father turns His back on His only son.

Is it any wonder the cross is a stumbling block to so many people: "For the word of the cross is to those who are perishing foolishness, but to us who are being saved it is the power of God" (1 Cor. 1:18).

The power of God. That is the topic Paul discusses in our lesson today in 2 Corinthians 4:7–12.

Power That Comes from God

Power to minister effectively and impact others comes from God. But His power is not displayed as humans would display it. There are no parades of military might. No bold headlines. No press conferences. No flexed muscles, or clenched fists, or angry threats. So how *does* God display His power? Paul tells us in 2 Corinthians 4:7a.

We have this treasure in earthen vessels.

Earthen vessels. Simple clay pots. Fragile and flawed. You and me. What a paradox. Power in pots . . . life in death.

Why would God place His priceless treasure in such unpretentious pottery?

> That the surpassing greatness of the power may be of
> God and not from ourselves. (v. 7b)

Like Mary's expensive perfume (John 12:3), the aroma of Christ inside our heart cannot be experienced by others until it is poured out. And often, God's way of pouring out that fragrance is to break the earthen vessel that holds it.

> We are afflicted[1] in every way, but not crushed; perplexed,[2] but not despairing; persecuted,[3] but not forsaken; struck down, but not destroyed. (2 Cor. 4:8–9)

Commenting on this passage, William Barclay says that "we are sore pressed at every point but not hemmed in . . . persecuted by men but never abandoned by God . . . at our wit's end but never at our hope's end . . . knocked down but not knocked out."[4]

But that's not what we want in life, is it? We want to be glazed and polished, displayed on some safe shelf. God, however, wants us to be a fragrant aroma of Christ (2:14–16). And that means we have to be taken off the shelf, poured out, even broken.

The spiritual battle is real, but we don't want real battles. We want life to be like Disneyland's "Pirates of the Caribbean" ride. We want to float through the water in little boats, watching from a distance the cannon fire and splashing water. But we don't want real cannonballs, we just want a safe thrill.

Life, however, isn't Disneyland. It's a war zone with real battles, real bullets, and real blood. Sickness, disease, heartache, disappointment, crippling accidents, crushing experiences, tears, and death touch each one of us.

Life is no joy ride.

But does God put us through all this just to watch us squirm . . . to make us miserable . . . to prove that He's in charge?

No. Instead, this all points back to the cross.

1. The word *afflicted* carries with it the idea of pressure. They were under pressure, like grapes squeezed by a winepress.

2. The word *perplexed* means "without a way." It suggests the idea of being lost and disoriented.

3. Compare John 15:20 with Romans 8:35–39.

4. William Barclay, *The Letters to the Corinthians*, rev. ed., The Daily Study Bible Series (Philadelphia, Pa.: The Westminster Press, 1975), pp. 198–200.

Life That Is in Jesus

We come now to another paradox: Experiencing the life of Jesus requires an acceptance of death.

> Always carrying about in the body the dying of Jesus, that the life of Jesus also may be manifested in our body. (4:10)

There is no abundant life without first an abasing death. And this reality should be displayed in our lives not only clearly but continually.

> For we who live are constantly being delivered over to death for Jesus' sake, that the life of Jesus also may be manifested in our mortal flesh. (v. 11)

What does Paul mean by "death" here? It includes acceptance of those four painful experiences mentioned in verses 8–9: "afflicted . . . perplexed . . . persecuted . . . struck down." When we accept those struggles as part of the process of releasing our fragrance, we're not destroyed. Rather, His power is perfected in our weakness. For when we die, He lives. When we lose, He wins. When we're weak, He is strong. When we are dependent, He is powerful. That is the beauty of the paradox. That is the power in clay pots.

"Delivered over to death." Doesn't sound like Disneyland, does it? But there is divine wisdom in the paradox. We are constantly being delivered to the point of death so that God's message will leak out. Then people who watch us will realize there isn't anything significant about the vessel—it's what's inside that counts.

When other people see this death in us, it changes them, as Paul states in verse 12.

> So death works in us, but life in you.

When others see God's power perfected in our weakness, it dawns on them that maybe God could use them too.

Do you want to make an impact where you work? Do you want to reach your school? Do you want to touch your neighborhood? Then merely live out the dying message of the Lord Jesus. Let it out. Don't hide the cracks in the clay. Let your humanity show. It's the cracks in the clay that allow people to see through and focus on the Lord. You'll be amazed how often God honors a weak, broken piece of pottery—and how seldom He uses the fine china.

Paradoxes That Must Be Remembered

At least three paradoxes splinter off from the paradox of the cross. First, when God displays His power, it flows through weakness. Second, when we model the death of Jesus, others see His life. And third, when the cross is lifted high, even the arrogant are brought low.

Let's conclude our study with the words of Jesus, calling out to us.

> "If anyone wishes to come after Me, let him deny himself, and take up his cross daily, and follow Me. For whoever wishes to save his life shall lose it, but whoever loses his life for My sake, he is the one who will save it." (Luke 9:23–24)

His words meet us at a juncture. Will you take the road to Calvary? Or will it be the off-ramp to Disneyland? The choice is yours.

Living Insights   STUDY ONE

Scripture is full of paradoxes: strength in weakness . . . much from little . . . life in death. Today we've seen how God's power is displayed in the broken clay pots of our lives. Let's review some of the Bible characters who found the same principle to be true.

- Think back over some of the Bible characters you've studied in the past. Many of them faced trials and even humiliation at times, and most of them have come to see that God's power shines through their brokenness. Look up the following characters in your concordance or a Bible encyclopedia, and fill in the chart as a reminder that great things can come from our worst moments.

Joseph

Trial: _____

_____

Results: _____

_____

_____

Ruth

Trial: _____

_____

Results: _____

_____

_____

Job

Trial: _____

_____

Results: _____

_____

_____

Daniel

Trial: _____

_____

Results: _____

_____

_____

 *Living Insights* _____ STUDY TWO

The principle of power in clay pots sounds noble and attractive on paper, but in real life, we often want to glue the chinks in our stoneware before they turn into leaky cracks. How is your pot holding up? Is it still intact, used only for decoration? Or is it chipped and scarred from years of service?

• Take some time to investigate your present circumstances. Are you protecting your porcelain finish when God wants you to spill a little perfume? There could be a purpose behind all those nicks and bumps you've been feeling lately. Spend a few moments pondering the possibilities of letting some of that aroma sweeten the air around you.

Chapter 9

THE RIGHT FOCUS

2 Corinthians 4:13–18

A ll of us would like to be remembered as people who didn't quit; who stayed at the task; who were, in a word, faithful.

Being faithful means more than starting well—more than a crowd-dazzling burst of speed off the starting block. It means ending well—crossing the finish line with your arms outstretched and your head held high.

Few examples of faithfulness are as inspiring as Paul's, and even fewer could etch his epitaph on their tombstones:

I have fought the good fight, I have finished the course, I have kept the faith. (2 Tim. 4:7)

From his blinding start on the Damascus road to his binding shackles in a Roman dungeon, Paul was faithful to the end.

To live like Paul doesn't require positive thinking or self-hypnosis, it requires the right focus.

Realistic Motivation

The most effective people for God are those who focus on their goal till the very end. They cross the finish line at full speed instead of slowing down to a comfortable trot or dropping out of the race altogether.

The race is long, the lanes are narrow, and it's easy to become discouraged. Yet Paul says in 2 Corinthians 4:1 and 16, "we do not lose heart." These clauses are like two pieces of bread sandwiching the meat of verses 2–15. Essentially, Paul is saying that we don't fade in the final stretch, we don't give in when the going gets rough.

One of the reasons for Paul's motivation is the enormity of the task before him. Whether you're Mother Theresa or Lee Iacocca, a realistic awareness of the challenges facing you is motivating. Winston Churchill knew that, and he used it to inspire England to stand firm against Hitler in World War II.

Upon this battle depends the survival of Christian civilization. . . . The whole fury and might of the enemy must very soon be turned on us. Hitler knows

that he will have to break us in this island or lose the
war. . . . Let us therefore brace ourselves to our du-
ties, and so bear ourselves that, if the British Empire
and its Commonwealth last for a thousand years, men
will still say: "This was their finest hour."[1]

Such is the stirring rhetoric of Paul in verse 1: "Since we have
this ministry, as we received mercy, we do not lose heart."

The ministry is indeed an enormous task, but that is not the
only support for Paul's motivation. The realization of debt forms the
other buttress.

The debt is mercy.

It costs nothing to receive, but it cost everything to give. It cost
the Savior His life. And the realization of our indebtedness to Him
along with the enormity of the challenge keeps us from losing heart.

Enthusiastic Determination

After addressing some of the paradoxes of serving in the Lord's
work (vv. 7–12), Paul stands tall and says:

But having the same spirit of faith, according to what
is written, "I believed, therefore I spoke," we also believe, therefore also we speak. (v. 13)

Paul doesn't throw in the towel in the face of the hardships of
verses 8–9. Instead he announces his enthusiastic determination.
His words, "I believed, therefore I spoke," are a reflection of Psalm
116:10.

It is particularly fitting that at this point Paul should
quote from Psalm 116 precisely because it is a hymn
of thanksgiving for deliverance from death: "The cords
of death compassed me. . . . I found trouble and sorrow. Then called I upon the name of Jehovah. . . . I
was brought low and He saved me. . . . Thou hast
delivered my soul from death, mine eyes from tears,
and my feet from falling. . . . I believed, and therefore
I spoke. . . . Praise ye Jehovah".[2]

---

1. *Bartlett's Familiar Quotations*, 14th ed., rev. and enl., ed. Emily Morison Beck
(Boston, Mass.: Little, Brown and Co., 1968), p. 921.

2. Philip Edgcumbe Hughes, *Paul's Second Epistle to the Corinthians* (Grand Rapids,
Mich.: William B. Eerdmans Publishing Co., 1962), pp. 146–47.

Paul's experience mirrors that of the psalmist. And also seen in that reflection is the same determination. But how can we hope to follow his example?

First: *Enthusiastic determination grows out of being delivered by the Lord.* When we come to an impasse in life, with the Red Sea before us and a horde of Egyptian chariots hot on our heels, nothing leaves such a lasting impression as when God parts the water. And just as Israel continually pointed back to that historic moment of deliverance, so we can point to the times when God has parted seas for us. And when we recall those times, we become filled with faith and resolve.

Second: *Enthusiastic determination also grows when we focus on our being resurrected.* As Paul states in 2 Corinthians 4:14,

> knowing that He who raised the Lord Jesus will raise
> us also with Jesus and will present us with you.

Death ends nothing. It merely closes the door on our earthly existence and opens the door of eternity. Knowing this with certainty keeps us at the task.

Not only is there a literal resurrection after we physically die, there is also a resurrection in a figurative sense. When we die to ourselves and invest our lives in the lives of others, we become resurrected in them. Teachers are resurrected in their students; pastors, in their congregations; and parents, in their children.

The fires of determination are fueled by such thoughts—He "will present us *with* you" (v. 14, emphasis added). When we live our lives for other people, the investment is lived out through them. That's what verse 15 is saying.

> For all things are for your sakes, that the grace which
> is spreading to more and more people may cause the
> giving of thanks to abound to the glory of God.

All this brings us to a third thought: *Enthusiastic determination grows by investing in the lives of others.* People who lose heart are usually those who have focused on themselves, who have turned inward and forgotten that the only truly happy life is the one lived for others (see Phil. 2:3–11).

Authentic Vision

In 2 Corinthians 4:16–18, Paul returns to where he started: "We do not lose heart."

Therefore we do not lose heart, but though our outer man is decaying, yet our inner man is being renewed day by day. For momentary, light affliction is producing for us an eternal weight of glory far beyond all comparison, while we look not at the things which are seen, but at the things which are not seen; for the things which are seen are temporal, but the things which are not seen are eternal.

Though we are losing our figure, our hair, our teeth—we are not losing heart. Why? Because of the renewal of the person on the inside, a person that is immortal. Though we are dying, the inner man is being renewed. And though we are afflicted, the affliction is light compared to the "eternal weight of glory."

All this relates directly to establishing the right focus in our lives. We are to focus not on the external but the internal (v. 16), not on the temporal but on the eternal (vv. 17–18).

Specific Application

We can keep the right focus by remembering that today's deeds are the threads in tomorrow's tapestry. Understanding that should give us the determination to *keep on weaving*—even when the pattern cannot be discerned.

Realizing that ordinary people are immortals in the making should give us the wisdom to *keep on investing*—for that is the most profitable way we can utilize the time and talents given us. C. S. Lewis underscores this thought in his essay "The Weight of Glory":

> It is a serious thing to live in a society of possible gods and goddesses, to remember that the dullest and most uninteresting person you talk to may one day be a creature which, if you saw it now, you would be strongly tempted to worship, or else a horror and a corruption such as you now meet, if at all, only in a nightmare. All day long we are, in some degree, helping each other to one or other of these destinations. It is in the light of these overwhelming possibilities, it is with the awe and the circumspection proper to them, that we should conduct all our dealings with one another, all friendships, all loves, all play, all politics. There are no *ordinary* people. You have never talked to a mere mortal. Nations, cultures, arts, civilization—these are mortal, and their life is to ours as the life of a gnat. But it is immortals whom we joke

with, work with, marry, snub, and exploit—immortal horrors or everlasting splendours. [3]

Finally, reflecting on the unseen rather than the seen should give us the courage to *keep on dreaming*—no matter how dark and dreary the "seen" world appears.

Keep on weaving. Keep on investing. Keep on dreaming. That's how you become a person who stays with it to the end.

Living Insights

This study provides for us three keys to gaining the right focus. These qualities are generously illustrated throughout the Scriptures. Let's study some of those illustrations.

• Name some biblical characters who possessed realistic motivation.

_____

_____

_____

_____

_____

• What was it that caused you to include these people on your list?

_____

_____

_____

_____

• Name some biblical characters who possessed enthusiastic determination.

_____

_____

3. C. S. Lewis, *The Weight of Glory* (Grand Rapids, Mich.: William B. Eerdmans Publishing Co., 1965), pp. 14–15.

_____

_____

_____

- What was it that caused you to include these people on your list?

  _____

  _____

  _____

  _____

- Name some biblical characters who possessed authentic vision.

  _____

  _____

  _____

  _____

- What was it that caused you to include these people on your list?

  _____

  _____

  _____

  _____

Living Insights STUDY TWO

One of our concluding applications spoke of the importance of continually investing in people. In whom are you investing, and how is it paying off in that person's life?

- Use the space on the next page to write your thoughts about your relationship investments: In whom are you investing your life? What is involved in your investment? Are you satisfied with your level of commitment to this person? What would you change if you could?

My Investment in People

_____

_____

_____

_____

_____

_____

_____

_____

_____

_____

_____

_____

_____

_____

_____

_____

_____

_____

_____

_____

HOPE BEYOND THE HEARSE

2 Corinthians 5:1–10

I n spite of all our quantum leaps in technology, one thing remains unchanged—death. Though technology may prolong our lives, it does not preserve us from this grim reality. Joseph Bayly discusses this paradox in his book *The Last Thing We Talk About:*

> This frustrates us, especially in a time of scientific breakthrough and exploding knowledge, that we should be able to break out of earth's environment and yet be stopped cold by death's unyielding mystery. Electro-encephalogram may replace mirror held before the mouth, autopsies may become more sophisticated, cosmetic embalming may take the place of pennies on the eyelids and canvas shrouds, but death continues to confront us with its blank wall. Everything changes; death is changeless.
>
> We may postpone it, we may tame its violence, but death is still there waiting for us.
>
> Death always waits. The door of the hearse is never closed.
>
> Dairy farmer and sales executive live in death's shadow, with Nobel prize winner and prostitute, mother, infant, teen, old man. The hearse stands waiting for the surgeon who transplants a heart as well as the hopeful recipient, for the funeral director as well as the corpse he manipulates.
>
> Death spares none.[1]

As Solomon says in Ecclesiastes, death is the great equalizer (2:14, 7:2, 9:2–3). No matter who we are, no matter how much money we have, no matter how much influence we exert, death is inescapable.

---

1. Joseph Bayly, *The Last Thing We Talk About*, rev. ed. (Elgin, Ill.: David C. Cook Publishing Co., 1973), pp. 11–12.

Because we cannot conquer death, we've come up with all sorts of comfortable, though misconceived, theories to soften its impact.

Popular Misconceptions about Death

Because they've been so widely espoused, three misconceptions stand out in particular.

Temporary Transition

Many believe that death simply moves us into a temporary state where others can pray to free us from punishment. This common doctrine teaches the existence of purgatory.[2] Ostensibly, it is "an intermediate place between heaven and hell, where the unfinished business of earth is settled."[3]

Repeated Reincarnations

Reincarnation is an Eastern philosophy that means a new birth into another body. Some people believe that we can be recycled eternally, reaching higher levels of happiness if we've lived a good life, or lower levels of misery if we haven't.

Although this takes the edge off death's sharpness, it is a lie. For the Bible says in Hebrews 9:27, "It is appointed for men to die *once* and after this comes judgment" (emphasis added).

Ultimate Conclusion

Some teach that death is the grand finale to life, there is no afterlife, this is all there is. This philosophy either leads a person to despair or to adopt the epicurean ethic: Eat, drink, and be merry, for tomorrow we die.

Even though these three theories are growing in popularity, and though their followers may be sincere, they are sincerely wrong.

The Scriptures clearly teach that death occurs to all (Eccles. 7:2); it is the ultimate result of sin (compare Gen. 2:17 and 3:19 with Rom. 3:23); we all will die only once and after death we will be judged by God (Heb. 9:27); and when we die, if there is a chasm between us and God, it will become unbridgeable (Luke 16:19–31, esp. v. 26).

2. Purgatory comes from the root word *to purge*, meaning "a place of spiritual purging." Those who believe in purgatory appeal to the apocryphal work of 2 Maccabees 12:39–45 along with Matthew 12:31–32 and 1 Corinthians 3:11–15 for their support.

3. David Steinmetz, "Purgatory," *The New International Dictionary of the Christian Church*, rev. ed., ed. J. D. Douglas (Grand Rapids, Mich.: Zondervan Publishing House, 1978), p. 814.

But that isn't all the Scriptures can teach about death. Second Corinthians 5:1–10 opens our understanding to this mystery like few other passages can.

Scriptural Insights regarding Death

When it comes to theories about death, we often hear the words "we think" . . . "we believe" . . . "we hope." But 2 Corinthians 5:1 begins with a confident "we know." Such is the certainty of Scripture regarding death.

An Earthly Tent . . . An Eternal House

Paul, a master of analogies, uses one here to help us understand this cryptic mystery.

> For we know that if the earthly tent which is our house is torn down, we have a building from God, a house not made with hands, eternal in the heavens. For indeed in this house we groan, longing to be clothed with our dwelling from heaven; inasmuch as we, having put it on, shall not be found naked. For indeed while we are in this tent, we groan, being burdened, because we do not want to be unclothed, but to be clothed, in order that what is mortal may be swallowed up by life. Now He who prepared us for this very purpose is God, who gave to us the Spirit as a pledge. (vv. 1–5)

A tent is a temporary place to dwell. It's fun to camp in a tent, but let's face it, it's not home. There's no fireplace, no cozy chair, no soft bed. It's cold in the winter, hot in the summer, and leaky when it rains. And the older it gets, the more it sags. Eventually it frays and tears and finally rots.

No wonder "we groan" (v. 2). Physicians make their living by listening to groaning tents. An orthopedic surgeon tries to keep the tent pegs from pulling loose, a dermatologist tries to keep the canvas in good shape, and general practitioners are always stitching and patching us up.

We groan because we are weary, rain-soaked campers longing for home (v. 2b). But when we shed this earthly tent from our shoulders, we will not be left naked and shivering (vv. 3–4). We will be clothed with immortality (1 Cor. 15:53–54). Like a huge down comforter, life—not death—will swallow us up (2 Cor. 5:4).

To assure us of this, God puts His seal of approval upon it all by giving us His Spirit as a deposit or down payment for our eternal home (v. 5).

Absent from the Body . . . At Home with the Lord

Since the Holy Spirit is given as a down payment, imagine what the full payment will be. If we have only the firstfruits now, the harvest should be incredible (Rom. 8:23). That is why we can live courageously by faith.

> Therefore, being always of good courage, and knowing that while we are at home in the body we are absent from the Lord—for we walk by faith, not by sight—we are of good courage, I say, and prefer rather to be absent from the body and to be at home with the Lord. (2 Cor. 5:6–8)

While we are here in our earthly tents, our relationship with Christ is from afar. Now, we neither see Him nor touch Him. But then, we will be at home with Him face-to-face (1 Cor. 13:12).

Verse 7 in 2 Corinthians 5 is parenthetical, as indicated by the dashes in the text, and instructs us how we are to live in the meantime—by faith, not sight.

Our Present Ambition . . . Our Future Reward

Whether we are here on earth or in heaven, the driving force of our life should be the same.

> Therefore also we have as our ambition, whether at home or absent, to be pleasing to Him. (v. 9)

To please the Lord. This is our top priority, not to be successful. Why? Verse 10 gives us the answer.

> For we must all appear before the judgment seat of Christ, that each one may be recompensed for his deeds in the body, according to what he has done, whether good or bad.

At the judgment seat, Jesus will look beyond the quantity of our work and judge its quality (1 Cor. 3:10–15). Not only will He assess our deeds but the motivation behind those deeds, as 1 Corinthians 4:4–5 reveals.

> I am conscious of nothing against myself, yet I am not by this acquitted; but the one who examines me is the Lord. Therefore do not go on passing judgment before

the time, but wait until the Lord comes who will both bring to light the things hidden in the darkness and disclose the motives of men's hearts; and then each man's praise will come to him from God.

Essential Considerations before Death

We began with three misconceptions about death. Let's close with three considerations that stem from three basic facts.

Fact number 1: *Birth initiates life.* That's as true in the spiritual realm as it is in the physical. Jesus' discussion with Nicodemus made that clear (John 3:3–6). Just as a tadpole can't survive on dry land until it undergoes a metamorphosis, so a person can't enter eternity without being born again. Consideration number 1: *Be certain you are born again.* You're not ready to live until you're ready to die. And you're not ready to die until you've been born from above.

Fact number 2: *Death terminates life.* Earthly life, that is. Consideration number 2: *Be certain you're ready to die.* No one can make reservations in heaven for you or pack your bags. You must make those crucial arrangements yourself—or the plane will leave without you.

Fact number 3: *Opportunity is limited to life.* Though life is short, it is eternally significant. What impact we make here ripples throughout the hereafter. Consideration number 3: *Be certain you realize you have no options after you die.* Purgatory, reincarnation, and death as an ultimate conclusion are not biblical options. Remember Hebrews 9:27? "It is appointed for men to die once and after this comes judgment."

In Catherine Marshall's book about her husband Peter, she cites a touching story of a young terminally ill son asking his mother what death was like, if it hurt.

With tears welling up in her eyes, the mother prayed silently for a moment to ask the Lord for a way to answer him.

> And the Lord did tell her.
> Immediately she knew how to explain it to him.

> "Kenneth," she said, . . . "you remember when you were a tiny boy how you used to play so hard all day that when night came you would be too tired even to undress, and you would tumble into mother's bed and fall asleep?

> "That was not your bed . . . it was not where you belonged.

71

"And you would only stay there a little while.
In the morning, much to your surprise, you would wake up and find yourself in your own bed in your own room.

"You were there because someone had loved you and taken care of you.
Your father had come—with big strong arms—and carried you away.

"Kenneth, death is just like that.
We just wake up some morning to find ourselves in the other room—our own room where we belong—because the Lord Jesus loved us."

The lad's shining, trusting face looking up into hers told her that the point had gone home and that there would be no more fear . . . only love and trust in his little heart as he went to meet the Father in Heaven.

He never questioned again.
And several weeks later he fell asleep just as she had said.[4]

 ## Living Insights

Earlier in our series, we took some time to observe the key words in the first chapter of 2 Corinthians. Since it's such a profitable method of Bible study, let's return to that technique here in this fifth chapter.

• Write down ten to twelve key words from 2 Corinthians 5:1–10 in the space below. Then define them by referring to a Bible dictionary or, better yet, by the context of the passage itself. Conclude your study by jotting down a summary statement as to why the word is significant.

2 Corinthians 5:1–10

Key Word _____

Definition _____

_____

4. Catherine Marshall, A Man Called Peter (New York, N.Y.: McGraw-Hill Book Co., 1951), p. 273.

Significance _____

_____

Key Word _____

Definition _____

_____

Significance _____

_____

Key Word _____

Definition _____

_____

Significance _____

_____

Key Word _____

Definition _____

_____

Significance _____

_____

Key Word _____

Definition _____

_____

Significance _____

_____

Key Word _____

Definition _____

_____

Significance _____

_____

Key Word _____

Definition _____

_____

Significance _____

_____

Key Word _____

Definition _____

_____

Significance _____

_____

Key Word _____

Definition _____

_____

Significance _____

_____

Key Word _____

Definition _____

_____

Significance _____

_____

Key Word _____

Definition _____

_____

Significance _____

_____

Two things are certain . . . birth and death. You had nothing to do with preparations for your birth, but you have everything to do with preparing to die. Are you prepared? Are all your accounts in order?

- These questions boil down to just one—have you received Jesus Christ as your personal Savior? If you have, use this time to pray for someone you know who is without the Lord . . . unprepared to die. If you haven't accepted the Lord, do it now. He hears your prayers. Make this all-important decision now, and in doing so, you'll be able to answer in the affirmative: "I am prepared to die."

Chapter 11

WHY CHRISTIANS ARE CONSIDERED CRAZY

2 Corinthians 5:11–21

C hristians are considered by many to be crazy. And with good reason, as A. W. Tozer notes:

> A real Christian is an odd number anyway. He feels supreme love for One whom he has never seen, talks familiarly every day to Someone he cannot see, expects to go to heaven on the virtue of Another, empties himself in order to be full, admits he is wrong so he can be declared right, goes down in order to get up, is strongest when he is weakest, richest when he is poorest, and happiest when he feels worst. He dies so he can live, forsakes in order to have, gives away so he can keep, sees the invisible, hears the inaudible, and knows that which passeth knowledge. [1]

Yes, Christians are different, but it's encouraging to know we're in good company.

Who's in the Company of the Crazy

Ever since New Testament times, Christians have been viewed as a peculiar breed of people (see 1 Pet. 2:9, KJV). In Mark 3 the multitudes said that Christ had "lost His senses" (v. 21) and was "possessed" (v. 22). In John 10, they said He had "a demon" and was "insane" (v. 20). Consequently, it's of little surprise that they treated His disciples with the same contempt. For example, after Paul gave his testimony before King Agrippa, he was accused of being out of his mind (Acts 26:24).

Such thoughts were not limited to the "fanatics" of the first century. We could trace our way through the history of the church and find numerous individuals who have been considered unbalanced because of their commitment to Christ. Those, for example, who tediously copied Scripture by hand before the age of the printing press. Those who lit the torch of the Reformation. Those who gave

---

1. A. W. Tozer, *The Root of the Righteous* (Camp Hill, Pa.: Christian Publications, 1986), p. 156.

their lives as martyrs. Those who stood in public places to speak openly of Christ. Those who set aside prestigious and lucrative careers to quietly serve the Savior in some obscure part of the world.

Hebrews 11 speaks of others the world thought were crazy.

> Others experienced mockings and scourgings, yes, also chains and imprisonment. They were stoned, they were sawn in two, they were tempted, they were put to death with the sword; they went about in sheep-skins, in goatskins, being destitute, afflicted, ill-treated (men of whom the world was not worthy), wandering in deserts and mountains and caves and holes in the ground. (vv. 36–38)

"Men of whom the world was not worthy." What an epitaph, etched on their tombstones by the very hand of God.

Yet if God is for us, why are so many in this world against us?

Why Are We So Misunderstood?

We Christians are misunderstood not only by those outside the family of God but even by those within it. That's exactly what happened to Paul. And that's what prompted him to send a second letter to the Corinthians.

In our last lesson we discussed the final judgment, when the Lord will assess our lives and reward us accordingly. Remember the verse?

> For we must all appear before the judgment seat of Christ, that each one may be recompensed for his deeds in the body, according to what he has done, whether good or bad. (2 Cor. 5:10)

It is with that judgment scene in mind that Paul goes on to write about our lives on this earth, because such a finale strikes fear in our hearts.

Our Mission Is Unique

One reason we are misunderstood is that our mission is unique.

> Therefore knowing the fear of the Lord,[2] we persuade men, but we are made manifest to God; and I hope

2. The fear referred to here is not the sense of being afraid of being clubbed or whipped by an angry God. Rather, it is an awesome reverence, a fear that grows out of respect. Proverbs 1:7 states that "the fear of the Lord is the beginning of knowl-edge," and 9:10 says that it is "the beginning of wisdom."

77

that we are made manifest also in your consciences. We are not again commending ourselves to you but are giving you an occasion to be proud of us, that you may have an answer for those who take pride in appearance, and not in heart. For if we are beside ourselves, it is for God; if we are of sound mind, it is for you. (vv. 11–13)

We are immersed in a live-and-let-live, I'm-OK-you're-OK society. But if we believe what we say we believe, we can't just sit in an easy chair with our remote control while the world races headlong to hell. We should get involved. We should intervene. We should persuade people that their lives *aren't* OK, that they need to be reconciled to God.

In verse 12, Paul makes it clear to his readers that he isn't bragging, isn't trying to impress them with his outward appearance. His mission is unique—it is from the heart, without pretense or hidden agenda. And people with such a mission have a different approach.

Our Approach Is Different

We are impelled by a supernatural force—the love of Christ—a force the world can neither see nor understand.

For the love of Christ controls us, having concluded this, that one died for all, therefore all died; and He died for all, that they who live should no longer live for themselves, but for Him who died and rose again on their behalf. (vv. 14–15)

Pulsating from our heart is a deep love for Christ. It throbs within us. It races through every artery of our existence down to the tiniest, most remote capillary.

This love is inextricably tied to a threefold message. One: Jesus died for all of us. Two: Since we all have died spiritually, we need someone to give us life. And three: Once we give Jesus our lives, we no longer desire to live for ourselves but for Him.

That's a crazy message to a world full of people looking out for number one. If we tell them number one is Jesus, they're going to roll their eyes and start whistling the theme to The Twilight Zone.

Ours is a different approach, no doubt about it. We're not only different in our motivation but in our value system as well.

Therefore from now on we recognize no man according to the flesh; even though we have known Christ according to the flesh, yet now we know Him thus no longer. (v. 16)

That type of approach is foreign to the world, but that's the way we are to live once we come to Christ. From now on we look beyond the sculpted physiques, the Caribbean tans, and the designer clothes . . . beyond the beggar's rags and the cancer patient's frail limbs. We look beneath the surface to the person inside, a person who not only needs Christ but in some ways represents Christ.

> "Then the King will say to those on His right, 'Come, you who are blessed of My Father, inherit the kingdom prepared for you from the foundation of the world. For I was hungry, and you gave Me something to eat; I was thirsty, and you gave Me drink; I was a stranger, and you invited Me in; naked, and you clothed Me; I was sick, and you visited Me; I was in prison, and you came to Me.' Then the righteous will answer Him, saying, 'Lord, when did we see You hungry, and feed You, or thirsty, and give You drink? And when did we see You a stranger, and invite You in, or naked, and clothe You? And when did we see You sick, or in prison, and come to You?' And the King will answer and say to them, 'Truly I say to you, to the extent that you did it to one of these brothers of Mine, even the least of them, you did it to Me.'" (Matt. 25:34–40)

Our Life Is Transformed

People whose mission is unique and whose approach is different are not people who have merely turned over a new leaf; they are people who have been transformed.

> Therefore if any man is in Christ, he is a new creature; the old things passed away; behold, new things have come. (2 Cor. 5:17)

The word "creature" is from the Greek word *ktisis.* The root term means "the act of creating" or "that which has been created."

When Christ invades a life, He performs a creative act . . . a miracle of metamorphosis . . . an inside-out transformation. Just as a caterpillar's whole body dissolves in the cocoon and is restructured into a butterfly, so our entire value system, our relationships, and our philosophy of life dissolve and are restructured around Christ.

This leads us to the question, Is this new life something Christians put on like a new suit of clothes? We find the answer in the next verse.

79

> Now all these things are from God, who reconciled us
> to Himself through Christ, and gave us the ministry
> of reconciliation. (v. 18)

We can't don this new wardrobe anymore than a caterpillar can clip on a set of wings and call itself a butterfly. An inward transformation has to take place—a transformation that comes from God and that we are to pass on to others. As He reconciled us, so we are to reconcile others. Verse 19 completes the picture.

> Namely, that God was in Christ reconciling the world to
> Himself, not counting their trespasses against them, and
> He has committed to us the word of reconciliation.

Our ministry is to show that Jesus' death on the cross appeased God's anger toward sin and replaced it with His acceptance of sinners. Human religions keep a running tab of sin. But with Christianity, Christ paid the debt and wiped the slate clean.

> And when you were dead in your transgressions and
> the uncircumcision of your flesh, He made you alive
> together with Him, having forgiven us all our trans-
> gressions, having canceled out the certificate of debt
> consisting of decrees against us and which was hostile
> to us; and He has taken it out of the way, having nailed
> it to the cross. (Col. 2:13–14)

In a world of debits and credits—a world that keeps score—this message sounds downright crazy.

Our Role Is Unusual

Another reason why the world thinks we are crazy is that we represent another authority. In serving an absent sovereign, we function in the role of ambassadors.

> Therefore, we are ambassadors for Christ, as though
> God were entreating through us; we beg you on behalf
> of Christ, be reconciled to God. (2 Cor. 5:20)

What is an ambassador? Think about that question for a minute. Ambassadors spend their lives on foreign soil. They speak a different language than the people. They have different traditions, customs, cultures, and lifestyles. They always feel somewhat like a stranger. They speak on behalf of their country, conveying its ideals, its policies, its decisions. And . . . the reputation of their country rests in their hands. For good or for bad, their country is judged by their words and by their actions.

In his commentary on 2 Corinthians, R. V. G. Tasker comments on this unusual role of privilege and honor.

> Ambassadors engaged upon human affairs are chosen especially for their tact, their dignity and their courtesy, and because they are gifted with persuasive powers. The ambassadors for Christ should show the same characteristics. They must never try to bludgeon men and women into the kingdom of God, but must speak the truth in love, just because it is a gospel of divine love that they are commissioned to proclaim.[3]

And this is the gospel we are commissioned to proclaim:

> He made Him who knew no sin to be sin on our behalf, that we might become the righteousness of God in Him. (v. 21)

How Can Crazy People like Us Be Effective?

In a world that's lost its way, we can be effective in three ways. First: *We need to maintain our mission.* As verse 11 says, because the fear of the Lord directs our steps, we need to keep on persuading a wayward world to be reconciled, to fall in step with the divine drumbeat.

Second: *We need to maintain our perspective.* We should never get impressed with illusions of success. Everybody needs Christ, whether the chief executive officer of a *Fortune 500* company or the shoeshine man on the corner. We need to train ourselves to look beneath the surface and not make judgments based on appearances.

Third: *We need to fulfill the role of a good ambassador.* Not to speak on our behalf but on the behalf of Christ. Not to act on our own authority but on the authority of Christ. Not to further our own little kingdom but the kingdom of Christ.

How in step are you with the Lord? One way to test yourself is to see how out of step you are with the world. If you are out of pace, and people look at you funny, don't worry. Keep on marching onward, Christian soldier. And let the words of Henry David Thoreau encourage you when others start calling you crazy.

> If a man does not keep pace with his companions, perhaps it is because he hears a different drummer. Let

---

3. R. V. G. Tasker, *The Second Epistle of Paul to the Corinthians* (Grand Rapids, Mich.: William B. Eerdmans Publishing Co., 1958), p. 90.

him step to the music which he hears, however measured or far away. [4]

 ## *Living Insights* STUDY ONE

You are a new creature. You've been reconciled. You are an
ambassador. You've received the righteousness of God. All of these
wonderful claims come from the passage we are presently studying.

• Pick out a favorite portion of 2 Corinthians 5:11–21 and mem-
orize it. Choose a realistic amount of text for the time you have
available for memorizing. Remember, write out the passage and
read it aloud over and over. Soon you'll be reciting from memory.

 ## *Living Insights* STUDY TWO

This topic that we're covering today could provide a fascinating
discussion between you and your family or your Christian friends.
Use the questions and statements that follow to guide your discussion. Encourage everyone to participate by being genuinely interested in what they share.

• Why are Christians considered crazy?

• Have you ever been considered crazy because of your faith? Share
it with the group.

• How has being "crazy" been a disadvantage?

• How has being "crazy" been an advantage?

• Share an experience when you really felt like an ambassador for
Christ.

• How do you maintain your mission in life?

• How do you keep your perspective?

---

4. Henry David Thoreau, *Thoreau: Walden and Other Writings*, ed. Joseph Wood
Krutch (New York, N.Y.: Bantam Books, 1971), p. 345.

Chapter 12

A REALISTIC PORTRAIT OF MINISTRY

2 Corinthians 6:1–10

M ost of us cringe when we have to show others our driver's license photograph. We look either washed out from too much light, or shadowy and suspicious from too little. Our eyes look either goofy and wide-eyed, or droopy and sleepy-eyed. Our hair is hopelessly out of place. And our smile? "Good grief," we say to ourselves, "do I really smile like that?"

Then there's the opposite extreme—the studio portrait. You know, when we make an appointment for a sitting and dress up and make sure every hair is in place. With the photographer's magic, the multitude of sins nature has inflicted are covered. The right background highlights our colors. The most flattering angle emphasizes our strong points. The lighting softens our features. And, as a last resort, the air brush can blow away any wrinkles or imperfections after the picture has been developed.

As radically different as they are, the driver's license photo and the studio portrait have one thing in common: neither is realistic. But if we want to be authentic people who impact others, it's important that the portrait others see is real.

The same is true of ministry.

Familiar Concepts of Ministry

The most familiar concepts of ministry can be almost clerically sorted into three files. First, many think ministry is an ivory-tower existence. They think of it as a place of stained-glass solitude and knee-worn prayer. They envision long hours of poring over the Scriptures by candlelight and meditating in a musty study. They see it as a monastic place where angels traffic and organ music pipes in the background.

Second, many think of ministry as a place of public manipulation and exploitation. These cynics look at the minister not as a pious monk but as a powerful mogul. He is pictured as one who likes to be in charge and be obsequiously followed. This driver's license photo of the ministry captures shades of Elmer Gantry and Jim Jones, but by and large, it's a distortion of the real picture.

Third, many think ministry is for an esoteric elite who have arrived spiritually and are models of perfection. This studio portrait of the ministry is too glowing and too flattering to be true. People in the ministry aren't perfect. They have wrinkles in their personality, age spots on some of their opinions, and a good share of sagging skin in their convictions. They aren't always loving or patient or unselfish or forgiving. Though ministers, they still are, in a word, human.

Necessary Commands to Ministers

Second Corinthians 5 states that if we have been reconciled to God, then we have been given a ministry of reconciliation (v. 18). It is a ministry God has committed to each of us, not to a select few (v. 19). Each are His ambassadors (v. 20).

Therefore, the portrait people see of ministry is a portrait of *us*. To make that portrait as positive as possible, Paul gives two commands to every minister, every Christian. The first command regards grace (6:1–2). The second regards credibility (vv. 3–4a).

Command #1

Paul's first command is "not to receive the grace of God in vain."

> And working together with Him, we also urge you not
> to receive the grace of God in vain—for He says,
> "At the acceptable time I listened to you,
> And on the day of salvation I helped you";
> behold, now is "the acceptable time," behold, now is
> "the day of salvation." (vv. 1–2)

For several paragraphs Paul has been urging us to model a New Covenant ministry, one that emphasizes the work of the Spirit as opposed to the work of the flesh. The work of the flesh is law-oriented; the work of the Spirit, on the other hand, is grace-oriented. The work of the flesh depends on self; the work of the Spirit depends on the Lord. The work of the flesh focuses on the external and the temporal; the work of the Spirit focuses on the internal and the eternal.

The "day of salvation" should never be relegated to a past-tense experience. It should be lived out "now," in the present, as we live by grace instead of by law.

Are your life and your ministry grace-oriented or law-oriented? Are you living freely by grace, or are you so afraid of license that you've become a legalist? If so, then God's grace is in vain. Ministry should be lived out freely and authentically, not rigidly and touched up.

Command #2

Paul's second command is "cultivate credibility in ministry."

> Giving no cause for offense in anything, in order that the ministry be not discredited, but in everything commending ourselves as servants of God. (vv. 3–4a)

How can we keep the ministry from being discredited? By not giving any cause for offense (v. 3a) and by being servants (v. 4a).

The Greek term for *discredited* is used only here and in 8:20. It means "to find fault or blame." The Hebrew equivalent is used in Proverbs 9:7 and is translated "dishonor."

The ministry can become discredited or dishonored when we break a promise, exploit people, live hypocritically, are unfaithful, compromise truth, become greedy, or expect special treatment.

Living out this ancient prayer will go a long way toward keeping your ministry from being discredited: "From the cowardice that shrinks from new truth, from the laziness that is content with half-truths, from the arrogance that thinks it knows all the truth, O God of truth, deliver us. Deliver me."

The apostle is urging *integrity* in ministry. But practically speaking, how does all this get worked out on a daily basis?

Realistic Characteristics of Ministering

In 2 Corinthians 6:4b–10, we have one of the clearest, most realistic descriptions of how to minister with integrity.

Realistic Circumstances

Verses 4b–5 rip to shreds the ivory-tower picture of the ministry:

> . . . in much endurance, in afflictions, in hardships, in distresses, in beatings, in imprisonments, in tumults, in labors, in sleeplessness, in hunger . . .

Those who minister effectively demonstrate "endurance." The word is *hupomonē*. In his commentary, William Barclay defines the sense of this word.

> It does not describe the frame of mind which can sit down with folded hands and bowed head and let a torrent of troubles sweep over it in passive resignation.

It describes the ability to bear things in such a triumphant way that it transfigures them.[1]

The list of things Paul endured can be categorized into three
groups of three.

First, there were inner struggles—afflictions, hardships, and distresses. The term for *afflictions* means "pressures," the things that
press in on us, weighing us down and crushing us. The word for
hardships refers to the painful discomforts of life. *Distresses* means
literally "narrow places," those tight spots that corner us and make
us feel trapped.

Second, there was the external treatment—beatings, imprisonments, and tumults. *Beatings* literally means "physical torture." *Tumults* has the idea of mob violence, of public outcry and assaults.

Third, there were the private disciplines of commitment—labor,
sleeplessness, and hunger. These descriptions show that the ministry
is hard work, often filled with nights of restlessness and days of
prayer and fasting (11:23–28).

How could anyone remain encouraged in the midst of such a
torrential downpour of circumstances? The next list Paul gives us
provides an umbrella of attitudes that are essential as we walk
through life's inclement situations.

Realistic Qualities

In 6:6–7, Paul lists nine qualities. Four can be seen by other
people, and five lie hidden beneath the surface.

> In purity, in knowledge, in patience, in kindness, in
> the Holy Spirit, in genuine love, in the word of truth,
> in the power of God; by the weapons of righteousness
> for the right hand and the left.

The visible qualities are purity—a clean, uncluttered lifestyle;
knowledge—a practical awareness of truth; patience—a calm in
the midst of the storm; and kindness—the opposite of severity and
meanness.

The unseen qualities are the Holy Spirit—our source of strength
who controls us; genuine love—seeking the highest good of others,
no matter what the consequences; the word of truth—honest and
accurate speech; the power of God—supernatural enablement; and
the weapons of righteousness—listed in Ephesians 6:10–20.

1. William Barclay, *The Letters to the Corinthians*, rev. ed., The Daily Study Bible
Series (Philadelphia, Pa.: The Westminster Press, 1975), pp. 212–13.

If we have these qualities in our ministry, certainly we can expect widespread revival, right?

Realistic Results

Wrong. Realistically, the results will be mixed.

> By glory and dishonor, by evil report and good report. (2 Cor. 6:8a)

Some will respect us; others will resent us. Some will adore us; others will attack us, just as they did Jesus (Mark 14:1–6).

Realistic Images

Some who enter the ministry are often confused about the image they should portray. For those people, Paul's list in 2 Corinthians 6:8b–10 offers a world of help:

> regarded as deceivers and yet true; as unknown yet well-known, as dying yet behold, we live; as punished yet not put to death, as sorrowful yet always rejoicing, as poor yet making many rich, as having nothing yet possessing all things.

A person in the ministry must be able to cope with contrasts— the irony of what appears to be and the truth of what is.

A Final Word on Ministry

A large group of people over the age of ninety-five were asked the question, If you could live your life over again, what would you do differently?

Their answers fell into three dominant categories. They said they would reflect more, risk more, and do more things that would live on after their death.

As we put the final brushstrokes on this realistic portrait of ministry, take a look at the canvas of your own life. What do you see? What would you paint over if you had the chance?

What is your life amounting to? Are you playing everything safe? Will anything you're doing now live on after your death?

Ministering to others is a great way to invest your life. It's a life of reflection. It's a life of risks. And it's a way of leaving something behind after you die.

Ministry is the noblest of endeavors. God had only one son . . . and God chose for Him a life of ministry.

The words before us in 2 Corinthians 6:1–10 are some of the most intimate, personal truths shared by Paul in his wonderful autobiographical style. But are these words sinking in? Can you fully appreciate what the apostle endured in his deep commitment to ministry?

- Let's return to paraphrasing. These ten verses in 2 Corinthians 6 are ideal for the depth that paraphrasing brings to a text. As you dig, you can feel the pain, the suffering, the emotion expended by the apostle Paul, and you can gain a new appreciation for his commitment.

2 Corinthians 6:1–10

Of the three concluding applications, perhaps you find the middle one the scariest—risk. By its very definition it is frightening. What have you done in the way of taking risks lately?

- Use the space below to jot down your recollections of your most current risks. Why did you take those risks? What were your fears? Have there been drawbacks? How about the positive— what good has come out of them? Has it ministered to others? What have you learned from them?

Reviewing Recent Risks

Chapter 13

GOOD RELATIONSHIPS AND BAD PARTNERSHIPS

2 Corinthians 6:11–18

A happy life and good relationships go hand in hand. People who find fulfillment and satisfaction in life have learned how to get along with other people.

Author and psychologist Alan Loy McGinnis makes it clear that the secret doesn't lie in having a good profession. Even doctors, in the most honored of professions, struggle with relationships.

> One evening a neurosurgeon and I stood silently at the window, watching the lights of the city come on far below us. It was not easy for him to begin counseling. . . .
> Finally, he took a deep breath, like a man about to dive into a cold swimming pool, and said:
> "I guess I'm here because I'm messing up all my relationships. All these years I've fought to get to the top of my profession, thinking that when I got there people would respect me and want to be around me. But it just hasn't happened."
> He crushed the empty Styrofoam cup in his fist, as if to emphasize his desperation.
> "Oh, I suppose I do command some respect down at the hospital," he went on, "but I'm not close to anybody, really. I have no one to lean on. But I'm not sure you can help me either—I've been shy and re-served all my life. What I need is to have my person-ality overhauled!"[1]

Contrary to that doctor's opinion, the secret to successful rela-tionships is not a new personality. Again, McGinnis illustrates.

> In my hometown an obscure nurseryman died re-cently. His name was Hubert Bales, and he was the

---

1. Alan Loy McGinnis, *The Friendship Factor* (Minneapolis, Minn.: Augsburg Pub-lishing House, 1979), pp. 12–13. Reprinted by permission.

shyest man I ever met. When he talked, he squirmed, blinked his eyes rapidly, and smiled nervously.

Hubert never ran in influential circles. He grew shrubs and trees, working with his hands the plot of land left him by his father. He was anything but an extrovert.

Yet when Hubert died, his funeral was the largest in the history of our little town. There were so many people that they filled even the balcony of the church.

Why did such a shy man win the hearts of so many people? Simply because, for all his shyness, Hubert knew how to make friends. He had mastered the principles of caring, and for more than 60 years he had put people first. Perhaps because they recognized that his generosity of spirit was an extra effort for someone so retiring, people loved him back. By the hundreds. [2]

If it isn't a good profession or a bubbly personality, what is it that contributes to a person having good relationships? In our passage today we'll examine some important principles in forging good relationships. But first, let's take a little time to review.

Where Have We Been?

Paul was a person who knew that relationships have both positive and negative aspects. In opening his letter, he explains himself in an attempt to clear up some negatives in his relationship with the Corinthians. He addresses the problem of a lack of understanding (2 Cor. 1:13–14), the problem of others accusing him of vacillating and talking out of both sides of his mouth (vv. 17–18), and the problem of being suspected of wielding dictatorial control (vv. 23–24).

Later in the letter, beginning at 2:14 and going to 6:10, Paul digresses and speaks about an effective ministry. And as there are two sides to relationships, so there are two sides to ministry—a bright side and a dark side (6:8–10).

When Is It Right to Be Free?

Regarding those relationships in his ministry, Paul reminds the Corinthians in 6:11 that he has been forthright and candid with them.

> Our mouth has spoken freely to you, O Corinthians, our heart is opened wide.

2. McGinnis, *The Friendship Factor,* p. 14. Reprinted by permission.

Literally, he says "our mouth is open to you" and "our heart is opened wide." He has been open and vulnerable to them. And how have they responded? They have withdrawn.

> You are not restrained by us, but you are restrained in your own affections. (v. 12)

The term "affections" is the Greek word *splagchna*, meaning "bowels." It literally means the upper viscera—that is, the heart, liver, and lungs. In ancient days, it was believed that the emotions emanated from these organs. Paul is saying that all the past emotions in their relationship have been one-sided. Now he urges a reversal.

> Now in a like exchange—I speak as to children—open wide to us also. (v. 13)

A successful relationship can never be a one-way street. The emotional traffic must travel both ways. The apostle is not saying anything deep or mysterious. He speaks to the Corinthians "as to children." He puts his message on the bottom shelf, within reach: "We opened up to you; now you open up to us."

Have you ever hugged someone who didn't hug back? Ever kissed someone who didn't kiss back? Ever tried to talk with a person who just gave anemic, one-word answers? What these responses are telling you is that the person doesn't want a close relationship. When is it right to be free and open with another person? When the person you're free with is free with you. There must be reciprocity.

But on the heels of his admonition to be free and vulnerable, Paul talks about holding back.

When Is It Wrong to Be Bound?

This is the opposite side of the relational coin. There are times when it is appropriate to hold back, when it is actually wrong to bond with another person. Verse 14a speaks of such a case.

> Do not be bound together with unbelievers.

Notice that this is not a prohibition against associations or friendships with unbelievers. A casual glance at 1 Corinthians 5:9–10 assures us of this.

> I wrote you in my letter not to associate with immoral people; I did not at all mean with the immoral people of this world, or with the covetous and swindlers, or with idolaters; for then you would have to go out of the world.

Nor is Paul referring to a marriage already established in which one person has become a Christian. He dispels that notion in 1 Corinthians 7:13–15.

> And a woman who has an unbelieving husband, and he consents to live with her, let her not send her husband away. For the unbelieving husband is sanctified through his wife, and the unbelieving wife is sanctified through her believing husband; for otherwise your children are unclean, but now they are holy. Yet if the unbelieving one leaves, let him leave; the brother or the sister is not under bondage in such cases, but God has called us to peace.

The words *bound together* literally mean "unequally yoked," an agricultural metaphor. In Deuteronomy 22:10, the Jews were instructed not to yoke an ox and a donkey together for plowing. This passage emphasizes a working relationship. In Leviticus 19:19, the emphasis is sexual, where God prohibits the crossbreeding of different animal species. In each case, the result is a diverse yoke.

In occupational and marital relationships, becoming yoked in a partnership with an unbeliever is prohibited. This raises an important question: How close do two people have to be to form a bond? Read through 2 Corinthians 6:14b–16a to find the answer.

> For what partnership have righteousness and lawlessness, or what fellowship has light with darkness? Or what harmony has Christ with Belial, or what has a believer in common with an unbeliever? Or what agreement has the temple of God with idols?

Underscore the words *partnership, fellowship, harmony, common,* and *agreement.* Any agreement or partnership or fellowship you have with an unbeliever that might jeopardize your Christian walk or your witness should be avoided.

In these verses, there are five crucial questions, each stressing the incompatibility of a Christian with a non-Christian. The point of each question is that real intimacy and real freedom cannot be experienced in an unequally yoked relationship. Certain people, like certain species of animals, are essentially distinct and fundamentally incompatible and therefore not meant to be brought together in a binding partnership. To put the purity of the Christian and the pollution of the pagan in a double harness is to breed confusion and create an environment in which convictions can be easily broken down.

The underlying reason for this prohibition is found in verses 16b–18.

> For we are the temple of the living God; just as God said,
> "I will dwell in them and walk among
> them;
> And I will be their God, and they shall
> be My people.
> "Therefore, come out from their midst
> and be separate," says the Lord.
> "And do not touch what is unclean;
> And I will welcome you.
> "And I will be a father to you,
> And you shall be sons and daughters
> to Me,"
> Says the Lord Almighty.

The main reason we shouldn't become unequally yoked with an unbeliever is that we are the temple of the living God. As such, we belong to Him, serve Him, model Him, and represent Him. The Christian represents spiritual harmony (v. 16b), personal purity (v. 17), and familial intimacy (v. 18).

Previously, we talked about when it's right to be free: when the other person is free in return. We also talked about when it's wrong to be bound: when the other person is already in bondage—to a lifestyle you can't condone, to a philosophy you disagree with, or to values you stand against.

What Are Some Safe Guidelines to Follow?

Undoubtedly, what we've discussed in this lesson has rocked the boat in many of your relationships. So as not to leave you bobbing in the wake, here are a couple of guidelines to steer you out of the choppy waters.

First: *Unless there is an emotional bond, we cannot be free in a relationship.* Where there is restraint in your relationships—whether parental, marital, or professional—bonding cannot take place. You can be friends with those people, but only on the surface. You can't form deep relationships without reciprocal vulnerability.

Second: *Unless there is spiritual freedom, we dare not be bound in a partnership.* Unless there is mutual agreement on certain spiritual values and goals, it will be like yoking an ox and a donkey together. They will always be out of step with each other. And chances are, the row they plow together is going to turn out crooked.

Paul admonished the Corinthians not to be bound with unbelievers because "we are the temple of the living God" (2 Cor. 6:16b). What does it mean to be a temple of God? Let's study that concept further, because understanding God's perspective will help us understand why we must keep our relationships centered on Him.

- Webster defines *temple* as "a place devoted to a special purpose."[3] To uncover other definitions, look up *temple* in a Bible dictionary. Then select some passages from a concordance to see how the word is used in Scripture. Record your findings below.

A Word Study on *Temple*

Definitions: _____

_____

_____

_____

Verses: _____

Observations: _____

_____

Verses: _____

Observations: _____

_____

_____

Verses: _____

Observations: _____

_____

_____

3. *Webster's Ninth New Collegiate Dictionary,* see "temple."

In this lesson, we learned two guidelines to follow concerning good relationships and bad partnerships. Use the space provided to evaluate how these principles apply to your relationships. If you are involved in a group study, discuss together what these principles mean.

• Unless there is an emotional bond, we cannot be free in a relationship.

_____

_____

_____

_____

_____

_____

_____

_____

• Unless there is spiritual freedom, we dare not be bound in a partnership.

_____

_____

_____

_____

_____

_____

_____

_____

Chapter 14

REVERENCE FOR GOD, RESPECT FOR OTHERS

2 Corinthians 6:11–7:4

B arbara Walters, a noted television interviewer, has written a book titled *How to Talk with Practically Anybody about Practically Anything*. In it, she gives a basic formula that acts as a catalyst in the chemistry of human relationships.

> The most consistently endearing human trait is warmth. *Everybody* responds to the person who radiates friendliness from a serene core. Such people are lovely to be around because they don't reject or belittle and, best of all, they bring out the best, most generous qualities in the people they encounter. [1]

The world is big, and lonely, and often cold. When we find someone who radiates warmth, it's like stepping out of the cold to warm our palms at a crackling fire. The fire chases away the chill and invites us to shed our coats and gloves and earmuffs.

In the same way, warm people invite us into their lives. Inside that space we feel cozy, accepted, and understood. And we shed our wraps naturally, becoming transparent before them.

We all need warmth in relationships as surely as we need fireplaces in winter. And we'll go to any lengths to find someone in whose presence we feel loved and accepted.

But just as a runaway child can wander down a wrong alley, looking for that type of warmth, so we can take a wrong turn regarding the relationships we enter into.

Guidelines for Living Fulfilled Lives

In our previous lesson, we uncovered some important guidelines to steer us into proper relationships and clear of potentially detrimental ones. The first one comes from 2 Corinthians 6:11–13.

---

1. Barbara Walters, *How to Talk with Practically Anybody about Practically Anything* (New York, N.Y.: Dell Publishing Co., 1970), p. 142.

Our mouth has spoken freely to you, O Corinthians, our heart is opened wide. You are not restrained by us, but you are restrained in your own affections. Now in a like exchange—I speak as to children—open wide to us also.

Guideline #1: *Unless there is an emotional bond, we cannot be free in a relationship.*

The second bit of advice comes in verses 14–18.

Do not be bound together with unbelievers; for what partnership have righteousness and lawlessness, or what fellowship has light with darkness? Or what harmony has Christ with Belial, or what has a believer in common with an unbeliever? Or what agreement has the temple of God with idols? For we are the temple of the living God; just as God said,
"I will dwell in them and walk among them;
And I will be their God, and they shall be My people.
Therefore, come out from their midst and be separate," says the Lord.
"And do not touch what is unclean;
And I will welcome you.
And I will be a father to you,
And you shall be sons and daughters to Me,"
Says the Lord Almighty.

Guideline #2: *Unless there is spiritual freedom, we dare not be bound in a partnership.*

Living Out Those Guidelines Day after Day

It's one thing to acknowledge the guidelines. It's quite another to apply them. To do that, we must first have a vertical reverence—a reverence for God. The exhortation of verse 1 in chapter 7 is based on "having these promises," that is, the promises delineated in 6:16–18.

Therefore, having these promises, beloved, let us cleanse ourselves from all defilement of flesh and spirit, perfecting holiness in the fear of God. (7:1)

Out of a reverence for God we should do two things: cleanse ourselves from all defilement, and perfect holiness. *Perfect*, in this text, means "to bring to completion." That should be our goal in life—not finding the right mate, the right job, the right school, or even the right church. Our goal should be revering God, first and foremost, as Eugene Peterson so eloquently states.

> A relationship with God is not something added on after we complete our basic growth, it is the essential core of that growth. Take that core out, and there is no humanity at all but only a husk, the appearance but not the substance of the human. [2]

Gordon MacDonald provides a timely warning that has universal application.

> Those with natural talents, like musicians, are quite vulnerable here. They can mistake the applause of the admiring crowds for God's blessing. Thinking that their ability to raise the emotions of people in an artistic setting is the same as being a tool in the hand of God, they begin to abandon any sense of need for spiritual passion or energy and move ahead on their own instincts. More often, what power they appear to have is sheer theatrics, not spiritual passion. Often the system seems to work for a long time, and then—disaster.
>
> Some people are good with words, able to put concepts and stories together with ease. The words form into testimonies, Bible studies, sermons. Again, the crowd's response dulls the speakers into thinking that they are God's servants and that a schedule that leaves no time for the refueling of spiritual energy is justified by the apparent results—again, disaster. [3]

How honest are you when it comes to reading your spiritual thermometer? Do you have a feverish and infectious love for Christ? Or is it room temperature? Even worse, has it grown cold?

In a painfully honest look at his own life, W. E. Sangster wrote in his journal that although he was a minister, the spiritual passion in his private life had languished. He made the following observations.

> *a.* I am irritable and easily put out.
>
> *b.* I am impatient with my wife and children.

2. Eugene H. Peterson, *Run with the Horses* (Downers Grove, Ill.: InterVarsity Press, 1983), p. 47.

3. Gordon MacDonald, *Restoring Your Spiritual Passion* (Nashville, Tenn.: Thomas Nelson Publishers, 1986), pp. 48–49. Reprinted by permission.

c. I am deceitful in that I often express private annoy-ance when a caller is announced and simulate pleasure when I actually greet them.

d. From an examination of my heart, I conclude that most of my study has been crudely ambitious: that I wanted degrees more than knowledge and praise rather than equipment for service.

e. Even in my preaching I fear that I am more often wondering what the people think of *me,* than what they think about my Lord and His word.

f. I have long felt in a vague way, that something was hindering the effectiveness of my ministry and I must conclude that the "something" is my failure in living the truly Christian life.

g. I am driven in pain to conclude that the girl who has lived as a maid in my house for more than three years has not felt drawn to the Christian life because of me.

h. I find slight envies in my heart at the greater suc-cess of other young ministers. I seem to match myself with them in thought and am vaguely jealous when they attract more notice than I do.[4]

For that minister, the fire in his heart had died. If the same is true in your life, don't increase your activity to try to generate warmth. Instead, rekindle the fire. For as a blazing fireplace is the focal point around which the family huddles to knit, to read, or to play, so spiritual passion should be at the center of all our activity.

And just as the heat rises vertically through the chimney, so it radiates horizontally to warm others gathered around the hearth. Respect for others leaps from the flame of our reverence for God.

Back in 2 Corinthians 7, notice how Paul's subject jumps from his relationship with God to his relationship with people, like a spark jumping from the fireplace.

Make room for us in your hearts; we wronged no one, we corrupted no one, we took advantage of no one. I do not speak to condemn you; for I have said before that you are in our hearts to die together and to live

4. As quoted by MacDonald, in *Restoring Your Spiritual Passion,* pp. 49–50.

together. Great is my confidence in you, great is my boasting on your behalf. (vv. 2–4a)

Remember how Paul began this section in 6:11–13? He had reached out to the Corinthians, but they refused to reach back. They restrained themselves. Now he returns to that same issue and, in doing so, makes three statements about respect for others.

One: *When you respect others, you make room for them in your heart* (7:2). Paul felt he deserved a place in the Corinthians' lives because he didn't wrong them, corrupt them, or exploit them. When we do any of those things, people who come to us for warmth get burned. And when that happens, they back away.

Two: *When you respect others, you don't speak words that condemn them* (7:3). Even though the Corinthians had thought evil things about Paul, he didn't reciprocate. When you have someone in your heart, condemnation is the farthest thing from your mind.

Three: *When you respect others, you have confidence in them* (7:4a). With all their flaws and faults, the Corinthians were people of great potential and immense worth in Paul's eyes. He believed in them . . . even when they failed.

Remember Peter's failure? Before the disciple's denial, Jesus put His arm around him and said: "Simon, Simon, behold, Satan has demanded permission to sift you like wheat; but I have prayed for you, that your faith may not fail; and you, when once you have turned again, strengthen your brothers" (Luke 22:31–32). That's confidence. That's believing in someone . . . even when he's failed.

That's how Christ sees you. Do you see yourself that way? Do you see your children that way? Your mate? Your friends? The people you work with?

Filled-to-Overflowing Benefits We Can Anticipate

Neatly tucked away in the folds of 2 Corinthians 7:4 are two benefits we can anticipate when we have the proper reverence for God and respect for others.

First: *When our relationships are right, there is comfort.* Paul says, "I am filled with comfort." When relationships ember away to ashes, a shivering discomfort takes place. But when relationships are in full blaze, it's like curling up with a quilt in a comfortable easy chair in front of the fireplace.

Second: *When we have respect for others, there is joy even when things go wrong.* Paul says, "I am overflowing with joy in all our

101

affliction." Contrary to popular perception, pain—not pleasure—is our greatest friend. Because pain is instructive. It clears away the veil that obscures reality.

Think about that for a moment. Remember your good times. Then remember your hard times. Which ones proved to be the better teacher? Which ones taught you more? Which ones matured you? Which ones drove you back to God?

The hard times. The crosses you've had to bear. The nails. The thorns. The dying to self. Our vertical and horizontal relationships intersect at the cross. Because it's only through the cross that we come to terms with reverence for God and respect for others.

 ## Living Insights

To have respect for others, we must first have reverence for God, a reverence that involves cleansing ourselves from sin and perfecting holiness. Have you made reverence for God a priority in your life? Are you allowing the Holy Spirit to cleanse and purify you daily? How has your relationship with God changed and grown during this process?

• Examine your heart and write an honest prayer to the Lord about your spiritual condition. If your spiritual passion is high, thank Him for the specific ways you've grown. If you're not as close to Him as you'd like, express those feelings and ask Him to rekindle your passion. He is there, waiting eagerly for you to renew your relationship with Him.

A Prayer from My Heart

_____

_____

_____

_____

_____

_____

_____

In our last lesson we evaluated two relational principles. In this lesson we learned three more. Think about the people close to you, and write out ways you can apply these principles to those relationships. But don't leave your thoughts on paper—put them into practice.

- When you respect others, you make room for them in your heart.

_____

_____

_____

_____

_____

- When you respect others, you don't speak words that condemn them.

_____

_____

_____

_____

_____

- When you respect others, you have confidence in them.

_____

_____

_____

_____

_____

Chapter 15

SINGIN' IN THE RAIN

2 Corinthians 7:1–7

R ainy days and Mondays always get me down." Those lyrics from a once-popular song by the Carpenters strike a familiar chord in all of us. If we're honest, we have to admit that life is full of pain and disappointment and heartache, full of rainy days and Mondays. Psychiatrist Scott Peck concurs:

> Life is difficult.
> This is a great truth, one of the greatest truths. It is a great truth because once we truly see this truth, we transcend it. Once we truly know that life is difficult—once we truly understand and accept it—then life is no longer difficult. Because once it is accepted, the fact that life is difficult no longer matters.
> Most do not fully see this truth that life is difficult. Instead they moan more or less incessantly, noisily or subtly, about the enormity of their problems, their burdens, and their difficulties as if life were generally easy, as if life *should* be easy. They voice their belief, noisily or subtly, that their difficulties represent a unique kind of affliction that should not be and that has somehow been especially visited upon them, or else upon their families, their tribe, their class, their nation, their race or even their species, and not upon others. I know about this moaning because I have done my share.
> Life is a series of problems. Do we want to moan about them or solve them?[1]

Into all of our lives periodic rain must fall, and into some lives the downpour is torrential. We can't stop the rain, but we can decide whether we're going to stand there, soaking and moaning, or sing in the rain instead.

The Painful Rain

We find the cause of some of our rainy days in Galatians 5. Just as the collision of a cold front and a warm front results in a tornado,

1. M. Scott Peck, *The Road Less Traveled* (New York, N.Y.: Simon and Schuster, 1978), p. 15.

104

so the clash of the Spirit and the flesh stirs up a tempestuous vortex within the heart. The effect can knock us off our spiritual feet.

> For the flesh sets its desire against the Spirit, and the Spirit against the flesh; for these are in opposition to one another, so that you may not do the things that you please. (v. 17)

The flesh brings with it the most carnal of climates, as verses 19–21a indicate.

> Now the deeds of the flesh are evident, which are: immorality, impurity, sensuality, idolatry, sorcery, enmities, strife, jealousy, outbursts of anger, disputes, dissensions, factions, envying, drunkenness, carousing, and things like these.

Though you may have lost ground in a stormy battle between the Spirit and the flesh, all is not gray and wet. First John 1:9 shines like a ray of hope.

> If we confess our sins, He is faithful and righteous to forgive us our sins and to cleanse us from all unrighteousness.

No matter how muddy we get, there is cleansing. A great promise. And on the basis of the promises of God, Paul exhorts us to seek that cleansing.

> Therefore, having these promises, beloved, let us cleanse ourselves from all defilement of flesh and spirit, perfecting holiness in the fear of God. (2 Cor. 7:1)

Sadly, another cause for the storms we experience in life is other Christians. In his book *Restoring Your Spiritual Passion*, Gordon MacDonald remarks on this all too common weather pattern within the church.

> One of the great literary pieces that came out of the Vietnam War was a book called *Friendly Fire*. It detailed the events surrounding the death of a soldier and the failure of the defense department to account for what had actually happened. Only after the dead soldier's persistent parents demanded disclosure did it become clear that the young man had not lost his life to the enemy but to misdirected artillery fire from American guns. Friendly fire, it was called.
>
> Friendly fire is not unusual among Christian leaders. The wounds incurred in spiritual battle come,

unfortunately, all too often from friendly guns. When we fire those guns at our fellow soldiers or receive fire from them, spiritual passion is often destroyed.[2]

MacDonald goes on to describe four different spirits that cut away at spiritual vitality: a competitive spirit, a critical spirit, a vain spirit, and an adversarial spirit. It was the critical spirit that MacDonald found in his own life.

> The competitive spirit was not the only poisoned spirit I found in the recesses of my inner life. A critical spirit that often squelches spiritual passion also lurked inside. It was there, in abundance, and while I despised it in others, I was embarrassed to discover it was also ready and waiting in me. When tired or unguarded, I found it easy to find a flaw in every person in my world. I found something to carp about in the reading of every magazine or in the watching of or listening to a Christian presentation on television or radio.
>
> The tendency to emphasize the negative in every situation, to find the ideological or doctrinal difference, to see the character fault, to major in locating the weakness of the program prevented me from generating the positive energy I needed to get on with my part of the work to which I'd been called.[3]

Paul had encountered this critical spirit in the Christians at Corinth. But despite the problems between them, Paul could still say:

> Great is my confidence in you, great is my boasting on your behalf; I am filled with comfort. I am overflowing with joy in all our affliction. (v. 4)

The Joyful Song

Though Paul's life was one of great accomplishment, it was also one of great stress, both internally and externally.

> For even when we came into Macedonia our flesh had no rest, but we were afflicted on every side: conflicts without, fears[4] within. (v. 5)

---

2. Gordon MacDonald, *Restoring Your Spiritual Passion* (Nashville, Tenn.: Thomas Nelson Publishers, 1986), pp. 95–96. Reprinted by permission.

3. MacDonald, *Restoring Your Spiritual Passion*, pp. 100–101. Reprinted by permission.

4. The Greek word is *phobos*. We get our term *phobia* from it. Yes, even Paul had phobias lurking within him, raising doubts and producing extreme introspection and insecurity.

Yet in the midst of this downpour, God opened an umbrella for the apostle.

> But God, who comforts the depressed, comforted us
> by the coming of Titus. (v. 6)

Not only was the apostle sprinkled with fears (v. 5), he was drenched with depression.[5] All of us get depressed from time to time. Some depressions hover over us like a lingering cloud. Other types are more transitory, varying in degree and duration.

Many Christians deny their depression. They may feel that if they aren't positive and sunny all the time, they are letting Christ down. But by denying their depression, they deny reality. Just as every day isn't filled with sunshine, so our lives aren't continually filled with the radiance of Christ. We have to face the facts of darkness, long shadows, and rainy days in our lives.[6]

God does indeed love us and have a wonderful plan for our life. But we'll still have days that get rained out. So instead of giving you four spiritual laws, here are four spiritual *flaws* to look out for. Because if you can avoid these four misconceptions about the Christian life, your storms will be easier to deal with.

Flaw #1—*When you become a Christian, all your problems are solved.* That is simply not true. As a matter of fact, becoming a Christian complicates your life. For then you come into the spirit-versus-flesh conflict, a problem you never had when you operated solely in the flesh.

Flaw #2—*All the problems you will ever have are specifically addressed in the Bible.* They are not. Some are specifically addressed. Others have their resolution in carefully and prayerfully applied biblical principles. Still others may go unresolved, leaving you with a question mark until you reach heaven.

Flaw #3—*If you're having problems, it's a sign that you're unspiritual.* Sometimes this is true, since we do reap consequences for the sins we sow. But other times the problems entering our lives are signs of spiritual activity, that God is alive and at work (Rom. 5:3–4, James 1:2–4).

5. The word *depression* comes from the Greek root meaning "to make low." It carries with it the nuances of "downcast . . . blue . . . humiliated."

6. When depression begins to interfere with our sleep, appetite, work, or relationships, it's time to seek professional treatment. For further reference, consult Archibald D. Hart's book *Counseling the Depressed* (Waco, Tex.: Word Books, 1987).

Flaw #4—*Being exposed to sound Bible teaching automatically solves your problems.* It doesn't, any more than immersing yourself in water makes you a fish.

No, the joyful song in Paul's life didn't come from a lack of problems. It came in the midst of and in spite of the rain—"overflowing with joy *in* all our affliction" (2 Cor. 7:4, emphasis added). His comfort was not in the warmth and shelter of sunny circumstances. He was comforted with the arrival of Titus, sent to him by God.

> And not only by his coming, but also by the comfort with which he was comforted in you, as he reported to us your longing, your mourning, your zeal for me; so that I rejoiced even more. (v. 7)

The news from Titus was like a refreshing wind to blow away the clouds that had gathered over Paul's life. So refreshing was it that it caused Paul to rejoice (v. 7b).

In between the lines of these verses are written two important secrets for singing during the rainy days of our lives. One: *Denial of difficulties complicates our lives.* If we deny the rain, we also deny the warmth and comfort God wants to give us. The result? We'll end up all wet with nowhere to dry off. Two: *Resentment of the rain stunts our growth.* Instead, we should follow James' prescribed attitude: "Don't resent [trials] as intruders, but welcome them as friends!" (James 1:2).[7]

The Next Time It Rains

The next time it rains, stop, look, and listen.

Stop feeling sorry for yourself or blaming others. *Look* for lessons to be learned. *Listen* to the silent lyrics from God. And he will put a song in your heart as He did for David.

> I waited patiently for the Lord;
> And He inclined to me, and heard my cry.
> He brought me up out of the pit of destruction, out of the miry clay;
> And He set my feet upon a rock making my footsteps firm.
> And He put a new song in my mouth, a song of praise to our God. (Ps. 40:1–3a)

---

7. J. B. Phillips, The New Testament in Modern English (New York, N.Y.: The Macmillan Co., 1958).

Living Insights STUDY ONE

Doesn't 2 Corinthians 7:1–7 bring a smile to your face? Even in great personal trial, the apostle Paul knew how to tap into the eternal source of joy. Let's meditate on some Scriptures that will remind us that He's still our source of joy today.

• Choose a passage of Scripture that speaks of the joy found in the Lord. Psalm 100 is a good place to start, or you can use your Bible concordance to find others. When you have decided on one, commit it to memory. It will serve you well when you, like Paul, find yourself in the midst of trials.

Living Insights STUDY TWO

When we set our worries aside and think of all that God's done for us, joy bubbles to the surface of our hearts like an overflowing spring. Let's find a way to express that joy as we focus on what God means in our lives.

• How are you most comfortable expressing joy? Is it through music or laughter, or are you more comfortable with quieter means, like prayer or meditation? Whatever your favorite method, use it today as you thank the Father for His presence in your life.

109

Chapter 16

REPROOFS THAT RESULT IN REPENTANCE

2 Corinthians 7:8–16

G od's goal for all of His children is *wisdom*—which is not the same as academic intelligence or street smarts or the accumulation of trivial facts. Wisdom is divine perception, the ability to see life from God's point of view and to respond accordingly.

Paul uses the word in that sense in 1 Corinthians 2.

> And when I came to you, brethren, I did not come with superiority of speech or of wisdom, proclaiming to you the testimony of God. For I determined to know nothing among you except Jesus Christ, and Him crucified. And I was with you in weakness and in fear and in much trembling. And my message and my preaching were not in persuasive words of wisdom, but in demonstration of the Spirit and of power, that your faith should not rest on the wisdom of men, but on the power of God. Yet we do speak wisdom among those who are mature; a wisdom, however, not of this age, nor of the rulers of this age, who are passing away. . . . Now we have received, not the spirit of the world, but the Spirit who is from God, that we might know the things freely given to us by God, which things we also speak, not in words taught by human wisdom, but in those taught by the Spirit, combining spiritual thoughts with spiritual words. (vv. 1–6, 12–13)

According to these verses such wisdom is not something we're born with or something we can glean from a book or a seminar. It comes from God, as the book of James affirms.

> But if any of you lacks wisdom, let him ask of God, who gives to all men generously and without reproach, and it will be given to him. (1:5)

Proverbs, more than any other biblical book, is a storehouse of wisdom (1:1–6). Frequently in that book, Solomon personifies wisdom as if it were a woman speaking to us:

Wisdom shouts in the street,
She lifts her voice in the square;
At the head of the noisy streets she cries out;
At the entrance of the gates in the city, she utters her
    sayings:
"How long, O naive ones, will you love simplicity?
And scoffers delight themselves in scoffing,
And fools hate knowledge?" (1:20–22)

Verse 22 addresses three kinds of people: the naive, or simple—those who are gullible, easily deceived and enticed; scoffers—those who are skeptical and cynical; and fools—those who think they can get along without God.

Where should we turn for wisdom? The following verse tells us.

"Turn to my reproof,
Behold, I will pour out my spirit on you;
I will make my words known to you." (v. 23)

Reproof is a rebuke, God's censure for a fault. It's His corrective measure, which may be painful initially but which, in the long run, leads us to righteousness. In today's lesson, we'll examine the reproofs that draw us to repentance.

Ancient Proverbs on Receiving God's Reproofs

To become people of wisdom, we must heed God's reproofs. How do we do this? When we learn from our mistakes, when we're grateful for corrections, when we're open to rebuke, when we're quick to admit our wrongs, and when we're receptive to the well-intended wounds of a friend (Prov. 27:5–6). Solomon, the wisest of the wise, has some fitting advice for all who desire to obtain wisdom.

Strike a scoffer and the naive may become shrewd,
But reprove one who has understanding and he will
    gain knowledge. . . .
Cease listening, my son, to discipline,
And you will stray from the words of knowledge.
(19:25, 27)

We all know people who are stubborn, stiff-necked, and who scoff at any form of criticism. Time and again we see these people resisting reproof, and we ask ourselves, "What's it gonna take to bring them to their senses?"

The answer? Repentance. They must come to a point where they change their mind and submit. All this prepares us for our passage in 2 Corinthians 7.

111

A Lost Letter That Resulted in Repentance

In 2 Corinthians 7, we see the process of repentance at work.

> For though I caused you sorrow by my letter, I do not re-
> gret it; though I did regret it—for I see that that letter
> caused you sorrow, though only for a while . . . (v. 8)

Paul refers to a previously sent letter that, since it does not
appear in the New Testament, must have been lost. In that letter,
he apparently rebuked the Corinthians for failing to condemn the
sin of a man who was living in an immoral relationship with his
stepmother (1 Cor. 5). The letter was strong and severe. After
sending it, Paul had second thoughts about inflicting the pain he
did—much like some parents feel after spanking their errant child.

But as the rod and reproof give wisdom to a child (Prov. 29:15),
so the sharp rap of rebuke on the spiritual knuckles of the Corinthians led to a change of heart.

> I now rejoice, not that you were made sorrowful, but
> that you were made sorrowful to the point of repen-
> tance; for you were made sorrowful according to the
> will of God, in order that you might not suffer loss in
> anything through us. For the sorrow that is according
> to the will of God produces a repentance without re-
> gret, leading to salvation; but the sorrow of the world
> produces death. (2 Cor. 7:9–10)

The difference between the sorrow inflicted by God and the
sorrow inflicted by the world is that the one is purposeful pain while
the other is pointless pain. Sorrow according to the will of God is
not an end in itself. It is a means to an end. It is redemptive.
Nothing is lost, only gained (see Rom. 8:28).

Sorrow that leads to repentance, a definite and deliberate change
in our thinking, is redemptive. It delivers us, often saving us from
catastrophic consequences. But when sorrow is just a hot rush of
tears without producing change, something withers and dies in us,
having the deadly effect of producing bitterness.

What makes suffering remedial is not its pain but our reaction to
it. A reaction of repentance opens the door to wisdom. A reaction of
resentment bolts the door on ever learning anything from our pain.

Verse 11 provides a checklist to find out if we're showing godly
repentance.

For behold what *earnestness* this very thing, this godly sorrow, has produced in you: what *vindication* of yourselves, what *indignation,* what *fear,* what *longing,* what *zeal,* what *avenging of wrong!* In everything you demonstrated yourselves to be innocent in the matter. (emphasis added)

All of us need friends who are close enough to reach below the surface and wound us with the truth—friends like the one Solomon speaks of in Proverbs 27:6.

Faithful are the wounds of a friend,
But deceitful are the kisses of an enemy.

Most of us have friends we talk with about spiritual things. But few are those whose words enter deep enough into our hearts to change us.

People who have our highest good in mind won't let us chatter our way through life. All through life there are necessary reproofs. They are essential for growth. And seeking them is a sign of maturity—it's what made David a man after God's own heart.

Search me, O God, and know my heart;
Try me and know my anxious thoughts;
And see if there be any hurtful way in me,
And lead me in the everlasting way. (Ps. 139:23–24)

Back in 2 Corinthians 7, Paul lifts the issue of reproof above its limited application to a certain person or to a select few.

So although I wrote to you it was not for the sake of
the offender, nor for the sake of the one offended, but
that your earnestness on our behalf might be made
known to you in the sight of God. (v. 12)

Besides the breach between the offender and the offended, a chasm had also widened between Paul and the Corinthians. Only reproof would bring the repentance necessary to bridge both gaps.

The clearest passage in the New Testament on the subject of reproof is Hebrews 12:5–11.

And you have forgotten the exhortation which is addressed to you as sons,
"My son, do not regard lightly the discipline of the Lord,
Nor faint when you are reproved by Him;

113

> For those whom the Lord loves He disci-
> plines,
> And He scourges every son whom He re-
> ceives."

It is for discipline that you endure; God deals with you as with sons; for what son is there whom his father does not discipline? But if you are without discipline, of which all have become partakers, then you are illegitimate children and not sons. Furthermore, we had earthly fathers to discipline us, and we respected them; shall we not much rather be subject to the Father of spirits, and live? For they disciplined us for a short time as seemed best to them, but He disciplines us for our good, that we may share His holiness. All discipline for the moment seems not to be joyful, but sorrowful; yet to those who have been trained by it, afterwards it yields the peaceful fruit of righteousness.

Isn't it wonderful when a defiant boy responds to discipline by throwing himself in his father's arms and, through his tears says, "I'm sorry, Daddy." That's what Hebrews 12 is all about. That's the "afterwards" of it all, that's the harvest, that's the "peaceful fruit of righteousness."

Interpersonal conflict produces anxiety (2 Cor. 2:4), but reproof leading to repentance can resolve conflict. And when conflict is resolved, a flood of good things rushes into the relationship.

> For this reason we have been comforted. And besides our comfort, we rejoiced even much more for the joy of Titus, because his spirit has been refreshed by you all. For if in anything I have boasted to him about you, I was not put to shame; but as we spoke all things to you in truth, so also our boasting before Titus proved to be the truth. And his affection abounds all the more toward you, as he remembers the obedience of you all, how you received him with fear and trembling. I rejoice that in everything I have confidence in you. (7:13–16)

There is relief, rejoicing, and refreshment (v. 13). There is affirmation, a liberating knowledge of the truth, and confidence (v. 14). There is affection, obedience, and acceptance (v. 15). And finally, there is more rejoicing and greater confidence (v. 16).

What a change! All brought about because reproofs were heeded. Remember where we started? To become people of wisdom, we must heed God's reproofs.

114

Timely Reminders regarding Reproofs and Repentance

First: *Godlike wisdom is still available, but without reproof it remains distant.* Wisdom from God comes in packages, some in the form of reproof. And each is opened by means of repentance.

Second: *God's reproofs come in many ways, but they fall flat without repentance.* From whom do these packages of reproof come? From parents, at home. From *children*, at home. From teachers, coaches, and counselors, at school. From friends. From failures. From Scripture. From sickness. By letter. By loss. By disaster. By disappointment. They come in all shapes and sizes.

Third: *Godly repentance unlocks the door, but only one can enter at a time.* God deals with each of us individually, so that when we come through wisdom's door, we come through it single file. It's a door that's open to you right now. Won't you leave your pride on the porch and cross the threshold that leads to wisdom, the peaceful fruit of righteousness, and growth?

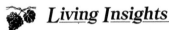 *Living Insights* STUDY ONE

Rebuke is always a tough pill to choke down. But what's even more difficult is that, to get it down, we first have to swallow our pride.

- Take a minute to humble yourself before God by praying the same prayer David prayed in Psalm 139:23–24.

> Search me, O God, and know my heart;
> Try me and know my anxious thoughts;
> And see if there be any hurtful way in me,
> And lead me in the everlasting way.

- Now spend some time listening to God, and write down anything He reveals in your life that is worrisome or destructive.

_____

_____

_____

_____

_____

_____

The second section of each set of Living Insights is devoted to practical application of the truths we've learned in each lesson. Let's review the most significant applications we've made in our study.

- Look back over your Bible and study guide and record below one significant application from each message.

A Ministry Anyone Could Trust

Telling It Like It Is _____

_____

_____

Unraveling the Mystery of Suffering _____

_____

_____

In Defense of Integrity _____

_____

_____

When Forgiveness Really Means Probation _____

_____

_____

What Is That Fragrance? _____

_____

_____

What's a New Covenant Ministry? _____

_____

_____

Checklist for an Effective Ministry _____

_____

_____

BOOKS FOR
PROBING FURTHER

S econd Corinthians offers a kaleidoscope of themes to reflect on: suffering . . . integrity . . . forgiveness . . . death . . . reverence . . . reproof. All are part of a colorful but fragmentary picture of Paul's ministry to the Corinthians.

As we turn these varicolored flecks over in our minds, new light is shone on our own circumstances. Through Paul's pain, we gain perspective. Through his struggles, we gain the strength to persevere. Through his firm yet tender admonitions, we gain a whole new respect for relationships.

The following books will help bring into focus many of the themes Paul touches on only briefly in his heartfelt letter to the Corinthians. Together they form a mosaic of a ministry anyone could trust.

Augsburger, David. *The Freedom of Forgiveness.* Revised and expanded. Chicago, Ill.: Moody Press, 1988. The author combines personal testimonies with Scripture for a highly motivational guide to applying forgiveness in your life.

Baldwin, Stanley C. *When Death Means Life.* Portland, Oreg.: Multnomah Press, 1986. Many of Paul's exhortations in 2 Corinthians are based on the cross. In this immensely practical book on theology, the author shows us how choosing the way of the cross is the only way to find true fulfillment.

Bayly, Joseph. *The Last Thing We Talk About.* Revised edition. Elgin, Ill.: David C. Cook Publishing Co., 1973. Death is the last thing we want to talk about. Yet Bayly manages to do it in both a compelling and concise way in this short but poignant book.

Fenton, Horace L., Jr. *When Christians Clash.* Downers Grove, Ill.: InterVarsity Press, 1987. Paul repeatedly clashed with the Corinthian church on subjects ranging from immaturity to immorality. In this book the author presents key principles from Scripture that can help all Christians work through the doctrinal disputes and tensions every church faces. He shows us how to keep from jumping to unwarranted conclusions, as well as how to confront others when necessary.

Hughes, Philip Edgcumbe. *Paul's Second Epistle to the Corinthians.* Grand Rapids, Mich.: William B. Eerdmans Publishing Co., 1962. Serving the interests of both pastor and scholar, this text is an excellent commentary for anyone wanting to dig deeper into 2 Corinthians.

Mowday, Lois. *The Snare.* Colorado Springs, Colo.: NavPress, 1988. In both letters to the Corinthians, Paul addresses the problem of immorality in the church. In this book, the author shows how emotional and sexual entanglements are really a snare. And she offers help to those wanting to escape its grasp.

Peterson, Eugene H. *Working the Angles.* Grand Rapids, Mich.: William B. Eerdmans Publishing Co., 1987. In this insightful work on pastoral integrity, Peterson exhorts fellow pastors to follow the basic but often neglected responsibilities of praying, reading Scripture, and giving spiritual direction.

Stedman, Ray C. *Authentic Christianity.* Portland, Oreg.: Multnomah Press, 1975. The author takes us through the heart of 2 Corinthians to discover that Jesus died *for* us in order that He might live *in* us. This is the hope of glory that Paul talks of in his second letter to the Corinthians.

Wiersbe, Warren W. *The Integrity Crisis.* Nashville, Tenn.: Thomas Nelson Publishers, 1988. In this book, the author asks some penetrating questions. What gospel is the church proclaiming? Is it the gospel of success? The gospel of prosperity? The gospel of whatever feels right? How are compromised lifestlyes affecting today's church? How can an individual Christian help change the situation? Answering these questions, Wiersbe points the way to a renewed church, a church that will once again have the right to be heard.

Yancey, Philip. *Disappointment with God.* Grand Rapids, Mich.: Zondervan Publishing House, 1988. This book offers comfort to any who have suffered loss. It also advances a carefully reasoned explanation of why God allows such losses to occur in the first place. Yancey tackles the crises of faith born out of real-life situations, situations Paul confronted so many times in his dealings with the Corinthians.

NOTES

NOTES

NOTES

NOTES

Insight for Living
Cassette Tapes
A Ministry Anyone Could Trust

More than a few chapters in the church's history book contain stories of leaders who failed or deviated from sound doctrine. Recent history is no exception. Fortunately, though, God's Word has a remedy for our disappointment over ministries gone to seed. Paul's second letter to the church at Corinth reminds us of traits that characterize a trustworthy ministry. The implications are clear . . . these are the qualities we need to focus on when disillusionment strikes.

			U.S.	Canada
MAT	CS	Cassette series—includes album cover	$44.50	$56.50
		Individual cassettes—include messages A and B	5.00	6.35

These prices are subject to change without notice.

MAT 1-A: *Telling It Like It Is*—A Survey of 2 Corinthians
     B: *Unraveling the Mystery of Suffering*—2 Corinthians 1:1–11

MAT 2-A: *In Defense of Integrity*—2 Corinthians 1:12–2:4
     B: *When Forgiveness Really Means Probation*—
2 Corinthians 2:5–11

MAT 3-A: *What Is That Fragrance?*—2 Corinthians 2:12–17
     B: *What's a New Covenant Ministry?*—2 Corinthians 3

MAT 4-A: *Checklist for an Effective Ministry*—2 Corinthians 4:1–6
     B: *Power in Pots . . . Life in Death*—2 Corinthians 4:7–12

MAT 5-A: *The Right Focus*—2 Corinthians 4:13–18
     B: *Hope Beyond the Hearse*—2 Corinthians 5:1–10

MAT 6-A: *Why Christians Are Considered Crazy*—
2 Corinthians 5:11–21
     B: *A Realistic Portrait of Ministry*—2 Corinthians 6:1–10

MAT 7-A: *Good Relationships and Bad Partnerships*—
2 Corinthians 6:11–18
     B: *Reverence for God, Respect for Others*—
2 Corinthians 6:11–7:4

MAT 8-A: *Singin' in the Rain*—2 Corinthians 7:1–7
     B: *Reproofs That Result in Repentance*—
2 Corinthians 7:8–16

How to Order by Mail

Simply mark on the order form whether you want the series or individual tapes. Mail the form with your payment to the appropriate address listed below. We will process your order as promptly as we can.

United States: Mail your order to the Sales Department at Insight for Living, Post Office Box 4444, Fullerton, California 92634. If you wish your order to be shipped first-class for faster delivery, add 10 percent of the total order amount (not including California sales tax). Otherwise, please allow four to six weeks for delivery by fourth-class mail. We accept personal checks, money orders, Visa, and MasterCard in payment for materials. Unfortunately, we are unable to offer invoicing or COD orders.

Canada: Mail your order to Insight for Living Ministries, Post Office Box 2510, Vancouver, British Columbia V6B 3W7. Please add 7 percent of your total order for first-class postage and allow approximately four weeks for delivery. Our listeners in British Columbia must also add a 6 percent sales tax to the total of all tape orders (not including postage). We accept personal checks, money orders, Visa, or MasterCard in payment for materials. Unfortunately, we are unable to offer invoicing or COD orders.

Australia, New Zealand, or Papua New Guinea: Mail your order to Insight for Living, Inc., GPO Box 2823 EE, Melbourne, Victoria 3001, Australia. Please allow six to ten weeks for delivery by surface mail. If you would like your order sent airmail, the delivery time may be reduced. Whether you choose surface or airmail, postage costs must be added to the amount of purchase and included with your order. Please use the chart that follows to determine correct postage. Due to fluctuating currency rates, we can accept only personal checks made payable in U.S. funds, international money orders, Visa, or MasterCard in payment for materials.

Overseas: Other overseas residents should contact our U.S. office. Please allow six to ten weeks for delivery by surface mail. If you would like your order sent airmail, the delivery time may be reduced. Whether you choose surface or airmail, postage costs must be added to the amount of purchase and included with your order. Please use the chart that follows to determine correct postage. Due to fluctuating currency rates, we can accept only personal checks made payable in U.S. funds, international money orders, Visa, or MasterCard in payment for materials.

Type of Postage	Cassettes
Surface	10% of total order
Airmail	25% of total order

For Faster Service, Order by Telephone

To purchase using Visa or MasterCard, you are welcome to use our **toll-free** numbers between the hours of 8:30 A.M. and 4:00 P.M., Pacific time, Monday through Friday. The number to call from anywhere in the United States is **1-800-772-8888.** To order from Canada, call our Vancouver office at **1-800-663-7639.** Vancouver residents should call (604) 272-5811. Telephone orders from overseas are handled through our Sales Department at (714) 870-9161. We are unable to accept collect calls.

Our Guarantee

Our cassettes are guaranteed for ninety days against faulty performance or breakage due to a defect in the tape. For best results, please be sure your tape recorder is in good operating condition and is cleaned regularly.

Note: To cover processing and handling, there is a $10 fee for *any* returned check.

Order Form

MAT CS represents the entire *A Ministry Anyone Could Trust* series, while MAT 1–8 are the individual tapes included in the series.

Series or Tape	Unit Price U.S.	Canada	Quantity	Amount
MAT CS	$44.50	$56.50		$
MAT 1	5.00	6.35		
MAT 2	5.00	6.35		
MAT 3	5.00	6.35		
MAT 4	5.00	6.35		
MAT 5	5.00	6.35		
MAT 6	5.00	6.35		
MAT 7	5.00	6.35		
MAT 8	5.00	6.35		
Subtotal				
Sales tax 6% for orders delivered in California or British Columbia				
Postage 7% in Canada; overseas residents see "How to Order by Mail"				
10% optional first-class shipping and handling U.S. residents only				
Gift to Insight for Living Tax-deductible in the U.S. and Canada				
Total amount due Please do not send cash.				$

If there is a balance: ☐ apply it as a donation ☐ please refund

Form of payment:

☐ Check or money order made payable to Insight for Living

☐ Credit card (circle one):   Visa   MasterCard

   Card Number _____ Expiration Date _____

   Signature _____
   We cannot process your credit card purchase without your signature.

Name _____

Address _____

City _____

State/Province_____ Zip/Postal Code _____

Country _____

Telephone _(____)_____ Radio Station ___ ___ ___ ___
If questions arise concerning your order, we may need to contact you.

Mail this order form to the Sales Department at one of these addresses:
Insight for Living, Post Office Box 4444, Fullerton, CA 92634
Insight for Living Ministries, Post Office Box 2510, Vancouver, BC, Canada V6B 3W7

Order Form

MAT CS represents the entire *A Ministry Anyone Could Trust* series, while MAT 1–8 are the individual tapes included in the series.

Series or Tape	Unit Price U.S.	Unit Price Canada	Quantity	Amount
MAT CS	$44.50	$56.50		$
MAT 1	5.00	6.35		
MAT 2	5.00	6.35		
MAT 3	5.00	6.35		
MAT 4	5.00	6.35		
MAT 5	5.00	6.35		
MAT 6	5.00	6.35		
MAT 7	5.00	6.35		
MAT 8	5.00	6.35		
Subtotal				
Sales tax 6% for orders delivered in California or British Columbia				
Postage 7% in Canada; overseas residents see "How to Order by Mail"				
10% optional first-class shipping and handling U.S. residents only				
Gift to Insight for Living Tax-deductible in the U.S. and Canada				
Total amount due Please do not send cash.				$

If there is a balance: ☐ apply it as a donation   ☐ please refund

Form of payment:

☐ Check or money order made payable to Insight for Living

☐ Credit card (circle one):   Visa   MasterCard

Card Number _____   Expiration Date _____

Signature _____
We cannot process your credit card purchase without your signature.

Name _____

Address _____

City _____

State/Province_____ Zip/Postal Code _____

Country _____

Telephone _( )_____ Radio Station ___ ___ ___ ___
If questions arise concerning your order, we may need to contact you.

Mail this order form to the Sales Department at one of these addresses:
Insight for Living, Post Office Box 4444, Fullerton, CA 92634
Insight for Living Ministries, Post Office Box 2510, Vancouver, BC, Canada V6B 3W7